P9-CES-833

Write to Be Read

Reading, Reflection, and Writing

William R. Smalzer

CAMBRIDGE
UNIVERSITY PRESS

PUBLISHED BY THE PRESS SYNDICATE OF THE UNIVERSITY OF CAMBRIDGE
The Pitt Building, Trumpington Street, Cambridge, United Kingdom

CAMBRIDGE UNIVERSITY PRESS
The Edinburgh Building, Cambridge CB2 2RU, United Kingdom
40 West 20th Street, New York, NY 10011–4211, USA
10 Stamford Road, Oakleigh, Melbourne 3166, Australia

© Cambridge University Press 1996

This book is in copyright. Subject to statutory exception
and to the provisions of relevant collective licensing agreements,
no reproduction of any part may take place without
the written permission of Cambridge University Press.

First published 1996
Fifth printing 2000

Printed in the United States of America

Typeset in Times

Library of Congress Cataloging-in-Publication Data
Smalzer, William R.
Write to be read : reading, reflection, and writing / William
R. Smalzer
p. cm.
ISBN 0-521-44991-X (pbk.)
1. English language – Textbooks for foreign speakers. 2. English
language – Rhetoric. 3. College readers. I. Title.
PE1128.S5816 1996   95–1856
428.2'4 – dc20   CIP

A catalogue record for this book is available from the British Library

ISBN 0-521-44991-X Student's Book
ISBN 0-521-48476-6 Teacher's Manual

Book design and text composition by
    Leon Bolognese & Associates, Inc.
Manuscript development and production by Jane Mairs.
Illustrations by Randy Jones.
Line drawing by Suffolk Technical Illustrators, Inc.

Contents

PLAN OF THE BOOK

IMPROVING WRITING SKILLS	CORE WRITING ASSIGNMENT
▶ Paraphrasing sentences ▶ Writing paragraphs with topic sentences ▶ Identifying parts of sentences, correcting fragments	Paragraph on birth order
▶ Summarizing passages ▶ Distinguishing patterns of organization ▶ Correcting run-together sentences	Paragraph on theme(s) from the readings: prejudice, jealousy, decision making
▶ More paraphrasing sentences ▶ Writing essays, making logical assertions ▶ Following the rules of subject-verb agreement	Essay on friendship
▶ Summarizing a story ▶ Writing introductions and conclusions ▶ Adding coherence	Essay on people and work
▶ Summarizing an article ▶ Outlining ▶ Using a variety of sentence types	Essay on a topic related to manners
▶ Summarizing a newspaper column ▶ Writing persuasive essays ▶ Achieving consistency in tense, person, number, and tone	Persuasive essay *for* or *against* arranged marriages
▶ Summarizing conclusions ▶ Avoiding logical fallacies ▶ Making segments parallel	Argument essay on the relationship between development and quality of life
▶ Writing one-sentence summaries ▶ Taking essay exams ▶ Achieving pronoun agreement and clear reference	Essay exam answers

Preface

OVERVIEW

Write to Be Read is a high-intermediate to advanced writing text designed to teach ESL/EFL students to write convincing English paragraphs and academic essays with greater fluency. Influenced by the whole language approach, it focuses primarily on meaning, rather than discrete skills, in both reading and writing. The methodology is a blend of both the process and product approaches to writing. The process approach encourages students to develop their thinking about a topic. The product approach, relying heavily on student essays as models, helps writing students meet the expectations of educated native readers of English.

Though much of writing is a solitary activity, *Write to Be Read* makes ample use of collaborative activities in discussion of readings and topics, in prewriting activities, and in peer review. The educational design of the book encourages students to think more clearly and critically and to develop their own voices as writers. The text also stresses the importance of summarizing and paraphrasing when using others' writing.

Readings include selections from nonfiction books, short stories, poems, and magazine articles. Of the eight chapters, the first two are devoted to the paragraph, the next five to essays, and the final chapter to essay exam answers. The text concentrates on the academic essay because it is seen as the basis for other forms of academic writing. An appendix with additional exercises on specific grammar and punctuation problems is included for students who need such work.

After becoming familiar with the topic of each chapter through reflection, discussion, and reading, students build up to a formal core writing assignment in stages. They begin with expressive writing and progress to objective academic writing in each chapter. First, in private journals, students respond subjectively to the main reading. Then they share more objective responses with an audience of peers. Next, students do additional reading and think more critically about the topic. After attention to writing skills, students begin the core writing assignment. They prepare a first draft after prewriting and collaborative activities. Then they revise their first draft, get feedback from peers, revise further, and edit their papers.

Progressing from private, subjective writing to public, objective writing in each chapter helps students develop their thinking about topics one step at a time. It also develops a sense of audience and purpose in writing. The thinking/writing process is enhanced by collaborative work in which comprehension of meaning (the reader's goal) and expression of meaning (the writer's goal) guide most tasks.

FORMAT

Each of the eight chapters in *Write to Be Read* contains these five parts:

1 GETTING A GRIP ON THE TOPIC

This first part includes three sections with activities and text designed to develop schema and prepare students for the main reading selection. Comprehension questions which accompany the main reading lead students to read for the main idea first and then delve more deeply and bring their own experience to the text.

2 RESPONDING TO THE MAIN READING

Students develop a sense of audience and voice by writing first for themselves and then for their classmates. In "Journals: A Private Audience" they use journals to record their personal reactions to the main reading and what it made them think about. Then, in "Shared Writing," they write on topics that are more objective in nature, and which require them to consider issues of logic and support. This work is shared and discussed in small groups. To foster attention on content and ideas rather than on mechanics and spelling, students read their "shared writings" aloud.

3 GOING MORE DEEPLY INTO THE TOPIC

This part contains a reading selection on the same topic as the main reading, but usually from a different genre and with an opposing point of view. Students negotiate the meaning of this second reading more independently, through a reader response approach. Part 3 ends with discussion questions designed to promote critical-thinking skills such as comparison, analysis, inference, and evaluation.

4 IMPROVING WRITING SKILLS

"Using Another's Writing," the first section in Part 4, contains a summary or paraphrase exercise intended to help students incorporate others' ideas without plagiarizing them. This exercise also serves as a review of one of the main reading selections as well as a challenging language exercise. Students study matters of form, organization, and logic in "Meeting Reader Expectations." They review common problems of sentence structure in "Language Conventions."

5 CORE WRITING ASSIGNMENT

Parts 1–4 help familiarize the students with the content and skills needed to write a formal, objective piece in this final part. Because *Write to Be Read* aims to help students improve their writing by developing their thinking, "Generating Ideas" and "Expanding Your Point of View" are important preliminaries to the core writing assignment. In the "Initial Drafts" section, students are given guidelines for first drafts and early revisions. "Review, Revision, and Assessment" guides students through further revision of their work. Also in this section, teachers review students' papers and may evaluate them or allow further revision, ideally at a later date, before assigning a grade.

RECOMMENDATIONS FOR TEACHING AND ASSESSMENT

1. Given the choice between reworking the same paper over and over and going on to a new topic, teachers and students will find it more productive to go on to a new topic. Students will benefit more from reading, thinking, and writing about a new topic than from continuing to revise an old paper. Revision of writing is important, of course; consider using the *portfolio approach* to evaluation (see item 11) so that several weeks elapse before a final revision on a paper is due.

2. Resist the temptation to take ownership of students' writing. Lead students to think, but do not think for them. If you wish, write the same assignments that your students do. Use your writing to illustrate revision, assessment, or other points. (Sharing your writing with students takes courage but makes a valuable point: Even "good" writers need to revise.)

3. Promote cooperation and collaboration among students by keeping the same small groups for "Feedback on Your Writing" (in Part 2), "Negotiating the Meaning" (in Part 3), "Expanding Your Point of View" (in Part 5), and "Peer Feedback" (also in Part 5) within the same chapter.

4. Though the schedule may not always allow, try to have a writing conference with each student, even for just two or three minutes, at some point during the drafting of each core writing assignment. Students can learn to "run" the conference by being ready to explain what stage they have reached in the writing process and what problems they are facing. The time is better spent if students ask you questions rather than vice versa.

(In a quick conference, it is better not to read a student's draft; there isn't enough time for you to judge the work fairly, and absence of comments may be taken by students as tacit approval of their writing.)

5. Help students realize that the course focuses more on clear writing than on correct grammar. Grammar does need to be dealt with, but it will keep the focus clearer if you refrain from marking every error. Instead, individualize grammar work by identifying for each student a few kinds of errors that occur in his or her work and assigning tasks that focus on these errors. A set of tasks for a given student might look like this:

    Write two new sentences with each of the following constructions:

    1. *even though*
    2. *look at* and *look for*
    3. *because* . . . (adjective + *er*) *than* . . .
    4. *more* (adjective) *than* . . .
    5. . . . ; *for example,* . . .
    6. *went* . . . *ago* and *has gone* . . . *since*

    Teaching grammar outside the context of the students' papers keeps the course focus on thinking and writing about ideas. Your specific and positive written comments on content, word choice, organization, and other points will assure students that you have read their papers carefully. Positive comments are also more motivating than lots of grammar corrections.

6. Help students understand the revision process by revising together in class. Use a former student's paper or your own.

7. Make a distinction between assessment, pointing out strengths and weaknesses, and evaluation, assigning a holistic letter grade. Once a letter grade is put on a paper, students will give it little further serious thought or work.

8. Use analytical assessment based on the guidelines provided so that students understand what is expected and how a weak paper can be improved. Paragraph assessment guidelines are provided at the ends of Chapters 1 and 2, and essay assessment guidelines are provided at the ends of Chapters 3–7. (Elements are added to these guidelines in each succeeding chapter.)

    Appendix B includes more complete essay assessment guidelines with the characteristics of very good, average, and weak essays in all three areas of assessment: (1) content and ideas, (2) organization and form, and (3) writing conventions. Revise or replace the guidelines if they do not fit your teaching or your students.

9. In assessing a paper, give three separate scores, one each for content and ideas, organization and form, and writing conventions so that students understand their strengths and weaknesses. An analytical assessment of 8/10 (8 out of a possible score of 10) for content and ideas, 4/5 for organization and form, and 1/5 for writing conventions, for example, indicates that the student has done well in two out of three areas. (Weighting content and ideas twice as heavily as the other two categories lets students know that you feel that the logic, clarity, and sincerity of the thoughts expressed are the most important aspects of their papers.)

10. As a class, assess an outside paper or one of the student models in the book so that students will know how to use the guidelines when they revise their own papers. Alternatively, give your students examples of what you consider high, medium, and low papers. Use papers from a previous class to avoid embarrassment.

11. If it works for your class, use a *portfolio approach* for evaluation. Rather than evaluate the core writing assignments with a letter grade, assess them using the assessment guidelines and numerical scores. Then allow students to revise a selection of already-assessed papers for a midterm grade and another selection of papers for a final grade. The portfolio approach allows students to come back to their writing later with more insights into the topic, perhaps, and with a better idea of rhetorical and language conventions because of intervening study. To avoid inflated grades, some teachers average the scores on successive revisions rather than considering only the last, best effort.

William R. Smalzer

Acknowledgments

TEXT CREDITS

Page 5: From Lucille K. Forer, *Birth Order and Life Roles,* 1969. Courtesy of Charles C. Thomas, Publisher, Springfield, Illinois.

Page 13: From "Born for Each Other?" by Pamela Withers, *McCall's Magazine,* February 1989. Reprinted by permission of Pamela Withers.

Page 35: From "As It Was in the Beginning" by E. Pauline Johnson, in *Moccasin Maker,* University of Arizona Press, 1987.

Page 42: Modified and reproduced by special permission of the Publisher, Consulting Psychologists Press, Inc., Palo Alto, CA 94303 from *Gifts Differing* by Isabel Briggs Myers and Peter B. Myers. Copyright 1980 by Consulting Psychologists Press, Inc. All rights reserved. Further reproduction is prohibited without the Publisher's written consent.

Page 66: From *Translations from the Chinese* by Arthur Waley. Copyright 1919 and renewed 1947 by Arthur Waley. Reprinted by permission of Alfred A. Knopf, Inc. and HarperCollins Publishers Ltd.

Page 75: From *The Prophet* by Kahlil Gibran. Copyright 1923 by Kahlil Gibran and renewed 1951 by Administrators C.T.A. of Kahlil Gibran Estate and Mary G. Gibran. Reprinted by permission of Alfred A. Knopf, Inc.

Page 100: "The Ant and the Grasshopper," from *Aesop & Company.* Text copyright © 1991 by Barbara Bader. Reprinted by permission of Houghton Mifflin Co. All rights reserved.

Page 102: Excerpted from "The Ant and the Grasshopper," from *The Complete Stories of W. Somerset Maugham.* Reprinted by permission from A. P. Watt Literary Fund on behalf of the Royal Literary Fund, and Reed Consumer Books, Ltd.

Page 131: Peale, Dr. Norman Vincent. *Saturday Evening Post,* May/June 1975. Reprinted with permission from the Ruth S. Peale Marital Trust.

Page 137: From *Lies, Deception and Truth.* Copyright © 1988 by Ann E. Weiss. Reprinted by permission of Houghton Mifflin Co. All rights reserved.

Page 163: From "Choosing Mates – The American Way" in *Society,* March/April 1992. Copyright © 1992 by Transaction Publishers. Reprinted by permission from Transaction Publishers.

Page 171: Andrea B. Rugh, *Family in Contemporary Egypt* (Syracuse: Syracuse University Press, 1984), pages 121–122, 124, 125–126, 135. By permission of the publisher.

Page 175: *The Ann Landers Encyclopedia: A to Z* by Ann Landers. Reprinted by permission of Doubleday and Co., Inc.

Page 194: From *Ancient Futures* by Helena Norberg-Hodge. Copyright © 1991 by Helena Norberg-Hodge. Reprinted with permission of Sierra Club Books.

Page 222: From *Filters Against Folly* by Garrett Hardin. Copyright © 1985 by Garrett Hardin. Used by permission of Viking Penguin, a division of Penguin Books USA Inc.

Page 228: Simon, Julian; *The Ultimate Resource*. Copyright © 1981 by Princeton University Press. Reprinted by permission of Princeton University Press and Blackwell Publishers.

Pages 81, 115, 142, 177, and 207: The essays on these pages were contributed by students whose names appear following their work.

PHOTOGRAPHIC CREDITS

Cover photo: © Inner-Visions

Page 12: *(from top)* © Ron Chapple/FPG International Corp., © Christopher Bissell/Tony Stone Images.

Page 31: © Ron Chapple/FPG International Corp.

Page 41: *(from left)* © Peter Angelo Simon/The Stock Market, © Richard Gross/The Stock Market, © Michael Rosenfeld/ Tony Stone Images.

Page 65: *(clockwise from left)* © Mug Shots/The Stock Market, © Anthony Edgeworth/ The Stock Market, © Arthur Tilley/FPG International Corp.

Page 74: © Bob Krist/Tony Stone Images.

Page 108: *(clockwise from upper left)* © Mark Kozlowski/FPG International Corp., © Spencer Grant/FPG International Corp., © Spencer Grant/FPG International Corp.

Page 159: © Roy Morsch/The Stock Market.

Page 191: *(from top)* © Robert E. Daemmrich/Tony Images, © Paul Chesley/Tony Stone Images.

Page 199: © Dave Bartruff/FPG International Corp.

Page 219: *(from top)* © Vanessa Vick/Science Source/Photo Researchers, Inc., © Alon Reininger/Contact Press/The Stock Market, © Michael Tamborrino/FPG International Corp.

Page 227: *(from left)* © Ron Chapple/FPG International Corp., © Spencer Grant/FPG International Corp.

ILLUSTRATIONS

Pages 99, 127, and 136: Randy Jones.

Birth Order
Your place in the family, your place in life

Do children raised in the same family end up with the same personalities? Why or why not?

1 GETTING A GRIP ON THE TOPIC

A. Reflection

Make a list of the children in your family, from oldest to youngest, and include your name in the list.

_____   _____

_____   _____

_____   _____

_____

Now look at the adjectives and phrases that follow. Read each one and decide which child in your family it describes best. (The words may apply to more than one child, but assign them to the child who comes to mind first.) Write the words after the name they describe.

a fast learner   capable
a tattletale (one who informs   confident
    on his brothers and sisters)   sometimes lonely
parental   protected by parents
flexible   responsible
independent   dependent on parents

Follow-up   Check your list against a classmate's. Is there any similarity in the descriptions you chose for the oldest child? The youngest?

B. Discussion

Read each statement, and write *A* if you agree with it and *D* if you disagree.

_____ 1. Older children in a family are often parental and bossy toward the younger children.

_____ 2. Parents are more relaxed and less excited about children after the first one.

_____ 3. Older children are more responsible because the younger siblings depend on them.

_____ 4. The youngest child is often spoiled because of all the care and attention he or she receives.

_____ 5. In most families, there is competition among the children for their parents' love and attention.

_____ 6. When there is a fight between an older and younger sibling, parents will usually take the side of the younger one and protect him or her.
_____ 7. Parents are stricter with their first children than with their later ones.
_____ 8. Most children who are difficult and demand a lot of attention will grow up to be difficult people.

Follow-up Compare your answers in pairs or small groups. Explain why you agree or disagree with each statement.

C. Notes on the main reading

It is interesting to notice that in a family of several children, the children are usually very different from each other. To explain the differences, psychologists point out that even with the same parents, each child's environment is a bit different. Furthermore, each child reacts to his or her environment differently because of differences in personality. Other people explain the differences between children in the same family by destiny: God has made each of us the person we are.

In "How Your Birth Order Influences Your Life Adjustment," Lucille K. Forer explains the differences between siblings by looking at their *birth order*. According to this article, whether one is an only, an oldest, a middle, or a youngest child determines to a great extent the kind of person that one will become.

Though not technical, this almost scientific reading is dense, with many separate ideas in a few pages. Make it easier to read by breaking very long sentences up into meaningful parts like this:

> The first and most obvious effect / of taking a certain position in the family / is the relationship we have / with respect to the people / already there.

After a brief introduction, Forer discusses two main points about the effects of birth order. These main points appear as boldface headings in the text. Preview the article by looking at the title and the headings.

VOCABULARY EXERCISE

To become familiar with some of the new vocabulary, work in pairs or small groups and suggest how each word or expression in the list that follows might be used in the reading. Check a dictionary for the meanings if necessary. One sample answer has been done for you.

hierarchy   unconscious
ploy   peer
imitate   barrier
loneliness

> hierarchy: Forer might use "hierarchy" to describe the authority
> each child has in the family, from highest to lowest, according to
> the child's birth order. She probably means the children in a family
> are not equal in the power or authority that they have.

Sample answer for "hierarchy."

GLOSSARY

Review the glossary before reading the selection, for help with some of the
more difficult vocabulary.

hovering (line 9): waiting nervously nearby
verbalize (line 15): say
perception (line 21): understanding
suppress (line 25): stop, keep inside
struggles (line 26): tries hard
delight (line 35): pleasure, joy
benefit (line 38): receive advantage or help
tendency (line 38): likelihood of acting a certain way
judgments (line 40): decisions
barrier (line 44): wall
sustenance (line 46): food and care
standards (line 51): requirements or expectations
identification with the parents (line 53): feeling of being like them
diluted (line 54): weaker
self-concept (line 68): view of oneself
adequate (line 71): good enough, satisfactory

D. Read for the main idea

Try to predict what Forer will say by changing the headings in this reading
into questions. For example, the first heading, "Relationship with Parents,"

might become, "What is each child's relationship with the parents?"

Read the whole selection to answer this main idea question: *In what three important ways does birth order affect a person?*

How Your Birth Order Influences Your Life Adjustment*
Lucille K. Forer

When we are born into a family unit or brought into it through adoption or as a step-child, we take a certain place in the family hierarchy. We become *only* child, *oldest* child, *middle* child, or *youngest* child.

The first and most obvious effect of taking a certain position in   5
the family is the relationship we have with respect to the people already there. If there are only adults present, we are in a very close and often intense relationship with them, as anyone knows who has had a child or who has watched first-time parents hovering over their infants. This constant and close relationship gives the first child in the   10
family an opportunity to imitate and learn from these adults to the fullest possible extent. The first child imitates their physical mannerisms and learns speech from them. He learns many more things and much of the learning takes place on an *unconscious* level. That is, neither the parents nor the child verbalize that thus and so is the way to   15
do something. The child observes and imitates.

Relationship with Parents

From the beginning the parents treat the child in accordance with his place in the family and soon the child recognizes that place. He is *the child* in the family, and he tends to think of himself as a child in relation to adults. The only child never has any reason to change such   20

*REPRINTED WITH PERMISSION FROM *PSYCHOLOGY TODAY* MAGAZINE, Copyright ©
1979 (Sussex Publishers, Inc).

perception of his role and he tends to carry into adulthood a strong feeling of being a child in relation to other people.

The first child, who becomes the older or oldest child, does not have this unlimited time to view himself as the child in the relationship with his parents. When a sibling arrives, he tries to suppress the view of himself as a child and he struggles to be *parental*. We shall find that in both childhood and adulthood the older or oldest child's emphasis upon being "parental" offers him both advantages and problems.

Children who follow the first child in the family come into a situation where the relationship with the parent is, except in most unusual cases, shared with another child. The parents themselves have been changed by the preceding child or children in many ways. They are more experienced as parents. They may not welcome their later children with as much delight as they did their first child, but they are probably less tense and anxious about being able to care for them properly. The later children enjoy many advantages as a result of having more relaxed parents. They benefit from the tendency of parents to try out ideas on their first child and to be more tolerant with later children. After testing judgments about matters ranging from when to toilet train a child to attitudes taken about dating, parents are relatively certain of approaches to take with later children and they are usually more relaxed (and exhausted) ones.

The first child serves as a barrier between later children and the parents. He is one of the models for his siblings. Later children in a family do not feel the same dependency on the parents for sustenance and companionship as did the first child. They have a "peer" to turn to when the parents are not available. Consequently they do not have such intense feelings of loneliness when the attention of the parents is directed elsewhere, nor do they seem to feel so inadequate when they do not meet the standards of their parents.

Extremely important to differentiating later children from first children is the extent to which direct identification with the parents is diluted for the later children. The later children seem more content to move gradually from child to adult. They do not seem to try as hard, as does the oldest child, to be parental and adult even during childhood.

How Children See Themselves and Others

The child becomes known as the family's only child, oldest child, middle child, or youngest child, depending on his birth order. He is thought and talked about as having that place in the family. Both in his mind and in the minds of other people an important part of his identity is his family position.

The other members of the family assume certain attitudes toward each child in terms of his birth order. Parents usually expect their oldest child to be more capable and more responsible than the younger children. The oldest child comes to think about himself in the same way. These ways of seeing himself, of thinking about himself because of his sibling role, become part of his self-concept.

Older or oldest brother or sister tends to develop a self-concept that includes the belief that "I can do many things better than my siblings can. I am more adequate than other people in many situations."

The middle child comes to think of himself as sometimes better able to do things than other people because he is usually more capable than his younger sibling or siblings. Sometimes, though, he must turn to his older sibling or to his parents for help and so he comes to think of himself as able to obtain help when he needs it.

The youngest child tends to think, "I am less able to do many things than other people. But I need not be concerned because there are always others around to take care of me."

The role we take as the result of being in a certain place in the family not only causes us to think about ourselves in certain ways, but it also causes us to think about other people in certain ways. The oldest tends to expect other people to be relatively less capable. The middle child has less specific expectations about the capabilities of other people. The youngest may see others as more adequate while the only child tends to think, "I am most secure when there are parents around to take care of me, but when they are not there, I have no one to turn to for help. So I'd better learn to take care of myself as much as possible."

The place in the family establishes for the child a specific role to be played within the family group. It influences him to develop certain attitudes toward himself and toward other people and helps him develop specific patterns of behavior.

Follow-up Answer the main idea question here: _____

_____

_____

E. Read for more detail

Read the article a second time. Use the questions to go more deeply into the reading and to bring your experience to it.

1. As you read, take notes by filling in the grid with phrases that characterize each birth order.

oldest child:
middle child:
youngest child:
only child:

2. Which birth order is yours? How accurate is the author's description of your birth order? (Check one.)

   _____ very accurate   _____ somewhat accurate

   _____ not accurate at all   _____ a little accurate

3. Think of family members or friends for the other birth orders. How well do the author's descriptions fit them?
4. Which birth order results in the most responsible child? The least responsible?

5. In what ways might an only child become more independent than a middle or youngest child?
6. *Key words* Make a list of six words that seem important to the article. Write down why each word is important, and what it means, if necessary.

> unconscious: This is an important word because it characterizes how children learn their birth-order behavior, without parents realizing they're actually teaching this to the child. "Unconscious" means without being aware, without knowing.

Follow-up Discuss your answers in small groups or as a class.

2   RESPONDING TO THE MAIN READING

A. Journals: A private audience

Choose two of the following topics. Write at least 75 words on each of them in your journal notebook. Express your opinions and feelings honestly. These journal entries are for your eyes only, so do not spend a lot of time using a dictionary or worrying about grammar.

1. Did you like this article? Why or why not?
2. If you had a choice, would you prefer another birth order to the one that you have? Which one? Why?
3. Did the author's descriptions remind you of anyone you know? Who? In what ways?
4. Does this reading make sense to you? Do you find it believable and logical?

B. Shared writing

Choose at least two topics and write for a total of 30 minutes. Your audience is your classmates, with whom you will share your writing. Your classmates will be interested not only in *what* you feel but also in *why* you feel that way. Therefore, you will want to express your views clearly and support them.

1. Do you think the author's discussion applies more to the typical nuclear family of the United States than to families in general?
2. Is Forer's discussion of birth order accurate or inaccurate for the children in your family? Explain.
3. The author devotes much more time to the oldest, only, and youngest children than to middle children. Does she mean that middle children are less influenced by birth order? Explain.
4. Do you prefer another explanation of the differences between children in the same family? If yes, explain.

C. Feedback on your writing

Get feedback on how clear and logical your thinking and writing are. Select one of your writings from the previous section, "Shared Writing," and read it to a group of two or three classmates. Each member of the group will read one of his or her writings. Follow the procedure in "Peer Feedback Guidelines" at the end of this chapter.

Follow-up In 5 minutes, evaluate in writing how well your audience received your paper. Could they summarize it accurately? Did they understand your points? How could you make your paper clearer? More interesting to your audience?

3 GOING MORE DEEPLY INTO THE TOPIC

One of these couples doesn't seem to be getting along well.
Do you think that the birth order of each partner might play a role
in the success of relationships?

A. Preparing to read

"Born for Each Other?", an article from *McCall's*, a popular magazine, has a
lighter style than the main reading. The writer, Pamela Withers, has two purposes here: to inform and to entertain the reader. The subject itself is perhaps
more interesting to us – which birth orders are the best combinations in marriages. The title of the article borrows from an expression one hears often
when people talk of a good match. If a man and a woman were "born for each
other," they are perfect for each other in every way.

Notice how Withers introduces the text with an example to grab our attention. Then she discusses each birth order and its best marital matches.

Before you read, think of couples you know (and whose birth orders you know). Choose one couple that is happily married and another couple that is not happily married. Keep the couples in mind as you read "Born for Each Other?"

B. First reading

Read the selection to answer this main idea question: *Does the article explain why the two marriages you chose above are happy or unhappy marriages?*

Born for Each Other?
Pamela Withers

Ronald and Lois, married for two decades, consider themselves a happy couple, but in the early years of their marriage
5 both were disturbed by persistent arguments that seemed to fade away without ever being truly resolved. They uncovered clues to what was going wrong
10 by researching a fascinating subject: how birth order (whether you came along first, second or later in your family) affects not only your personal-
15 ity, but also how compatible you are with your mate!

Ronald and Lois are only children, and "onlies" grow up accustomed to being the apple
20 of their parents' eyes. They're not necessarily spoiled – just used to constant attention and approval. Match two onlies and you have partners who subcon-
25 sciously expect each other to continue fulfilling this expectation, while neither has much experience in the "giving" end. The habit of trying to dominate
30 a relationship and taking it personally when your spouse does the same can result in quarrels that sound alike from one onlies household to another.

35 All those patterns set in motion by birth and gender order don't prescribe what must occur; they simply describe tendencies that may need to be rec-
40 ognized or overcome.

Here's a list of common birth-order characteristics – and some thoughts on the best (and worst) marital matches for each:

Oldest Child

45 The oldest tends to be self-assured, responsible, a high achiever and relatively serious and reserved, with parental qualities as a result of caring for

50 younger siblings. He may become a perfectionist and worrier who finds it difficult to take criticism or tolerate others' mistakes, and he may be slow to

55 make friends, perhaps content with only one companion.

The more "same sex" siblings an oldest has, the more independent and domineering he or

60 she is and the more difficult it may be for him or her to find a suitable mate. The best matches are with a youngest, an only, or a mate raised with a large num-

65 ber of opposite-sex siblings. The worst match is with another oldest of same-sex siblings, since the two will be too sovereign to share a household com-

70 fortably. The oldest sister of brothers is popular because she values men and is a good sport. She matches well with a youngest, whom she can lead

75 and nurture. The oldest brother of sisters tends to be easygoing, fun-loving, considerate and very fond of women. He is good at pleasing all females and

80 is especially well matched with the youngest sister of brothers.

Youngest Child

The baby of the family thrives on attention and tends to be outgoing, adventurous,

85 optimistic, creative, easygoing and less ambitious than others in the family. He may lack self-discipline and have difficulty making decisions on his own.

90 The youngest may learn to manipulate, either by pouting or by being charming.

A younger sister of sisters will match best with an oldest

95 sibling, who will see through her manipulation and is charmed by her playfulness. A youngest brother of brothers, often headstrong, unpredictable

100 and romantic, will match best with an oldest or middle sister of brothers, whom he will allow to control his life in an unobtrusive manner. The youngest of

105 same-sex siblings should avoid each other, since neither is nurturing, nor are they accustomed to members of the opposite sex. The youngest sister of brothers,

110 often a tomboy and a flirt, is best matched with an oldest brother of sisters, who will happily indulge these traits. She's smart to stay away from an old-

115 est brother of brothers or, worse, a youngest brother of brothers. The youngest brother of sisters is popular because he

enjoys women who are sup-
120 portive, admiring and eager to
please.

Middle Child

The middle child is influenced by many variables; however, middles are often intro-
125 verted, less likely to take
initiative or achieve high academic standards and more anxious and self-critical than others.
130 The middle child's most comfortable marriage duplicates a
relationship with a close sibling.
Middles often successfully
marry other middles, since both
135 are strong on tact, not so strong
on aggressiveness and tend to
crave affection.

Only Child

The only child picks up characteristics of her same-sex par-

140 ent's birth order, and this may
influence who represents her
best match. She is often most
comfortable when alone, but
since an "only" tends to be a
145 well-adjusted individual, she'll
eventually learn to relate to any
chosen spouse.
The male only child expects
his wife to make life easier
150 without getting much in return;
he is sometimes best matched
with a younger or middle sister
of brothers, or a maternal, oldest sister of brothers. His most
155 difficult match is with another
only. The female only child,
who tends to be slightly more
flexible, is well matched with
an older man, who will indulge
160 her tendency to test his love.
Any birth order will do, but her
best match is apt to be a brother
of sisters. Her worst match?
Another only, of course.

Follow-up   Answer the main idea question here: _____

_____

_____

C. Additional readings

Read the selection again. Mark any places in the text that are still unclear to
you. Then read these passages once more to improve your understanding of
them.

D. Negotiating the meaning

Write at least 75 words on this selection. Write on any or all of the following:

▶ whether you liked it or not, and why
▶ whether you prefer it to the previous selection
▶ what you have trouble understanding

Follow-up   To a group of two or three, read what you have written. Read your reaction a second time if necessary.

   Each group member will respond with (1) a question, (2) a comment, and/or (3) clarification. Every group member should read what he or she has written. As a group, choose one response to share with the whole class.

E. Discussion: Critical thinking

Discuss these questions in pairs, small groups, or as a class.

1. Which writer, Forer or Withers, is more informative? Which one is more entertaining? What can you conclude about each writer's profession or background from their writing?
2. Some psychologists criticize birth-order theory as wrong and unscientific. They feel there are many other more important influences on people's personalities. Are you a supporter or critic of birth-order theory? Explain.
3. Which influences or factors other than birth order might explain why children in the same family often have very different personalities?
4. Do Forer and Withers basically agree or disagree with each other in how they look at birth order? Explain.

4 IMPROVING WRITING SKILLS

A. Using another's writing: Paraphrasing

For your core writing assignment in this chapter, you will be asked to write a paragraph on a topic related to birth order. You may want to use some of Forer's or Wither's ideas in your writing. Use their ideas, but express them in your own words, for two reasons: First, you want your audience to know that you understand the ideas and are not just copying them from the text. Second, direct quotations from other writers do not belong in pieces of paragraph length. (Quotations can be used effectively in essays and other longer pieces.)

To express an author's ideas in your own words is to paraphrase. Practice paraphrasing Forer effectively by doing Exercise 1.

 EXERCISE 1   Paraphrasing sentences

Work with a partner and follow these guidelines to paraphrase the quotations that follow.

a.   Find the sentence in the main reading text, "How Your Birth Order Influences your Life Adjustment," and read the whole context (the lines before and after, too) several times.
b.   With your partner, rewrite the sentence in your own words. To benefit more from the exercise, change the structure of the original sentence and do not use the words given in italics in your paraphrase.
c.   If necessary, revise your first try to make your paraphrase clear, economical, and grammatical.

1.   (lines 17–18) ". . . the parents *treat* the child *in accordance with his place* in the family and soon the child recognizes that place."

> *1. Paraphrase: The child in a family learns his place in the family from the way that his parents behave with him, which is determined by that child's birth order. (28 words)*
>
> *Revision: The child soon learns his role in the family from his parents' behavior with him, which is influenced by the child's birth order. (23 words)*

2. (lines 25–26) "When a sibling arrives, he tries to *suppress the view* of himself as a child and he *struggles* to be parental."
3. (lines 38–40) "[Later children] *benefit* from the *tendency* of parents to *try out ideas* on their first child and to be more tolerant with later children."
4. (lines 60–62) "Both *in his mind* and *in the minds* of other people an important part of his *identity* is his family position."

B. Meeting reader expectations: Writing paragraphs with topic sentences

Simply put, a paragraph is an indented block of writing that expresses one *main idea.* Not all writers actually express the main idea in every paragraph, but for students trying to improve their writing, it is useful to express the main idea in a *topic sentence.* Beginning your paragraphs with a topic sentence helps you decide what details you will choose to support the topic sentence. By letting your topic sentence guide the choice of support, you will write a *unified* paragraph: a paragraph that sticks to its main idea without losing the point.

✎ EXERCISE 2 The main idea

Read the model paragraph and answer the questions that follow.

There are obviously factors other than birth order that affect how we deal with other people. Our society plays a big role. Some societies are very communal, and people other than parents are very involved in raising the children. Heredity is also important in differentiating siblings from each other. Many experts accept that characteristics like temperament, sensitivity to the environment, and intelligence are inherited. These characteristics vary from child to child in the same family; they also play a role in the child's personality. Last, our parents themselves are a big factor in what kind of people we are. From them we learn to be cheerful, kind, helpful people – or not. The issue of how we are as people is a complicated one; birth order plays a role, but so do factors like society, heredity, and parents.

1. Is the main idea expressed in a topic sentence by the author? If so, underline it.

2. How many main points support the topic sentence? Number them. Is the paragraph *complete*, that is, are there enough details to convince you of the author's main idea? Briefly, what are the main points of support?
3. Is this paragraph unified? Explain.
4. What is the function of the last sentence in the paragraph?

✎ EXERCISE 3   Topic sentences

A good topic sentence satisfies the following two criteria:

a. The topic is *narrow* enough to cover in a paragraph.
b. The statement about the topic is *specific*, but general enough to lead to a well-developed paragraph.

Look at these examples with a partner. Discuss whether they meet the two criteria.

1. Psychology is an interesting subject to study.
2. I wanted to sign up for the adolescent psychology course during course registration yesterday, but the class was already full.
3. B. F. Skinner was a famous American psychologist who studied the learning process.
4. Children who grow up without siblings usually learn to play well by themselves.
5. The three most important ingredients in a successful marriage are good communication, shared goals, and a willingness to compromise.
6. Research has shown that children from happy marriages are more likely to have successful marriages themselves.

✎ EXERCISE 4   Narrowing the topic

Practice narrowing these general topics into more specific topics that are suitable for single paragraphs. Do this in two steps, narrowing more with each step.

1. work   *teaching*   *teaching foreign students*

2. food   _____   _____

3. people   _____   _____

4. recreation   _____   _____

5. relationships   _____   _____

✎ **EXERCISE 5   Judging the topic sentence**

Judge these topic sentences. Write *Good* if the topic is narrow and specific enough to be covered in one paragraph, but still general enough to be developed into a good paragraph. Write *Weak* if the topic sentence would not lead to a good paragraph. Discuss why.

_____ 1. Children are always interesting to watch.
_____ 2. Americans don't seem to make their children behave in public.
_____ 3. A little boy I know, Tommy, slapped his mother in the supermarket yesterday.
_____ 4. When a boy in my country turns eight, he faces a number of new responsibilities.
_____ 5. Children in my country are more dependent than children in the United States.

✎ **EXERCISE 6   Completing the topic**

Complete each of these topics with a specific statement to make a good topic sentence. Each topic sentence should have the potential to lead to a well-developed paragraph. (Your topic sentences do not have to relate to the readings in this chapter.)

1. An only child . . .
2. A middle child . . .
3. The oldest child . . .
4. Parents with a first child . . .
5. A child with many siblings . . .

C. Language conventions

CLAUSES, PHRASES, AND SENTENCES

A clause contains a subject and a complete verb that has tense:

(1) Not everyone agrees about the effects of birth order.
(2) . . . because there are many influences on personality
(3) . . . who are born later
(4) But birth order helps to explain some differences in siblings.

Clauses can be *independent*, as in examples 1 and 4, or they can be *dependent*, as in 2 and 3. An independent clause can stand alone because it expresses a complete thought. It is a sentence.

A dependent clause cannot stand alone; it must appear with an independent clause. A dependent clause is not a sentence. Dependent clauses begin with *subordinators*, words like *because, when, while, although, if, whereas,* and *since,* and the relative pronouns *who, which,* and *that.*

A phrase is a group of related words that may include a subject or a verb, but not both. There are many kinds of phrases:

<u>Birth-order theory</u> has been used to explain differences in siblings.
noun phrase   *verb phrase*   *infinitive phrase*   *prepositional phrase*

Phrases together make up clauses and sentences. Of course, phrases cannot stand alone because they are not sentences; they are only parts of sentences.

Prepositional phrases are sometimes troublesome for students because they make it difficult to find subjects and verbs in a clause. They begin with prepositions, words like *from, with, in, without, by, at, for, of, because of,* and *in spite of.* They have a noun (e.g., *beginning, place, family*) or a gerund (e.g., *pouting, being*) as an object:

From the beginning the parents treat the child in accordance with his place in the family.

The youngest may learn to manipulate, either by pouting or being charming.

To identify dependent and independent clauses in sentences, first find the prepositional phrases. This will make it easier to identify the clauses because a prepositional phrase is never part of a subject or a verb in a sentence.

EXERCISE 7   Identifying phrases and clauses

Underline the prepositional phrases once. Underline clauses twice.

1. The Egyptian family is often an extended family and includes relatives beyond the nuclear family.
2. Grandparents, uncles, aunts, and cousins are more likely to live with a family than they are in many western countries.
3. This extended family configuration probably alters the effects of birth order.
4. There may not be as much competition among siblings for the parents' affection.
5. With other adult relatives in the household, there may be a larger source of attention and affection for the children.
6. It would be surprising if none of the conclusions of birth-order theory were correct for Egypt, however.
7. For example, we would still expect the oldest child to see himself as more capable and responsible in comparison with others.

FRAGMENTS

Unlike speech, more formal writing requires that what looks like a sentence actually be a grammatical sentence. Sometimes what looks like a sentence is not one. Look at these examples:

    (1) Because I got up late this morning.
    (2) Finishing my homework before going to bed.

A grammatical sentence needs a subject and a complete verb; it must also express a complete thought. Examples 1 and 2 are not sentences because:

▶ Example 1 is a dependent clause, which can't stand alone.
▶ Example 2 is a phrase with no complete verb or subject.

Although they are written as complete sentences with capital letters and periods, examples 1 and 2 are *fragments* because they are not independent clauses.

✎ EXERCISE 8   Identifying fragments

Underline any fragments in the following groups of items. Decide why each underlined item is a fragment; write the letter of the reason (*a* or *b*) in the blank. If there is no fragment, write *OK*.

a.   It is a dependent clause.
b.   It is a phrase that lacks a complete verb and/or a subject.

_____ 1. Parents try to give a fair share of the family's resources to each child. In order to distribute the resources evenly.

_____ 2. The children themselves are not so interested in an even distribution of resources. They compete. Because each one wants as much as possible of the parents' time and attention.

_____ 3. Smaller children usually learn that they can compete with older ones. Despite their small size.

_____ 4. Because they are smaller and weaker, younger children can usually count on the help of the parents in a dispute with siblings. Most parents will intervene.

_____ 5. Younger children learn to use their smallness and weakness to their advantage. They can easily become tattletales. Or even crybabies.

_____ 6. A tattletale reports misdeeds of a sibling to parents. For example, the tattletale will say things like, "Mommy, Bobbie hit me again!"

_____ 7. A crybaby soon learns the power of tears to get what he or she wants. And to win in a conflict with an older sibling.

HOW TO CORRECT FRAGMENTS

You can correct a fragment by (1) adding it to an independent clause that it logically goes with, or (2) making the fragment an independent clause. Look at these examples:

WRONG   In a dispute between siblings, parents usually take the side of the younger child. Because that child is weaker and smaller.

CORRECTION 1   In a dispute between siblings, parents usually take the side of the younger child because that child is weaker and smaller.

CORRECTION 2   In a dispute between siblings, parents usually take the side of the younger child. They do so because that child is weaker and smaller.

(*Note:* Correction 2 is better when correction 1 would result in a sentence that is too long.)

EXERCISE 9   Correcting fragments

Read each item and underline any fragments. Then rewrite the entire item, correcting the fragments using correction 1 or correction 2.

1. Two only children who marry each other may have problems. Because both are used to a lot of attention and approval.
2. An oldest child may find that another oldest is not a good marriage match. An oldest may be happier with an only child. Or with a youngest child.
3. A youngest sister of sisters matches best with an oldest brother. Who will appreciate her charm. Also tolerate her manipulation.
4. The best match for a middle child is often another middle child. Since both are tactful. And normally not aggressive.
5. Although only children find it easier to make good matches. There are bad matches for them. For example, another only.

EXERCISE 10   Editing for fragments

Read the paragraph at the top of the next page. Then do the following:

a. Underline all fragments.
b. Rewrite the whole paragraph, correcting the fragments by connecting them to other sentences or adding the necessary words to make them independent clauses.

Critics of birth-order theory say that it is not scientific. Because one cannot prove it. And because it is like astrology. Interesting, perhaps, but not to be taken seriously. Supporters of birth-order theory admit that it alone does not determine what kind of people we are. Our parents and society, for example, are very strong influences. Whether we are happy or gloomy, calm or nervous, or good-natured or bad-tempered people. However, birth order does play a role. Determining the degree to which a child is happy, calm, and good-natured, for example. It plays another role. In determining how a child uses his happiness, calmness, and good-naturedness in dealing with other people.

5 CORE WRITING ASSIGNMENT

A. Writing topics

Choose a topic (or topics) for writing from the following list. You will be asked to develop a paragraph on your topic in the remaining sections of this chapter.

1. *Comparison/contrast*   Summarize what Forer and/or Withers say about your birth order. Then compare that to how you actually see yourself. How closely do the authors' ideas match your view? Begin your paragraph with a topic sentence that characterizes the match between the theory and your reality.
2. *Description/example*   Which of the birth orders seems to have the easiest life? The most difficult one? The happiest one? The most attractive life? Choose one and describe it by telling what makes that life easy, difficult, happy, or attractive.
3. *Cause/effect*   Choose a couple you know well. Discuss how successful their relationship is and find causes in birth-order theory to support your evaluation.
4. *Narrative*   Relate a true incident that illustrates a point about birth order. Make that point clear in your topic sentence.

B. Generating ideas: Free writing

Write freely for 20 minutes on your topic. Write without worrying about grammar and vocabulary. Write whatever comes to your mind, without trying to judge or organize your ideas. You are writing to help yourself think about the topic at this point.

Follow-up   Read what you have written. What main idea about your topic has emerged from this free writing? Write that main idea down now. Circle the parts of your free writing that support your main idea directly.

C. Expanding your point of view

With your main idea in mind, reread sections of the readings that you will need in your paragraph. Take notes by paraphrasing the authors' words.

Then have a 5-minute conference with a classmate. Tell your partner (1) what your topic is, (2) what your main idea is, and (3) how you plan to support the main idea. When you finish, your partner will summarize orally, in two or three sentences, what you said.

D. Initial drafts

FIRST DRAFT

Begin with a topic sentence that expresses your main idea by narrowing the topic and making a specific statement about it. Support the topic sentence as effectively as you can. If you use an author's ideas, paraphrase them and mention the author's name. Feel free to use terminology and new vocabulary from the readings, of course.

REVISION

Leave your first draft for a while. Then revise it. When good writers revise, they do not check their spelling and grammar. Rather, they check their *thinking*. They check how clearly they have thought about the topic and how clearly they have expressed their thoughts.

When you revise your first draft, ask yourself these questions:

▶ Have I thought about this topic enough?
▶ Have I expressed my ideas about the topic clearly?
▶ Have I included enough points of support to convince my audience?

See (on the next page) the earlier draft of the model paragraph from Exercise 2 in Part 4 and how the writer revised it. For more direction in revising, use the criteria listed in the "Paragraph Assessment Guidelines" at the end of this chapter. Mark your revised draft "Revision 1."

E. Review, revision, and assessment

PEER FEEDBACK

Get feedback on how clear and logical your thinking and writing are. Read your paragraph to a group of two or three classmates. Each member of the group will read his or her paper to the group. Follow the "Peer Feedback Guidelines" at the end of this chapter.

FURTHER REVISION

How well did your group receive your paper? Could they summarize it accurately? Did they understand your main points? Secondary points? How could your paper be clearer and more interesting to your audience? Make notes of changes you need to make.

>   There are obviously factors other than birth order that
>   how we deal with other people.
> affect ~~what kind of people we are~~. Our society plays a big role.
>
> Some societies are very communal, and people other than
>   parents
> ~~the father and mother~~ are very involved in raising the children.
>   siblings from each other.
> Heredity is also important in differentiating ~~children from each~~
> ~~other, even within the same family.~~* Our parents themselves are
>   Last,
> a big factor in what kind of people we are. From them we learn to
>   not.
> be cheerful, kind, helpful people – or ~~gloomy, unhelpful people~~. The
>
> issue of how we are as people is a complicated one; ~~and~~ birth
>   plays a role, but so do factors like society, heredity, and parents.
> order ~~is just one of several factors~~.
>
> *Examples needed to make this clear: Many experts accept that
>
> characteristics like temperament, sensitivity to the environment,
>
> and intelligence are inherited. These characteristics vary from
>
> child to child in the same family; they also play a role in the
>
> child's personality.

Earlier draft of paragraph from Exercise 2 in Part 4.

If necessary, revise your paper using the feedback you got from your group. Edit your paper for fragments. Submit all drafts to your teacher, with the last one marked "Revision 2" at the top.

If you choose not to revise, write a paragraph to your teacher summarizing the feedback you received and explaining why you decided not to revise.

TEACHER ASSESSMENT

Your teacher will assess your paper using the "Paragraph Assessment Guidelines" at the end of the chapter. Your teacher may give you a grade on the paragraph or allow you to make further revisions before assigning a grade.

PEER FEEDBACK GUIDELINES

Writers

☐ Read the paper clearly, a second time if necessary.

☐ Respond to listeners' comments and questions.

☐ Ask for suggestions if you want them.

Listeners

☐ Listen quietly until the writer finishes reading.

☐ Briefly summarize what you understood, orally.

☐ Pick out parts of the paper (words, expressions, or ideas) that stand out for you. Share these parts with the group.

☐ If you wish, share with the group how the writing makes you feel and ask questions about parts that are not clear.

☐ Do not make negative comments or tell the writer what changes to make.

PARAGRAPH ASSESSMENT GUIDELINES

These are the criteria for a well-written paragraph. Use this checklist to critically examine your writing and determine how it can be improved. Your teacher will use it to evaluate your final draft.

Content and ideas

☐ The writer has thought about the topic and has a clear main idea.

☐ The paragraph is convincing because there are enough logical points to support the main idea.

☐ No important point is left out; no irrelevant point is included.

Organization and form

☐ The reader wants to continue reading and can understand the main idea and supporting points easily after one reading. Each sentence is where it belongs.

☐ The main idea is clearly expressed in a topic sentence.

☐ It is clear which are main points of support and which are secondary points.

☐ The paper has paragraph form: The first sentence is indented, and the remaining sentences follow each other, with no gaps in space or thought.

Writing conventions

☐ The paper is very readable. There are few errors in:

▶ word choice
▶ sentence structure
▶ grammar
▶ mechanics (spelling, capitalization, punctuation)

2

Head or Heart
Judgments and decisions

On the basis of arguments and evidence heard in court,
judges must make decisions that affect people's lives.
Do you think that most judges use logic or
feelings when making decisions and judgments in court?

1   GETTING A GRIP ON THE TOPIC

A. Reflection

Are you more emotional or more logical when you make decisions and judgments? Think of decisions you have made recently about education, work, friends, and family. Did you follow your head (logic) or your heart (feelings) in making these decisions? Read the descriptions below and decide which one describes you more accurately. Both paragraphs may describe you, but which one describes you *better*?

(1)   I like to decide things logically, and I want to be treated fairly. Sometimes I hurt other people's feelings without knowing it. Generally, ideas and things are more important to me than people. It doesn't bother me to argue; there are times when an argument is necessary.

(2)   I like to make decisions based on my feelings and values even if my decisions aren't so logical. It's important to me to please other people. I'm very aware of other people's feelings; in fact, I can often predict how someone will feel about something. I don't like arguments. Harmony is important to me.

If paragraph 1 describes you better, you are probably a *thinker:* cool and impersonal when you make a decision. If paragraph 2 describes you better, you are probably a *feeler:* Your feelings and values are more important in your decisions than logic is. We all make thinking and feeling decisions and judgments, but each person uses one judgment style more than the other. Which description fits you better, thinker or feeler?

Follow-up   Compare results as a class. How is the class divided into thinkers and feelers?

B. Discussion

Read this passage from "As It Was in the Beginning," a story about Esther, a young Canadian Indian woman who left her family and home to become educated and converted to Christianity as a young girl. Many years later she has learned the white man's ways but is very homesick. She longs for the more natural surroundings of her people.

Language notes: A *tepee* is a cone-shaped Indian house made of poles and animal skins. The literal meaning of *pagan* is a person who does not follow one of the world's major religions. The connotation here is of a wild, uncivilized person. *Buckskin* is deer leather, from which Esther's tribe made their clothing at the time of the story, the turn of the century. Animal skins, *tanned*, or made into leather through a process with smoke, were traded by the Indians for goods at an English company, the *Hudson's Bay Company*. Father Paul is a *missionary*, a Catholic priest whose mission, or job, it was to educate and convert the Indians to Christianity. *Father* is his title, not his relationship to anyone in the story.

Read to answer this question: *Is Esther's homesickness temporary, or will it continue after this episode?*

. . . I wanted my own people, my own old life, my blood called out for it, but they always said I must not return to my father's tepee. I heard them talk amongst themselves of keeping me away from pagan influences; they told each other that if I returned to the prairies, the tepees, I would degenerate, slip back to paganism, as other girls had done; marry, perhaps, with a pagan – and all their years of labor and teaching would be lost.

I said nothing, but I waited. And then one night the feeling overcame me. I was in the Hudson's Bay store when an Indian came in from the north with a large pack of buckskin. As they unrolled it a dash of its insinuating odor filled the store. I went over and leaned above the skins a second, then buried my face in them, swallowing, drinking the fragrance of them, that went to my head like wine. Oh, the wild wonder of that wood-smoked tan, the subtlety of it, the untamed smell of it! I drank it into my lungs, my innermost being was saturated with it, till my mind reeled and my heart seemed twisted with a physical agony. My childhood recollections rushed upon me, devoured me. I left the store in a strange, calm frenzy, and going rapidly into the mission house I confronted my Father Paul and demanded to be allowed to go "home," if only for a day. He received the request with the same refusal and the same gentle sigh that I had so often been greeted with, but this time the desire, the smoke-tan, the heart-ache, never lessened.

Discuss these questions in pairs.

1. Does Esther seem like a feeler or a thinker here?
2. What about Father Paul?
3. What can Esther do to overcome these feelings of homesickness? What do you think will make her feel less homesick?
4. How does reading this passage make you feel? Have you ever reacted so strongly to a smell as Esther did?

Follow-up   Share your answers with the class.

C.   Notes on the main reading

E. Pauline Johnson wrote "As It Was in the Beginning" at the turn of the century, so the way she depicts life is dated. Today Indians, or Native Americans, no longer live in tepees or wear buckskin clothes.

Although Johnson was half Canadian Indian/half English, her story is not important simply because of insights into Native American character or life. It is important because it deals with very human issues like homesickness, love, prejudice, and loss. The ending may surprise you.

In the continuation of the story, the author introduces another character, Laurence. Laurence is Father Paul's nephew. He grew up at the mission with Esther, who says of him: "He was my solace in my half-exile, my comrade, my brother, until one night . . ."

Something happened "one night" in the story to change Esther's mind about her homesickness. What do you think happened? Write for 10 minutes on how you think the story will continue. Then share your predictions in small groups.

GLOSSARY

Review the glossary before reading the selection, for help with some of the more difficult vocabulary.

long for (line 3): desire strongly
lodge (line 3): home, dwelling
prairie (line 24): wide area of flat grassland in Canada
dulcet cadence (line 27): sweet music
benediction (line 33): blessing, a prayer for God's good wishes
remonstrating (line 42): protesting, arguing
factor (line 43): merchant or agent
rollicking (line 44): noisy and full of humor
started (line 49): spoke suddenly with surprise

faltered (line 49): hesitated, spoke uncertainly

riveted (line 63): fixed, concentrated

venerable (line 66): deserving respect because of age or position

revered (line 66): respected greatly

saints (line 67): holy people

worshiped (line 69): loved deeply and respected

shuddered (line 80): trembled, shook

archfiend (line 87): worst enemy

kinsman (line 87): relative

blight (line 110): destroy

wound itself about me like the coils of a serpent (line 115–116): wrapped around me like the twisting body of a snake

beaded bag (line 116): decorated leather bag used by Indians mainly for medicine

slipped (line 125): sneaked, moved like a snake

bowed with grief (line 130) carrying great sadness

I was suspected (line 131): it was thought I might be guilty

D. Read for the main idea

Read the whole story at a quick comfortable pace to answer this main idea question: *Does Esther stay at the mission or return to her people?*

As It Was in the Beginning

E. Pauline Johnson

Night after night I would steal away by myself and go to the border of the village to watch the sun set in the foothills, to gaze at the far line of sky and prairie, to long and long for my father's lodge. And Laurence – always Laurence – my fair-haired, laughing, child playmate, would come calling and calling for me: "Esther, where are you? We miss you; come in, Esther, come in with me." And if I did not turn at once to him and follow, he would come and place his strong hands on my shoulders and laugh into my eyes and say, "Truant, truant, Esther; can't *we* make you happy?"

My old child playmate had vanished years ago. He was a tall, slender young man now, handsome as a young chief, but with laughing blue eyes, and always those yellow curls around his temples. He

was my solace in my half-exile, my comrade, my brother, until one
night it was, "Esther, Esther, can't *I* make you happy?"

15   I did not answer him; only looked out across the plains and
thought of the tepees. He came close, close. He locked his arms about
me, and with my face pressed up to his throat he stood silent. I felt
the blood from my heart sweep to my very finger-tips. I loved him.
Oh God, how I loved him! In a wild, blind instant it all came, just
20 because he held me so and was whispering brokenly, "Don't leave me,
don't leave me, Esther; my Esther, my child love, my playmate, my
girl comrade, my little Cree sweetheart, will you go away to your
people, or stay, stay for me, for my arms, as I have you now?"

    No more, no more the tepees; no more the wild stretch of prairie,
25 the intoxicating fragrance of the smoke-tanned buckskin; no more
the bed of buffalo hide, the soft, silent moccasin; no more the dark
faces of my people, the dulcet cadence of the sweet Cree tongue –
only this man, this fair, proud, tender man who held me in his arms,
in his heart. My soul prayed to his great white God, in that moment,
30 that He let me have only this. It was twilight when we re-entered the
mission gate. We were both excited, feverish. Father Paul was reading
evening prayers in the large room beyond the hallway; his soft, saint-
like voice stole beyond the doors, like a benediction upon us. I went
noiselessly upstairs to my own room and sat there undisturbed for
35 hours. . . .

    *(Laurence meets Father Paul, his uncle, and tells him of his love
for Esther and his desire to marry her. Father Paul is very upset.
Esther overhears the conversation.)*

    "Laurence, my boy, your future is the dearest thing to me of all
40 earthly interests. Why, you *can't* marry this girl – no, no, sit, sit until I
have finished," he added, with a raised voice, as Laurence sprang up,
remonstrating. "I have long since decided that you marry well; for
instance, the Hudson's Bay factor's daughter."

    Laurence broke into a fresh, rollicking laugh. "What, uncle," he
45 said, "Little Ida McIntosh? Marry that little yellow-haired fluff ball,
that kitten, that pretty little dolly?"

    "Stop," said Father Paul. Then with a low, soft persuasiveness,
"She is *white*, Laurence."

    My lover started. "Why, uncle, what do you mean?" he faltered.

"Only this, my son: poor Esther comes of uncertain blood; would   50
it do for you – the missionary's nephew, and adopted son, you might
say – to marry the daughter of a pagan Indian? Her mother is hope-
lessly uncivilized; her father has a dash of French somewhere – half-
breed, you know, my boy, half-breed." Then, with still lower tone
and half-shut, crafty eyes, he added: "The blood is a bad, bad mix-   55
ture, you know that; you know, too, that I am very fond of the girl,
poor dear Esther. I have tried to separate her from evil pagan influences; she is the daughter of the Church; I want her to have no other
parent; but you can never tell what lurks in a caged animal that has
once been wild. My whole heart is with the Indian people, my son;   60
my whole heart, my whole life, has been devoted to bringing them to
Christ, but it is a different thing to marry with one of them."

His small old eyes were riveted on Laurence like a hawk's on a
rat. My heart lay like ice in my bosom. . . .

I listened, sitting like one frozen. Could those words have been   65
uttered by my venerable teacher, by him whom I revered as I would
one of the saints in his own black book? Ah, there was no mistaking
it. My white father, my life-long friend who pretended to love me, to
care for my happiness, was urging the man I worshiped to forget me,
to marry with the factor's daughter – because of what? Of my red   70
skin; my good, old, honest pagan mother, my confiding French-Indian
father. In a second all the care, the hollow love he had given me since
my childhood, were as things that never existed. I hated that old mission priest as I hated his white man's hell. . . .

Laurence sat motionless, his face buried in his hands, but the old   75
man continued: "No, no; not the child of the pagan mother; you can't
trust her, my son. What would you do with a wife who might any day
break from you to return to her prairies and her buckskins? *You can't
trust her.* . . ."

Laurence shuddered, lifted his face, and said hoarsely: "You're   80
right, uncle; perhaps I'd better not; I'll go away, I'll forget her, and
then – well then – yes, you are right, it is a different thing to marry
one of them."

"Good-night, son," he said.

"Good-night, uncle, and thank you for bringing me to myself."   85

They were the last words I ever heard uttered by either that old archfiend or his weak, miserable kinsman. . . .

What were his years of kindness and care now? What did I care for his God, his heaven, his hell? He had robbed me of my native faith, of my parents, of this last, this life of love that would have made a great, good woman of me. God, how I hated him! I crept to the closet in my dark little room. I felt for a bundle I had not looked at for years – yes, it was there, the buckskin dress I had worn as a little child when they brought me to the mission. I tucked it under my arm and descended the stairs noiselessly. I would look into the study and speak good-bye to Laurence; then I would –

I pushed open the door. He was lying on the couch where a short time previously he had sat, white and speechless, listening to Father Paul. I moved towards him softly.

God in heaven, he was already asleep. As I bent over him the fullness of his perfect beauty impressed me for the first time; his slender form, his curving mouth that almost laughed even in sleep, his fair, tossed hair, his smooth, strong-pulsing throat. God! How I loved him!

Then there arose the picture of the factor's daughter. I hated her. I hated her baby face, her yellow hair, her whitish skin. "She shall not marry him," my soul said. "I will kill him first – kill his beautiful body, his lying, false heart." Something in my heart seemed to speak; it said over and over again, "Kill him, kill him; she will never have him then. Kill him. It will break Father Paul's heart and blight his life. He has killed the best of you, of your womanhood; kill his best, his pride, his hope – his sister's son, his nephew Laurence." But how? How?

What had that terrible old man said I was like? *A strange snake.* A snake? The idea wound itself about me like the very coils of a serpent. What was this in the beaded bag of my buckskin dress? This little thing rolled in tan that my mother had given me at parting with the words, "Don't touch much, but sometime maybe you want it!" Oh! I knew well enough what it was – a small flint arrow-head dipped in the venom of some strange snake.

I knelt beside him and laid my hot lips on his hand. I worshiped him, oh, how I worshiped him! Then again the vision of her baby

face, her yellow hair – I scratched his wrist twice with the arrow-tip.
A single drop of red blood oozed up; he stirred. I turned the lamp
down and slipped out of the room – out of the house.   125

I dream nightly of the horrors of the white man's hell. Why did
they teach me of it, only to fling me into it?

Last night as I crouched beside my mother on the buffalo-hide,
Dan Henderson, the trapper, came in to smoke with my father. He
said old Father Paul was bowed with grief, that with my disappear-   130
ance I was suspected, but that there was no proof. Was it not merely a
snake bite?

They account for it by the fact that I am a Redskin.

They seem to have forgotten I am a woman.

Follow-up Answer the main idea question here: _____

_____

_____

E. Read for more detail

Read the selection a second time. Use the questions to go more deeply into the
story and to bring your experience to it.

1. What ended Esther's homesickness? Do you find this fast change in her
   believable?
2. What ended her new happiness?
3. How did Father Paul convince Laurence? Do you agree with Father Paul's
   reasoning?
4. After Father Paul spoke to Laurence, how did Esther's feelings for them
   change?
5. What solution did Esther have for the jealousy and hatred she felt? Can you
   understand why she acted as she did?
6. Which of the characters are feelers? Which are thinkers?
7. *Key words* Make a list of six words that you feel are important to the story.
   Be ready to explain why each word is important, and what it means, if
   necessary.

Follow-up Discuss your answers in small groups or as a class.

2 RESPONDING TO THE MAIN READING

A. Journals: A private audience

Choose two of the following topics. Write at least 75 words on each of them in your journal notebook. Express your opinions and feelings honestly. These journal entries are for your eyes only, so do not spend a lot of time using a dictionary or worrying about grammar.

1. Which of the three main characters do you like the most? Why?
2. Which of the three do you like the least? Why?
3. How did you feel when you finished the story? Upset? Pleased for Esther? Satisfied that she'd taken revenge? Shocked by her actions?

B. Shared writing

Choose at least two topics and write for a total of 30 minutes. Your audience is your classmates, with whom you will share your writing. They will be interested not only in *what* you feel but also in *why* you feel that way. Therefore, you will want to express your views clearly and support them.

1. Can you understand why Esther killed Laurence? Can you accept that she did so?
2. What does Esther mean by the last two lines of the story, speaking about the murder?
3. Do you find this story believable? Explain.

C. Feedback on your writing

Get feedback on how clear and logical your thinking and writing are. Select one of your writings from the previous section, "Shared Writing," and read it to a group of two or three classmates. Each member of the group will read one of his or her writings. Follow the procedure in "Peer Feedback Guidelines" at the end of this chapter.

Follow-up In 5 minutes, evaluate in writing how well your audience received your paper. Could they summarize it accurately? Did they understand your points? How could you make your paper clearer? More interesting to your audience?

3 GOING MORE DEEPLY INTO THE TOPIC

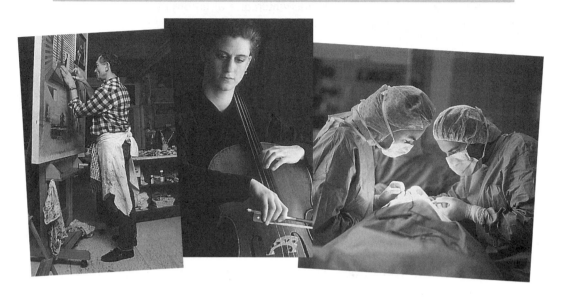

Do you think that the thinker/feeler difference helps determine the career a person chooses? If so, would most surgeons probably be thinkers or feelers? What would artists and musicians tend to be?

A. Preparing to read

In her book *Gifts Differing*, Isabel Briggs Myers presents her work on personality and learning types. In the chapter presented here, "Effect of the TF Preference," she explains the differences between thinkers (T) and feelers (F). The thinking/feeling difference is one of four dimensions. The other three are introvert/extrovert, intuitive/sensing, and perceptive/judging. Thus, "INFP" in the reading refers to an individual who is introvert/intuitive/feeling/perceptive. (One's profile, including all four dimensions, helps to describe what kind of person one is and how one learns.) This chapter deals with the TF preference only.

As you read "Effect of the TF Preference," see if you agree with Briggs Myers's characterization of your type. Keep a friend or relative in mind to help you judge whether her views of the other type are accurate in your opinion.

B. First reading

Read the excerpt a first time to decide which pair of antonyms best describes
the difference between thinkers' and feelers' judgments:

rational/irrational   personal/impersonal
successful/unsuccessful   intelligent/emotional

Effect of the TF Preference

ISABEL BRIGGS MYERS, with Peter B. Myers

Thinking and feeling are rival instruments of decision. Both are
reasonable and internally consistent, but each works by its own standards. Jolande Jacobi (1968)* says that thinking evaluates from the
viewpoint "true-false" and feeling from the viewpoint "agreeable-dis-
5   agreeable." This sounds like a thinker's formulation. "Agreeable" is
too pale a word for the rich personal worth of a feeling evaluation.

The important point to recognize is that each kind of judgment
has its appropriate field. To use feeling where thinking is called for
can be as great a mistake as to use thinking where feeling is needed.

10 Thinking is essentially impersonal. Its goal is objective truth,
independent of the personality and wishes of the thinker or anyone
else. So long as the problems are impersonal, like those involved in
building a bridge or interpreting a statute, proposed solutions can
and should be judged from the standpoint "true-false," and thinking
15 is the better instrument.

But the moment the subject is people instead of things or ideas –
and some voluntary cooperation from those people is needed – the
impersonal approach is less successful. People (even thinkers) do not
like to be viewed impersonally and relegated to the status of
20 "objects." Human motives are notably personal. Therefore, in the
sympathetic handling of people where personal values are important,
feeling is the more effective instrument.

To thinkers, the idea of evaluating by means of feeling sounds
flighty, unreliable, and uncontrolled, but thinkers are no judges of
25 feeling. They naturally judge all feeling by their own, and theirs is relatively underdeveloped and unreliable. When feeling is well-devel-

The Psychology of C. G. Jung. New Haven, Conn.: Yale University Press.

oped, it is a stable instrument for discriminating the worth of personal values, selecting as guiding stars those values that rank highest, and subordinating the lesser to the greater. . . .

Thus, in teaching, in acting and the other arts, in oratory and in the humbler branch of persuasion called salesmanship, in the relations of the clergy to their congregations, in family life, in social contacts, and in any sort of counseling, *it is feeling which serves as the bridge between one human being and another.*

The TF preference is the only one that shows a marked sex difference. The proportion of feeling types appears to be substantially higher among women than among men. This difference in the frequencies of the types for men and women has led to much generalization about the sexes. Women have been assumed to be less logical, more tenderhearted, more tactful, more social, less analytical, and more inclined to take things personally. All these are feeling traits. Feeling types (of either sex) will tend to have them. Thinking types (of either sex) will not. The generalization tends to pass over the women with thinking and the men with feeling, partly because types that do not fit the stereotypes have often learned the art of protective coloration.

The merits of the thinker's logical approach to life are so obvious and so well known that it has not seemed necessary to discuss them here. But it should never be assumed that thinkers have a monopoly on all worthwhile mental activity. They do not even have a monopoly on thinking. Just as thinkers may attain, on occasion, a very useful supplementary development of feeling that does not interfere with their thinking judgments, so too the feeling types may sometimes enlist their thinking to find the logical reasons needed to win a thinker's acceptance of a conclusion they have already reached by way of feeling. Before the publication of a cherished piece of work, undertaken from motives of feeling and carried out intuitively, thinking may be used to check for possible flaws and fallacies.

Conventional measures of mental ability, such as intelligence tests and scholarship, show some of the highest records belong to INFP and INFJ types, who relegate thinking to last place or next to last place. The preference for thinking appears to have far less intellectual effect than the preference for intuition, even in some technical fields,

such as scientific research, where its influence was expected to be
65 most important.

It would seem, therefore, that the mark of a thinker is not so
much the possession of greater mental powers but having them run
on a different track. Thinkers are at their best with the impersonal,
and they are the most able to handle things that need to be done
70 impersonally. The judge and the surgeon, for example, tend to rule
out personal considerations. One famous surgeon was so impersonal
that his wife could not even focus his attention on his own children
unless she took them to his office.

Finally, thinking is not always first-class thinking. Its product is
75 no better than the facts it started with (and they were acquired by
perception of unknown quality) and no better than the logic
employed. When a person once reportedly described logic as an organized way of going wrong with confidence, he voiced the distrust of
the out-and-out intuitives and the feeling types for such a cut-and-
80 dried method of decision. When feeling types know that they value an
idea or a person or a course of action, a thinker's argument designed
to confute that value leaves them cold. The thinker's judgment could
be wrong! Thinkers often contradict each other, each one claiming,
"This is truth." The feeling type need only say, "This is valuable to
85 me."

Follow-up Which pair of antonyms listed under the heading "First Reading"
best characterizes the thinker/feeler difference? Do you agree with Briggs
Myers's characterization of your type?

C. Additional readings

Read the article again. Mark any places in the text that are still unclear to you.
Then read these passages once more to improve your understanding of them.

D. Negotiating the meaning

Write at least 75 words on this selection. Write on any or all of the following:

▶ whether you liked it or not, and why
▶ whether you prefer it to the previous selection
▶ what you have trouble understanding

Follow-up To a group of two or three, read what you have written. Read your reaction a second time if necessary.

   Each group member will respond with (1) a question, (2) a comment, and/or (3) clarification. Every group member should read what he or she has written. As a group, choose one response to share with the whole class.

E. Discussion: Critical thinking

Discuss these questions in pairs, small groups, or as a class.

1. It is ironic that Father Paul, whose goal was to "deliver Esther from evil" by converting her, actually led her to kill Laurence. Can you think of examples from your own life in which someone's good intentions ended badly?
2. Johnson's story paints a picture of the prejudice of the whites against the Indians. This prejudice was based on the Indians' religion and possibly on their color. Given that this story is more than 80 years old, do you think these kinds of prejudice are more common or less common in the world today? Explain.
3. Common wisdom and author Briggs Myers say that more women are feelers and more men are thinkers. Do you agree with this? If your class has men and women, how did the class divide according to the survey in Part 1, Section A of this chapter?
4. Does Briggs Myers conclude that either thinkers or feelers are superior in their judgments? Do you think she would say that a balance between thinking and feeling leads to better judgments?
5. Esther's jealousy plays a role in her murder of Laurence. Is jealousy purely a feeling, or does it have an aspect of logic in it? Explain.

4 IMPROVING WRITING SKILLS

A. Using another's writing: Summarizing

In courses that you take, your teachers want you to learn from what you read. They want you to absorb new ideas from authors and to improve your English from exposure to new texts. Both new ideas and better language will come if you strive to put the new ideas into your own words rather than copy the author's words.

✎**EXERCISE 1 Summarizing passages from a story**

Practice putting Johnson's ideas into your words by summarizing passages from her story. In summarizing, you want to capture the essence of what the author has said, but in fewer words. There is no point in a summary that is as long as the original. To summarize, follow these steps:

a. Read the passage several times.
b. Decide on the essential points; write down key words and expressions that remind you of these essential points. (These may come from the text or from you.)
c. Expand your key words into a sentence or two. You can write in the third person (*she, he,* for example) even if the passage is in the first person (*I*). Limit your summary to 25–30 words.

(1)   My childhood recollections rushed upon me, devoured me. I left the store in a strange, calm frenzy, and going rapidly to the mission house I confronted my Father Paul and demanded to be allowed to go "home," if only for a day. He received the request with the same refusal and the same gentle sigh that I had so often been greeted with, but this time the desire, the smoke-tan, the heart-ache, never lessened.

(2)   No more, no more the tepees; no more the wild stretch of prairie, the intoxicating fragrance of the smoke-tanned buckskin; no more the bed of buffalo hide, the soft, silent moccasin; no more the dark faces of my people, the dulcet cadence of the sweet Cree tongue – only this man, this fair, proud, tender man who held me in his arms, in his heart. My soul prayed to his great white God, in that moment, that He let me have only this. It was twilight when we re-entered the mission gate. We were both excited, feverish.

> _Key words_
>
> _homesickness came upon Esther_
>
> _demanded to go home_
>
> _F. Paul refused_
>
> _desire remained_
>
> _Summary_
>
> _The homesickness Esther felt was so strong that she demanded to go home, but Father Paul refused. Her homesickness remained as strong as before. (25 words)_

Sample answer for Exercise 1, passage 1.

Father Paul was reading evening prayers in the large room beyond the hallway; his soft, saint-like voice stole beyond the doors, like a benediction upon us. I went noiselessly upstairs to my own room and sat there undisturbed for hours.

(3)   I listened, sitting like one frozen. Could those words have been uttered by my venerable teacher, by him whom I revered as I would one of the saints in his own black book? Ah, there was no mistaking it. My white father, my life-long friend who pretended to love me, to care for my happiness, was urging the man I worshiped to forget me, to marry with the factor's daughter – because of what? Of my red skin; my good, old, honest pagan mother, my confiding French-Indian father. In a second all the care, the hollow love he had given me since my childhood, were as things that never existed. I hated that old mission priest as I hated his white man's hell.

(4)   I knelt beside him and laid my hot lips on his hand. I worshiped him, oh, how I worshiped him! Then again the vision of her baby face, her yellow hair – I scratched his wrist twice with the arrow-tip. A single drop of red blood oozed up; he stirred. I turned the lamp down and slipped out of the room – out of the house.

Follow-up In small groups, share summaries by exchanging papers. Did your classmates choose the same details that you did?

B. Meeting reader expectations: Patterns of organization

The texts you have read so far are made up of paragraphs of varying lengths, some short and some long. The length of a paragraph depends on the writer's purpose and even on the audience. When you write for a formal audience, for academic purposes, for example, your paragraphs will often be different from those in the readings. Your paragraphs will usually be longer, able to stand on their own as answers to essay questions or as part of a formal essay.

Formal English writing has formal organization. There are a number of different *patterns of organization* that are conventional. They are patterns that readers are used to, if only unconsciously, in paragraphs and essays. Because these patterns of organization are familiar to readers, using them will help you communicate with an English-speaking audience more effectively.

Before going on to the exercise, think about the differences between the items in each of the following pairs. Discuss the differences as a class.

an example/a reason   a comparison/a contrast
a description/a definition   a narrative/a description

✎ EXERCISE 2   Model paragraphs: English patterns of organization

The following paragraphs represent the seven most common ways to develop a paragraph in English expository writing. To show the difference between the seven rhetorical modes, each paragraph is written on the same topic: *jealousy*. Some examples may seem to follow more than one pattern. To help see the difference between the paragraphs, keep in mind the author's purpose in writing each one. Read each paragraph and answer the questions that follow.

1. Examples

Literature gives us many examples of jealousy, but a look at daily life yields an ample supply closer at hand. Take the three-year-old child who lives upstairs. His parents have just brought home a newborn baby sister, and the three-year-old acts as if an enemy had entered the house. He is jealous of his sister. Or look at the wife whose husband is talking to another woman at a party. The more interested he seems in talking to the woman, the more unattractive and irritated his wife feels. The wife is jealous. For another example, picture a young computer programmer, considered a whiz, appreciated and praised by his co-workers and boss. In comes a new programmer, who starts to share some of the lime-light and accolades that were formerly given to the first programmer. The first programmer feels jealous. In all three cases, the people feel their relationships threatened by a rival: They feel jealous.

1. Is there a topic sentence in which the main idea is expressed? If so, which sentence is it?
2. How many examples are used to make the writer's point? What are they?
3. Is the paragraph complete, i.e., are there enough examples and do they make the meaning of jealousy clear? Explain.
4. If there are so "many examples of jealousy" in literature, why didn't the writer use them here? (Consider the audience.)
5. Does the author use real examples or hypothetical ones? If hypothetical, are they believable?

2. Cause and effect

An anthropological look for causes has led some experts to conclude that jealousy is biological – that it is instinctive behavior, in other words. A more interesting approach might be to look at why some people are more jealous than others. In surveys, psychologists have discovered three personality characteristics that the very jealous have in common. The first is insecurity in relationships, stemming from low self-esteem. The jealous person does not see him- or herself as worthy of the love and attention of the other person, perhaps. Another characteristic of the jealous person is a greater than normal discrepancy between how that person is and how he or she would like to be. Looking at it another way, we could say this person was quite dissatisfied with him- or herself. The last characteristic is that the very jealous tend to put a lot of stock in worldly items such as wealth, fame, popularity, and physical attractiveness. These are, of course, important to most people but not to the same degree that they are to the very jealous. That we might call these personality traits causes of jealousy is possible only because those with the characteristics exhibit abnormal levels of what is a normal human emotion, jealousy.

(Adapted from "The Heart of Jealousy," by P. Salovey and J. Rodin, *Psychology Today,* Sept. 1985.)

1. Is the topic sentence in the normal position as first sentence? Which is the topic sentence?

2. How many causes does the writer give? What are they?
3. How are causes different from examples?
4. Does the writer list all the causes of jealousy? Is the paragraph complete?
5. A paragraph does not always have a good conclusion, especially if it is part of a longer piece of writing. Does this paragraph have a conclusion? If so, what is it?

Note: In a single paragraph, it is impossible to discuss both causes and effects. As a writer, you will want to focus on one or the other as the author of paragraph 2 has done.

3. Definition

Although a subject of many songs and much literature, jealousy is not a topic that has a long life span in most daily conversations. What is this unmentionable emotion that all people feel at times, many suffer agony over, and some are led to crime by? Jealousy is the feeling of fear, unhappiness, or even ill will that arises when a person feels that an important relationship with someone is threatened. The negative feelings are a reaction to loss – real, potential, or imagined – of someone important in our lives. Some psychologists speculate that the origin of jealousy lies in biology, i.e., that jealousy is an instinctive response in humans. Others see an economic basis for jealousy; there is a limited amount of care a parent can give a child and a limited amount of emotional and sexual energy a spouse can give a partner. A new child in the family or a lover encroaches on these attentions. Still other theories exist to explain jealousy, the emotion difficult to talk about because it poisons the very relations that it wants to keep and nurture.

(Adapted from *Jealousy: What Is It and Who Feels It?*, by Peter Van Summers, Penguin Books, 1988.)

1. Is there a topic sentence that expresses the main idea of this paragraph? If so, what is it?
2. What definition does the writer give of jealousy?
3. To consider this paragraph one of definition, we have to look at the author's purpose in writing it. Is the purpose to make jealousy clearer by giving examples of it, as in paragraph 1 in this exercise? What is the writer's purpose?

4. Comparison and contrast

The terms *jealousy* and *envy* are often used in place of each other, but there is a basic distinction to be made between them. Envy is the feeling that we want to have something that we do not have. It could be the neighbor's car or the classmate's high score on a test. Jealousy, on the other hand, is the feeling or thought that we might lose something (more usually someone) that we already have. A jealous husband fears he will lose his wife; a jealous child fears losing a parent's love to a new sibling. If the distinction does not seem important, consider that society's reaction to the two is very different. Western society accepts jealousy but rejects envy. Westerners sympathize with the jealous lover's situation and may even secretly endorse the lover's rash actions against a rival. However, pity the person who is envious of a neighbor's swimming pool. That person is covetous according to Western religious and cultural values and receives no sympathy.

1. What is the topic sentence? Is the writer's purpose to compare (show similarities) or to contrast (show differences)?
2. What examples are used here? If this is a comparison/contrast paragraph, why are there examples?
3. In what two ways are jealousy and envy different?
4. In comparison/contrast paragraphs, you have a decision to make about organization: whether to (a) discuss the items being compared point by point with each other, or (b) discuss one item completely and then the second item completely, in blocks, often in separate paragraphs. Did this writer use point-by-point or block organization?
5. There is no conclusion in this paragraph. Write one.

5. Narration

The first time I remember feeling jealous was many years ago when I was three or four. I had been carefully choosing the right crayons to color pictures in a new coloring book on the floor in the dining room. Satisfied that I had done a good job, I wanted to show my new masterpieces to my mother, who was busy with morning chores in the kitchen. My father, too, might like the pictures, but he was sleeping. So into the kitchen I went carrying the new pictures. I found my mother there, but to my dismay, she was not waiting to "ooh" and "aah" at my artwork. Instead, she was in the arms of this man, who was kissing her. My attempt to interrupt this nonsense was met by, "We're busy, can't you see?" from my father. There was no response from that woman – that woman who preferred him to me, that nonsense to my masterpieces. I ran to my room broken-hearted.

1. Narration tells a story by carefully choosing details to make a point. Does this paragraph paint a picture of jealousy that you understand?
2. Is there a topic sentence here? If so, which sentence is it?
3. Which detail (which sentence) does not seem particularly relevant to the paragraph? Can it be omitted? Why or why not?
4. In terms of organization, the essential characteristic of a narrative is that events are in chronological order or the order in which they happened. Without looking back, can you relate the events of this narrative paragraph in order?

6. Description

John had no idea what to do about his feelings. He was ashamed of himself for how he felt when his wife spoke to another man, even the mail carrier or a clerk at the store. He could feel anger building in his head, which was like a bomb about to explode. Underneath the anger was an emptiness, a feeling that perhaps there was nothing in him to love. Were other men better-looking than he was? Somehow more attractive to his wife? He couldn't actually talk to her about it because she would think he was silly for feeling jealous. More often, he would just turn away so that she couldn't read the jealousy in his eyes. The one time he had confronted her with his feelings, she didn't know what he was talking about. And when she had found him snooping in her purse (was he looking for a tell-tale note or some sign of infidelity?), her reaction was a soft sigh of disbelief and then a look of confusion. Could he end this agony before it ended his marriage?

1. At first glance, this description might seem like a narrative paragraph. How is it different from a narrative?
2. There is no topic sentence in this paragraph, but certainly there is a main idea. Write out the main idea in your words.

3. In description, details "paint a picture" that conveys the writer's message. Good descriptive details often appeal to the senses of sight, hearing, smell, and feeling. What details has the author chosen to describe a jealous person here? Do any of them appeal to the senses?
4. Write a topic sentence for this paragraph, one that leads the reader to expect a description.

7. *Classification*

Though the basic feelings involved in jealousy may be the same no matter what the cause, it can be useful to look at the different faces jealousy can wear. All cases of jealousy probably fall into one of four categories. The first, the one that probably pops into most people's minds when jealousy is brought up, is sexual jealousy, between husband and wife or between lovers. Another kind of jealousy, found within the family unit, is jealousy among brothers and sisters. All children, with the possible exception of the youngest, have probably felt this kind of sibling rivalry. Professional jealousy is yet another kind of jealousy. Here we are talking not only about the jealousy that can exist among employees in relation to their boss or co-workers, but also about the jealousy that often exists between athletes on the same team or students in the same class. Last, and perhaps the slowest to be acknowledged by many people, is jealousy between friends, which develops when one friend feels threatened by another friend's other friendships. This kind of jealousy, possessiveness, would even include a husband who feels jealous because much of his wife's former time and affection for him is now going to the children. That we even attempt to classify jealousy is not to imply that the jealous feeling is different in people from one classification to another. Rather how a jealous person might try to deal with the jealousy is very likely influenced by its classification.

1. On the surface, a classification paragraph can seem like an example paragraph. What differences are there between the two?
2. A good classification should account for all possible occurrences of the thing being classified. Can you think of a type of jealousy that does not fit into the four categories named above? Can you think of a better way to classify jealousy?

3. If the first sentence is not the topic sentence, how does it function in the paragraph? Which sentence is the topic sentence?
4. Look at the last two sentences. Does this paragraph warrant such a long conclusion? If you find the conclusion too long, rewrite it in a shorter form.

C. Language conventions: Correcting run-together sentences

Look at the sentences below. Both contain errors that can occur in written English although they do not exist in spoken English. Can you identify the errors?

> WRONG   Student thinking types need order and achievement feeling types need approval and support.
>
> The preference for thinking or feeling goes with us in all aspects of life, the preference even affects how students react to instruction.

In the first example, two independent clauses are joined together, with no punctuation or conjunction. This error is a fused sentence. What are the two clauses?

In the second example, two independent clauses are separated by a comma alone. Commas are often used when we combine sentences, but a comma alone does not join two independent clauses. This error is a *comma-splice*.

Both fused sentences and comma-splices, often referred to as *run-together sentences*, become more common when students progress to writing longer sentences. To make sure you recognize run-together sentences, do this exercise now.

✎ EXERCISE 3   Recognizing run-together sentences

Each of the following sentences contains two clauses. In the blank, write *RT* for a run-together sentence or *C* for a correctly punctuated sentence.

_____ 1. Americans have great faith in education, they see it as the solution to many problems.
_____ 2. Education can help people get ahead; moreover, it helps citizens vote more intelligently.
_____ 3. Although some education obviously takes place in schools, we can learn many things outside of school.
_____ 4. Many parents read to their small children, their children are likely to enjoy reading as adults.

_____ 5. We learn from all kinds of experiences, so not even television should be overlooked.

_____ 6. Public television in particular offers intelligent programming people of all ages can benefit from the variety of programs shown.

GUIDELINES FOR CORRECTING RUN-TOGETHER SENTENCES

Guideline 1 If the two independent clauses of a run-together sentence are closely related and not too long, they can be separated with a semicolon.

> Student thinking types need order and achievement; feeling types need approval and support.

It is better to separate two longer or unrelated independent clauses with periods.

> The preference for thinking or feeling goes with us in all aspects of life. This preference even affects how students react to instruction.

Guideline 2 A coordinating conjunction (*and, but, so, nor, for, yet, or*) can be used to join the two independent clauses. (Place a comma before the coordinating conjunction.)

> Student thinking types need order and achievement, *but* feeling types need approval and support.

Guideline 3 A subordinator (*because, although, since, whereas, so that*) can be used to join the two clauses. If the dependent clause with the subordinator comes first, separate it from the independent clause with a comma.

> *Since* the preference for thinking or feeling goes with us in all aspects of life, it even affects how students react to instruction.

If the dependent clause comes after the independent clause, use no comma.

> Student thinking types need order and achievement *whereas* feeling types need approval and support.

Guideline 4 A transition word can be used to join the two independent clauses. (Note the use of the semicolon.)

> Student thinking types need order and achievement; *however*, feeling types need approval and support.

Since both clauses are independent, they can also be written separated by a period:

> The preference for thinking or feeling goes with us in all aspects of life. *For example,* this preference even affects how students react to instruction.

(Transition words include many of the longer and multiple-word conjunctions: *nevertheless, in addition, for example, moreover, therefore, consequently, also, on the other hand, in contrast, however, in other words, otherwise,* etc.)

✎ EXERCISE 4   Separating run-together sentences

Follow Guideline 1 to separate the two independent clauses and correct the run-together sentence errors. Rewrite the sentences. Use a semicolon if the clauses seem closely related; otherwise, it is better to use a period to separate them.

1. Thinking types need to achieve and to see their progress achievement is not so important to feeling types.
2. Thinking types need and look for order and logic in an assignment approval of their work is more important to feeling types.
3. Thinking types will not work simply to please the teacher their goal is to master the subject.
4. A teacher can help thinking types by organizing their work in a logical way these students are troubled if they don't see the logic of a task.

Follow-up Write two pairs of original sentences about education in your country, illustrating Guideline 1.

✎ EXERCISE 5   Using coordinating conjunctions

Identify the two independent clauses in each item. Then combine them according to Guideline 2. Choose appropriate coordinating conjunctions according to the meanings they give the combined sentences. Rewrite each item as one sentence.

1. Teachers can help feeling types by appreciating their work an impersonal grade is not as valuable to them as a warm remark.
2. The harmony of the group will be more important to feeling students than the task itself teachers may need to keep them focused on the task.
3. Feeling types want their work to be useful to other people they don't like memorization or routine exercises.

4. Teachers can help feeling types by instructing them to work with a friend this is the ideal "work situation" for feeling types.

Follow-up Write two original sentences about classrooms in your country, illustrating Guideline 2.

✏ EXERCISE 6   Using subordinators

Identify the two independent clauses in each item. Then combine them following Guideline 3. Choose subordinators for the meaning they give the combined sentences. Rewrite each item as one sentence.

1. Thinking types like to be right feeling types will often give in to keep peace in an argument.
2. They need support and appreciation feeling types work better in pairs and groups.
3. Thinking types can help the teacher analyze problems in the class their logic leads them easily to causes and effects.
4. Feelers will be quick to identify disharmony in the classroom thinkers will spot confusion very quickly.

Follow-up Write two original sentences on students' problems in your country, illustrating Guideline 3.

✏ EXERCISE 7   Using transition words

Identify the two independent clauses in each item. Then combine them following Guideline 4. Choose transition words according to the meaning they give the combined sentences. Rewrite each item as one sentence, with a semicolon or as two sentences separated by a period.

1. Thinking and feeling preferences influence how comfortable people are in their jobs people unconsciously often choose occupations that fit their preference for thinking or feeling.
2. Thinkers often choose more analytical occupations like law, engineering, management, or police work feelers are more likely to choose teaching, counseling, or the clergy.
3. It is easy for thinkers to offer criticism at work feelers will try to avoid saying unpleasant things.
4. It is important to thinkers to finish a task they will ignore other people's wishes to do so and may hurt others' feelings.

Follow-up Write two original sentences about teachers' problems in your country, illustrating Guideline 4.

EXERCISE 8 Editing for run-together sentences

Edit this paragraph to find run-together sentences. First underline areas where run-together sentences occur. Then rewrite the paragraph, making corrections according to Guidelines 1–4.

People reach judgments in two very different ways. One is by thinking and the other is by feeling. Thinking is logical and impersonal feeling is subjective and personal. Most people say they make decisions in both ways, sometimes they use thinking and other times they use feeling. Isabel Briggs Myers maintains that people prefer one way of judging they have a preference for one or the other, and this is the path they usually follow. People who prefer to make judgments through feeling are probably more skillful dealing with people and relationships, thinkers are especially good at organizing facts and ideas.

5 CORE WRITING ASSIGNMENT

A. Writing topics

Choose a topic (or topics) for writing from the list that follows. You will be asked to develop a paragraph on your topic in the remaining sections of this chapter. Use the pattern of organization specified for each topic.

1. *Definition* Write a paragraph defining *prejudice*.
2. *Cause/effect* Write a paragraph in which you discuss the causes of prejudice. Take prejudice as the effect; what are the causes?
3. *Comparison/contrast* Contrast two ways of making the same decision. Think of an important decision you must make now or in the future. Contrast the two ways you can make the decision: through thinking and through feeling. How would a thinker make the decision? A feeler?
4. *Narrative* Tell the story of a difficult decision you had to make in the past. Use chronological order. Make sure the story has a point; make that point clear in your topic sentence.
5. *Examples* "As It Was in the Beginning" has more than one theme, or message about life for the reader. One of Johnson's themes is about jealousy. Identify three of Johnson's themes in the story and explain what she wants to tell us about life through these themes.

B. Generating ideas: Free writing

Write freely for 15 or 20 minutes on your topic. Write whatever comes to mind at this point. Don't sit and ponder; write. The act of writing usually leads to more thinking about a topic.

Follow-up Read what you have written. Circle ideas and sentences that seem especially good to you. Write down three questions that remain in your mind about the topic.

C. Expanding your point of view: Group discussion

Get together with a small group of other students who chose the same topic. Take turns sharing the questions each of you wrote about the topic and discuss your answers.

Follow-up Quickly write down any new ideas that came out in the discussion. Were the other students' questions similar to yours?

D. Initial drafts

FIRST DRAFT

If a main idea has emerged in free writing and discussion, express it in a topic sentence. If no main idea has emerged, reread your free writing and think about your discussions with classmates. Formulate a topic sentence at this point to guide your writing of the paragraph.

Develop your topic, keeping the assigned pattern of organization in mind. Are you trying to define, compare, list causes, give examples, or tell a story? Keep this purpose in mind as you choose support for your topic sentence.

REVISION

Leave your paragraph for a while. Then look at it again with fresh eyes. As you revise your first draft, ask yourself these questions about the paragraph:

▶ Have I thought about the topic enough?
▶ Have I included enough relevant support to convince my audience?
▶ Does it sound like I wrote this or like a stranger wrote it? Give your paragraph your voice by honestly writing your thoughts, using your own examples, and keeping your audience in mind as you write. Let your goal be not to impress your audience but to let them get to know you and your thinking better.

For more direction in revising, look at your paragraph through the eyes of your teacher: Measure it against the "Paragraph Assessment Guidelines" at the end of this chapter. Label this latest draft "Revision 1."

E. Review, revision, and assessment

PEER FEEDBACK

Get feedback on how clear and logical your thinking and writing are. Read your paragraph to a group of two or three classmates. Each member of the group will read his or her paper to the group. Follow the "Peer Feedback Guidelines" at the end of this chapter.

FURTHER REVISION

How well did your group receive your paper? Could they summarize it accurately? Did they understand your main points? Secondary points? How could your paper be clearer and/or more interesting to your audience? Make notes of changes you need to make.

If necessary, revise your paper using the feedback you got from your group. Edit your paper for run-together sentences. Submit all drafts to your teacher, with the last one marked "Revision 2" at the top.

If you choose not to revise, write a paragraph to your teacher, summarizing the feedback you received and explaining why you decided not to revise.

TEACHER ASSESSMENT

Your teacher will assess your paper using the "Paragraph Assessment Guidelines" at the end of this chapter. Your teacher may grade the paper or allow you to make further revisions before assigning a grade.

PEER FEEDBACK GUIDELINES

Writers

☐ Read the paper clearly, a second time if necessary.

☐ Respond to listeners' comments and questions.

☐ Ask for suggestions if you want them.

Listeners

☐ Listen quietly until the writer finishes reading.

☐ Briefly summarize what you understood, orally.

☐ Pick out parts of the paper (words, expressions, or ideas) that stand out for you. Share these parts with the group.

☐ If you wish, share with the group how the writing makes you feel and ask questions about parts that are not clear.

☐ Do not make negative comments or tell the writer what changes to make.

PARAGRAPH ASSESSMENT GUIDELINES

These are the criteria for a well-written paragraph. Your teacher will use this checklist to evaluate your final draft. You can use it to critically examine your writing and determine how it can be improved.

Content and ideas

☐ The writer has thought about the topic and has a clear main idea.

☐ The paragraph is convincing because there are enough logical points to support the main idea.

☐ No important point is left out; no irrelevant point is included.

Organization and form

☐ The reader wants to continue reading and can understand the main idea and supporting points easily after one reading. Each sentence is where it belongs.

☐ The main idea is clearly expressed in a topic sentence.

☐ It is clear which are main points of support and which are secondary points.

☐ The paper has paragraph form: The first sentence is indented, and the remaining sentences follow each other, with no gaps in space or thought.

Writing conventions

☐ The paper is very readable. There are few errors in:
  ► word choice
  ► sentence structure
  ► grammar
  ► mechanics (spelling, capitalization, punctuation)

3

Friendship

Do you think it is important for people to be of the same sex in
order to have a true friendship? Must they be the same age?
Is it important for friends to share similar interests and background?

1 GETTING A GRIP ON THE TOPIC

A. Reflection

Read this Chinese poem written by one friend to another, to answer this question: *When will their friendship end?*

VOCABULARY

li (line 2): a peasant's straw hat
teng (line 5): the umbrella of a street seller or peddler

Oaths of Friendship

If you were riding in a coach
And I were wearing a li,
And one day we met in the road,
You would get down and bow.
5   If you were carrying a teng
And I were riding a horse,
And one day we met in the road,
I would get down for you.

Shang Ya!
10   I want to be your friend
For ever and ever without break or decay.
When the hills are all flat
And the rivers are all dry,
When it lightens and thunders in winter,
15   When it rains and snows in summer,
When heaven and earth mingle –
Not till then will I part from you.

(Chinese, 1st century)

Read the poem again to answer these questions:

1. What might come between these friends to break their friendship? Money? Time?

2. Which characteristic of friendship is this poem basically about – acceptance of each other, intimacy, loyalty, or honesty?
3. Does this poem remind you of a friend? Whom? How would you describe that friendship?

Follow-up Compare answers with a partner.

B. Discussion: Survey on friendship

Read these findings from a survey on friendship among Americans done by the popular magazine *Psychology Today*. Put a check (✔) by statements that you find "normal." Put an ✗ by statements that you find surprising.

_____ 1. Loyalty, warmth, and the ability to keep confidences are the qualities most valued in a friend; age, income, and occupation are less important.
_____ 2. People who have frequently moved have fewer casual friends than people who have stayed put.
_____ 3. Feeling betrayed by a friend is one of the main reasons for ending a friendship.
_____ 4. In a crisis, 51 percent of our sample say they would turn first to friends, not family.
_____ 5. Twenty-nine percent say they have a close friendship with someone who is a homosexual.
_____ 6. Only 26 percent think career success interferes with friendship opportunities.
_____ 7. Seventy-three percent agree that friendships with the opposite sex are different from those with the same sex.
_____ 8. Thirteen percent would lie for a friend in a divorce proceeding.

Follow-up In small groups or as a class, discuss your reactions to the findings. In general, does your group find these statements normal or surprising? Why?

C. Notes on the main reading

"The Friendship Bond," a report on the *Psychology Today* friendship survey, commands attention because the survey included a large sample of Americans (forty thousand). The writing is somewhat scientific in that the author, Mary Brown Parlee, reports the results of the survey by giving us the statistics for the answers to different questions. At the same time, she interprets the statistics and draws conclusions about friendship in the United States.

VOCABULARY EXERCISE

To preview the text and practice guessing word meaning from context, find the following words in the text, in the lines indicated. Write down what you think each word or expression means from its context. If you are very doubtful after making a guess, check your guess in a dictionary.

1. bonding (lines 12–13) _____

2. enhance (line 22) _____

3. impersonality (line 49) _____

4. deficits (line 73) _____

5. link (line 135) _____

6. consistency (line 217) _____

GLOSSARY

Review the glossary before reading the selection, for help with some of the more difficult vocabulary.

give cold comfort to (line 9): will not please
rationale (line 21): reason for being
trust (line 23): confidence
anomie (line 49): feeling of hopelessness, caused by breakdown of rules and
      values
self-indulgence (line 54): having or doing everything you enjoy
commitment (line 55): willingness to promise to give and be loyal to others
confide in (line 65): share private thoughts with
reciprocal (line 80): involving two friends who give equally to each other
presuppose (line 130): require, assume
self-disclosure (lines 141–142): sharing private thoughts and feelings
implicitly acknowledged (lines 188–189): understood and agreed upon
      without being stated directly
feeble (line 207): weak
striking contradictions (lines 210–211): large lack of agreement
glowing (line 217): enthusiastic and favorable

D. Read for the main idea

Read the whole selection to answer this main idea question: *According to this report, is the American view of friendship idealized and romantic, or is it realistic? Explain.*

THE FRIENDSHIP BOND*

Mary Brown Parlee

More than forty thousand readers told us what they looked for in close friendships, what they expected of friends, 5 what they were willing to give in return, and how satisfied they were with the quality of their friendships. The results give cold comfort to social 10 critics.

Friendship appears to be a unique form of human bonding. Unlike marriage or the ties that bind parents and children, 15 it is not defined or regulated by law. Unlike other social roles that we are expected to play – as citizens, employees, members of professional societies 20 and other organizations – it has its own subjective rationale, which is to enhance feelings of warmth, trust, love, and affection between two people.

25 The questionnaire on friendship appeared in the March issue of *Psychology Today*. The findings confirm that issues of trust and betrayal are central to 30 friendship. They also suggest that our readers do not look for friends only among those who are most like them, but find many who differ in race, sexual 35 preference, religion, and ethnic background. Arguably the most important conclusion that emerges from the data, however, is not something that we 40 found – but what we did not.

Social critics have pointed to the dislocation and isolation that they think grows out of the high mobility rate among 45 Americans and a loss of community supports. Ever since the work of sociologist Emile Durkheim, they have described the impersonality and anomie 50 of life in modern cities, where increasing numbers of people choose to live alone. They have written a good deal about a trend toward self-indulgence 55 and lack of commitment in our society, which could very well lead to tensions in friendships just as it may be contributing to the divorce rate among married 60 couples.

In the questionnaire responses, we looked for signs of dissatisfaction with the quality of people's friendships, but we 65 found few. Do people confide in their friends these days? Do they tend to turn to them in times of emotional crises? Do

*REPRINTED WITH PERMISSION FROM *PSYCHOLOGY TODAY* MAGAZINE, Copyright © 1979 (Sussex Publishers, Inc.).

70 friends become more important as one gets older? Turned around, all of these questions provide clues as to whether people today find deficits in their friendships. Most of the
75 responses to our survey strongly suggest they do not. When asked, for example, whether they felt that many of their friendships are not completely
80 reciprocal, almost 60 percent answered no. At least among our readers and others like them, friendship in America appears to be in sound health.

85 When we asked our readers to tell us what qualities they believe to be important in a friend, they valued, above all, loyalty and the ability to keep
90 confidences. Warmth, affection, and supportiveness were also high on the list, while external characteristics such as age, income, and occupation, were
95 not. Again, in the letters commenting on friendship in general, similar themes recurred: typical words and phrases were "trust," "honesty," "accepts me
100 even when he doesn't totally approve," "supportive," and "understanding."

Some insights into what holds friendships together can
105 be gained from looking at what drives them apart. When asked about reasons for a friendship's cooling off or ending, readers gave as the two most important

110 reasons feeling betrayed by a friend, and discovering that a friend had very different views on issues the respondent felt were important. The question-
115 naire answers thus confirm what many readers said explicitly in their comments: in a satisfying friendship, trust and feeling accepted are two of the
120 most essential components.

Activities of Friendship

Given the importance of trust, it is not surprising that "had an intimate talk" is the activity most or second-most
125 frequently mentioned by both men and women as something they have done with friends in the past month. Two other items high on the list of activi-
130 ties also presuppose a certain amount of trust and involvement: helping out a friend and turning to a friend for help.

Social psychologists have
135 proposed a link between trust and liking that seems to fit these friendship data. The theory suggests that trust encourages self-disclosure (revealing aspects of
140 yourself that are both precious and vulnerable). If self-disclosure meets with continued acceptance (not necessarily the same as approval of the feelings
145 or actions), liking and affection deepen – as well as trust. In this theory, self-disclosure and trust

must be reciprocated in order for the relationship to deepen.

Rules of Friendship

In addition to inquiring about actual activities, we asked some specific questions about what people would or would not do with friends, both in general and in certain hypothetical situations. We wanted our survey to give us an idea of some of the "rules" that govern, or perhaps define, behavior between friends.

As both theory and the data suggest, one rule of friendship is that friends confide in each other, sharing intimate aspects of their personal lives and feelings. Perhaps most significantly, bad as well as good news can be shared. Even though in our society, one's success is often equated with success at work, 89 percent of our sample said they would tell a close friend about a failure at work. Furthermore, over two-thirds (68 percent) said that if they had a terminal illness, they would tell a friend. Eighty-seven percent of the respondents say they talk with friends about sexual activities (60 percent discussing activities in general, 27 percent in detail).

Our respondents clearly indicated that in some situations, the rules of friendship involve the right to ask for help (presumably the obligation to help a friend is also implicity acknowledged). When asked who they would turn to first in a crisis, over half (51 percent) said they would turn to friends before family. This was true for all subgroups, even though older people in the sample said they tend to rely more on family and professional counselors in a crisis than do the younger age groups, and a higher proportion of men than women said they go it alone.

Yet friendship has limits. Only 10 percent of the sample said they thought a friend should help another commit suicide if the friend wanted to but was too feeble to do it alone (41 percent said no and 36 percent were opposed to suicide.)

In short, there are no striking contradictions between people's descriptions of actual friendships, their beliefs about friendship in general, and their perception of the rules that apply to these relationships. This consistency, and the glowing descriptions of friends and friendship we received, suggest that our readers are satisfied with their friendships, even though 67 percent of the respondents also acknowledge feeling lonely "sometimes" or "often."

Follow-up Answer the main idea question here:_____

_____

_____

E. Read for more detail

Read the article a second time. Use the questions to understand it better and to bring your own experience to the reading.

1. In what way would the results of the friendship survey surprise social critics?
2. What five qualities are important for Americans in a friend according to the survey? Would you list the same five qualities? In the same order?
3. Which of the two reasons for ending a friendship makes more sense to you?
4. What activities are most characteristic among friends? What are these activities based on?
5. What rules of friendship do Americans follow? In your friendships, do you talk about the same subjects that Americans do?
6. In what way do Americans put limits on friendship?
7. *Key words* Make a list of six words that you feel are important to the reading. Be ready to explain why each word is important, and what it means, if necessary.

Follow-up Compare your answers in pairs or small groups.

2 RESPONDING TO THE MAIN READING

A. Journals: A private audience

Choose two of the following topics. Write at least 75 words on each of them in your journal notebook. Express your opinions and feelings honestly. These journal entries are for your eyes only, so do not spend a lot of time using a dictionary or worrying about grammar.

1. Who is your closest friend? What makes the two of you close?
2. Can friends ever be more important to you than family?
3. Who has hurt you more in your life – a friend or a relative?
4. How important is friendship to you? Do you have different kinds of friends?

B. Shared writing

Choose at least two topics and write for a total of 30 minutes. Your audience is your classmates, with whom you will share your writing. They will be interested not only in *what* you feel but also in *why* you feel that way. Therefore, you will want to express your views clearly and support them.

1. What are the rules of friendship in your country?
2. In what ways is friendship in the United States similar to friendship in your country?
3. In what ways is friendship in the United States different from friendship in your country?
4. What would end a friendship in your country?

C. Feedback on your writing

Get feedback on how clear and logical your thinking and writing are. Select one of your writings from the previous section, "Shared Writing," and read it to a group of two or three classmates. Each member of the group will read one of his or her writings. Follow the procedure in "Peer Feedback Guidelines" at the end of this chapter.

Follow-up In 5 minutes, evaluate in writing how well your audience received your paper. Could they summarize it accurately? Did they understand your points? How could you make your paper clearer? More interesting to your audience?

3   GOING MORE DEEPLY INTO THE TOPIC

Which pair of friends do you think has a deeper friendship?
What makes you think so?
Is it important for friends to talk when they are together?

A. Preparing to read

Before reading a poem about friendship from *The Prophet*, by Kahlil Gibran, think about these questions. Discuss them with a friend if possible.

1. In his poem, Gibran tells us we "sow" and "reap" friendship the way a farmer sows seeds and reaps, or harvests, crops. In what way do you think we can sow and reap friendship?
2. Can you say no to a friend as easily as you say yes? Explain. (Gibran uses "nay" – pronounced like say – and "ay" – pronounced like I – for no and yes in his poem.)
3. Do you always "grieve," or feel very sad, when you leave a friend for a long time?
4. Gibran compares one's "purpose" in friendship to a fisherman casting a net to catch fish. Does real friendship bring personal gain the way that a net catches fish?

GLOSSARY

Review the glossary that follows before reading the poem, for help with some of the more difficult vocabulary.

your board and your fireside (line 4): used figuratively to mean food (and perhaps other material things) as well as comfort

seek (line 6): look for

unacclaimed (line 14): unspoken

save (line 21): except for

aught (line 22): anything

disclosure (lines 22–23): revealing, making known

the ebb of your tide . . . its flood also (lines 27–28): Literally, *ebb* and *flow* of the tide describe the daily coming in and going out of the ocean. What might they mean figuratively?

dew (line 36): the moisture left on plants and other objects by the night air

B. First exposure

If possible, listen to your teacher or a friend read Gibran's poem to you twice to answer this main idea question: *Is friendship more a matter of the mind or a matter of the heart for Gibran?*

On Friendship
BY KAHLIL GIBRAN

Your friend is your needs answered.
    He is your field which you sow with love
and reap with thanksgiving.
    And he is your board and your fireside.
5   For you come to him with your hunger,
and you seek him for peace.

    When your friend speaks his mind you
fear not the "nay" in your own mind, nor
do you withhold the "ay."
10   And when he is silent your heart ceases
not to listen to his heart;
    For without words, in friendship, all
thoughts, all desires, all expectations are born
and shared, with joy that is unacclaimed.
15   When you part from your friend, you
grieve not;
    For that which you love most in him may
be clearer in his absence, as the mountain
to the climber is clearer from the plain.

20   And let there be no purpose in friendship save the deepening of the spirit.
     For love that seeks aught but the dis-
closure of its own mystery is not love but
a net cast forth: and only the unprofitable
25   is caught.

     And let your best be for your friend.
     If he must know the ebb of your tide,
let him know its flood also.
     For what is your friend that you should
30   seek him with hours to kill?
     Seek him always with hours to live.
     For it is his to fill your need, but not
your emptiness.
     And in the sweetness of friendship let
35   there be laughter, and sharing of pleasures.
     For in the dew of little things the heart
finds its morning and is refreshed.

Follow-up   Answer the main idea question here: _____

_____

     Now read the poem to yourself and then work with a partner, if possible, to answer these questions. Answer the questions according to the views expressed in the poem.

1. How can I know how a friend feels if he or she doesn't tell me?
2. Should we show our friends only our good side? Or both our good and bad sides?
3. What does Gibran mean by "deepening of the spirit" (line 21)?
4. Express these lines in your own words: "For it is his to fill your need, but not your emptiness."

C. Additional readings

Read the poem again. Mark any places in the text that are still unclear to you. Then read these portions of the poem once more to improve your understanding of them.

D. Negotiating the meaning

Write for 15 minutes on the poem. Write on any or all of the following:

▶ whether you liked it or not, and why
▶ whether you prefer it to the previous selection
▶ what you have trouble understanding

Follow-up To a group of two or three, read what you have written. Read your reaction a second time if necessary.

   Each group member will respond with (1) a question, (2) a comment, and/or (3) clarification. Every group member should read what he or she has written. As a group, choose one response to share with the whole class.

E. Discussion: Critical thinking

Discuss these questions in pairs, small groups, or as a class.

1. Friends do not become relatives, but relatives can be friends. Can friends be as important to you as relatives?
2. Can you be as good friends with someone from another culture as with someone from your culture? Explain.
3. English has two contradictory sayings that can apply to friendship: "Birds of a feather flock together," and "Opposites attract." What do they mean? Which one describes friendship more accurately?
4. What would cause a break in friendship between you and a good friend?
5. Are friendships among women the same as friendships among men? Explain.

4 IMPROVING WRITING SKILLS

A. Using another's writing: Paraphrasing others' ideas

In your core writing assignment in this chapter, you may want to use some of the authors' ideas. Do so, but take their writing and put it into your own words by paraphrasing.

✎ **EXERCISE 1 More practice in paraphrasing sentences**

Work with a partner and follow these steps to practice paraphrasing portions of the main reading text, "The Friendship Bond":

a. Read each sentence in the following list and find it in the text. Read the whole context of the sentence (the lines before and after) several times.
b. With your partner, rewrite the sentence in your own words. To benefit more from the exercise, change the structure of the original sentence and do not use the italicized words in your paraphrase.
c. If necessary, revise your first try to make your paraphrase clear, economical, and grammatical.

1. (lines 13–16) "Unlike marriage or the ties that *bind* parents and children, it is not defined or regulated by law."
2. (lines 27–30) "The findings confirm that *issues* of trust and betrayal are *central* to friendship."
3. (lines 114–120) "The questionnaire answers thus *confirm* what many readers said explicitly in their comments: in a *satisfying* friendship, trust and feeling accepted are two of the most essential components."

---

1. Paraphrase: The law defines relationships between spouses and between parents and children and tells us how to act in them; it does not do the same for friendship. (27 words)

Revision: The law clearly states what family relationships are and how we should act in them; it does not do the same for friendships. (23 words)

Sample answer for Exercise 1, sentence 1.

4. (lines 210–216) "In short, there are no striking *contradictions* between people's descriptions of actual friendships, their *beliefs* about friendship in general, and their *perception* of the rules that apply to these relationships."

Follow-up Exchange paraphrases with at least one other pair of partners. Compare their work with yours for the accuracy of the paraphrasing, clarity, and economy of language.

B. Meeting reader expectations: Introducing the essay and logical assertions

COMPARING THE PARAGRAPH AND THE ESSAY

As you have seen, a good English paragraph expresses one main idea and provides the reader with enough logical support to be convincing. We can look at an essay the same way, with one difference: The main idea is more general, so it needs more support. Traditionally, an essay has four or more paragraphs, which correspond in function to the parts of the paragraph:

The parts of a paragraph

1. *Topic sentence*   Expresses the main idea in a sentence.
2. *Points of support (1, 2, 3, etc.)*   Secondary ideas to support the topic sentence.
3. *Conclusion*   One sentence, usually found in longer paragraphs.

The parts of an essay

1. *Thesis statement*   Expresses the main idea of the essay in a sentence. Usually located in the introduction, it is often the last sentence in this first paragraph.
2. *Body paragraphs (1, 2, 3, etc.)*   Each body paragraph will have its own main idea and therefore its own topic sentence. Secondary ideas support the topic sentences.
3. *Conclusion*   The last paragraph. A longer piece of writing needs a conclusion to end the essay.

✎ EXERCISE 2 Paragraph and essay: Correspondences

In the figure on the next page, draw arrows between the parts of the paragraph and the parts of the essay to show how the parts correspond. One arrow has been drawn for you.

ESSAY

INTRODUCTION

_____ .
_____ .
_____ .
_____ .
_____ .

Thesis statement _____ .

BODY PARAGRAPH 1

Topic sentence _____ .

_____ .
_____ .
_____ .
_____ .

_____ .

BODY PARAGRAPH 2

Topic sentence _____ .

_____ .
_____ .
_____ .
_____ .

_____ .

BODY PARAGRAPH 3

Topic sentence _____ .

_____ .
_____ .
_____ .
_____ .

_____ .

CONCLUSION

_____ .
_____ .
_____ .
_____ .
_____ .

_____ .

PARAGRAPH

Topic sentence _____ .

Support: Secondary idea 1 _____ .

Secondary idea 2 _____ .

Secondary idea 3, etc. _____ .

Conclusion _____ .

Figure for EXERCISE 2, Paragraph and essay: Correspondences.

✎ **EXERCISE 3   Student essay on friendship**

Read this student essay on friendship and answer the questions that follow.

AN INDISPENSABLE FRIENDSHIP

People have always tried to find something or
someone to trust in life. Everyone needs a good
friend to feel some kind of security and companionship. For example, many of us like to go out for
dinner on weekend nights with a friend who wants to
hear about how we feel and what our plans are.
Nowadays, it is not easy to find good and loyal
friends because there are many kinds of people with
different thoughts, feelings, and even intellect.
Despite these differences, friendship can be
classified into three categories: superficial,
selfish, and real. Even though true friendship is
to give and not to expect anything back, not all
friendships are based on this principle.

A superficial friendship is one that often makes
us fall into materialistic behavior against our
better judgment. When I was in junior high school
at the age of twelve, I had some girlfriends who
used to tell me I was quite conservative and that I
would have to dress like them if I wanted to continue being part of their group and to keep our
friendship. I thought, "I don't want to be lonely,"
and suddenly I turned into a very different person
who changed her own way of being and thinking.
Conversations between my girlfriends and me were
usually about new fashions, jewelry, singers, and
so on — mainly not very important things. I felt
uncomfortable pretending to be somebody that I
wasn't. This kind of relationship is not very deep
or sentimental and never lasts for a long time
precisely because it is superficial.

Another category of friend is the selfish
friend. An example of a selfish friendship is one

with a friend that tries to take advantage of you.
The selfish friend starts out seeming very interested in what you have to say and trying to make
you feel like an important person in his life.
After this friend gets enough confidence, he will
begin to ask you for some help or will unload his
problems on you and expect you to solve them for
him. This relationship makes you feel obligated to
your friend and not free to make friends with
others. The main reason that these relationships
occur is that we sometimes need someone to depend
on and are deceived by the selfish friend's initial
interest in us. The problem is that selfish people
may not be able to show sincere feelings of friendship to others. My personal opinion is that if we
have given our friendship sincerely, even to a
selfish friend, there is nothing to regret.

When there is a real friendship, you are always
willing to share all kinds of sadness and joy with
your friend. You can trust a real friend completely
and feel free to be just the way you are without
pretending. Real friendship gives a satisfaction
that money cannot buy and makes you feel very
important to someone you respect and love.
Actually, it is as important as the love of family.
In a real friendship, you find endless loyalty,
confidence, and security any time you need support
or even protection. Also, real friendship places no
limits on friends helping each other to reach all
their goals and desires.

These days, the need for the security and understanding of a good friend is essential for everybody. Even though we may have many kinds of friends
in our life, once we find a real one, it allows us
to give the best of ourselves to make our friends
feel good. I am sure this is the only kind of
friendship that will be everlasting.

(Elizabeth Ontiveros, Mexico)

1. How many paragraphs does the essay have?
2. Does the introduction grab your attention? Underline the thesis statement.
3. How many categories does Ms. Ontiveros classify friendship into? Do you agree with her classification?
4. Does each body paragraph have its own main idea? Is each main idea supported adequately?
5. Has Ms. Ontiveros convinced you of her thesis? Explain.

✎ EXERCISE 4   Topic sentence or thesis statement?

Look at the following main idea sentences. For each one, decide whether:

a. it is fairly specific and can be well developed in a single paragraph,
b. it requires an essay to be developed well, or
c. it could be either a paragraph or an essay topic, with modifications.

Write *P* for paragraph and *E* for essay, or *P/E* for both, and be ready to defend your choices. (*Hint*: Think of the information in the reading and your own knowledge that you would use to support these main idea sentences.)

_____   1. Friendship and kinship are different relationships in terms of loyalty, obligation, and feeling.
_____   2. Men and women cannot be real friends for a number of reasons.
_____   3. We choose our friends but not our relatives: This is the basic difference between friendship and kinship.
_____   4. There are definite qualities that Americans look for in a friend.
_____   5. There are three important characteristics that all real friendships share.
_____   6. A good friend taught me a valuable lesson about loyalty.
_____   7. There are two kinds of friends: fair-weather friends and real friends.
_____   8. Two reasons for the break-up of an American friendship stand out in research findings.
_____   9. A friend becomes part of the family in my country.
_____ 10. We have different kinds of friends for different parts of our lives.

OBJECTIVE WRITING

The writing that you do in the "Journals" and "Shared Writing" sections in Part 2 of each chapter is personal and subjective. The topics ask you to discuss what you like and dislike, to recall similar incidents from your own life, and sometimes to write about subjects that might be too intimate for a formal audience. This expressive writing is an important step to take in developing your writing. It allows you to express informally your immediate reactions to what you read.

Later, in Part 5 of each chapter, you are asked to write more formally and objectively, to move beyond what the reading means to you personally and to express your views on issues that have meaning for others as well. At this stage, your purpose is more *informative* and *persuasive* than expressive.

In Part 5, your opinion is still important, but the reasons behind your opinion are equally important and more interesting to your readers: your teacher, your classmates, or some other formal audience. Your teacher will look at your composition to see how logically you present your thoughts. He or she will look at what statement you make about the topic and what proof you use to support your view. In other words, as you move from Part 2 of each chapter to Part 5, your thinking and writing will progress from the *subjective* to the *objective*.

MAKING LOGICAL ASSERTIONS

Writing objectively for a formal audience requires a slightly different approach to a topic. One way to bring objectivity to your writing is to make sure that your thesis statement makes a *logical assertion*.

A logical assertion is a statement of opinion or judgment that you can support logically. Consider the following statements:

(1) My father is my best friend.
(2) Italy won the World Cup in 1990.
(3) The food in my country is the most delicious in the world.
(4) There is intelligent life on other planets.
(5) Computers create more employment than unemployment.

Statement 1 may be true, but it is a subjective assertion, one that cannot be supported logically. Statement 2 is a matter of fact; there is nothing in it that is arguable. Either it is true or it isn't.

Statement 3 may also be true, but it is simply an expression of taste. There is no arguing with taste, so even a researched attempt to prove the assertion logically would have no point. Statement 4 may be true, but there is no way to verify it; thus, it is impossible to support logically.

Only statement 5 is a logical assertion. It expresses an opinion about computers that a reader may disagree with. Logical support is necessary to convince the reader, who might easily take the opposite view without proof. Even if the reader agrees with the assertion, he or she will probably be interested in why the writer has made the assertion.

In making sure that the thesis statement of your essay is a logical assertion, you are building your composition on a firm foundation. You have a reason to think and write about the topic, and the reader has a reason to read your writing.

✎ EXERCISE 5   Logical assertions

Read the statements. Decide whether each one is a logical assertion that could serve as the thesis statement in an essay.

If a statement is a good logical assertion, write *LA* in the blank. If you decide a statement is not a logical assertion, find the reason why in the following list of choices, and write the letter of the reason in the blank.

a. It is a subjective assertion.
b. It is not a matter of judgment or opinion; it is a matter of fact.
c. It is a question of taste.
d. It may be true, but it cannot be verified.

_____ 1. Soccer is the world's best sport.
_____ 2. Women do not drive as well as men.
_____ 3. More men than women were involved in car accidents last year.
_____ 4. Money can't buy happiness.
_____ 5. The wrong diet can lead to health problems.
_____ 6. A woman has no hope of being elected president of the United States.
_____ 7. The late John F. Kennedy would not approve of the present U.S. president's foreign policy.
_____ 8. Women and men can be friends under certain circumstances.
_____ 9. I like classical music better than popular music.
_____ 10. Friendship between people of two different cultures presents obstacles to overcome.

C. Language conventions: Subject-verb agreement

SUBJECT-VERB AGREEMENT

To be good English sentences that are easy to read, the sentences you write must have subjects and verbs that agree. Simply put, this means singular subjects should have singular verbs, and plural subjects should have plural verbs, as in the examples that follow. Note that the subjects are underlined, and verbs appear in italics.

Friendship *is* unlike other relationships
(A non-count noun takes a singular verb.)

A friend in need *is* a friend indeed.
(A singular noun takes a singular verb.)

Most people *feel* that good friends *are* necessary to their lives.
(Plural nouns take plural verbs.)

<u>Being able to confide in one another</u> *is* an important component of true friendship.

(A gerund phrase is singular by definition.)

To help make subjects and verbs agree in your writing, follow the eight guidelines presented on the following pages.

Guideline 1   Subjects connected by *and* are plural.

<u>Friendship</u> and <u>kinship</u> *are* very different relationships.

A <u>friend</u> and a <u>relative</u> *occupy* important but different places in our lives.

Guideline 2   Phrases that come between the subject and verb do not affect the verb (examples: *in addition to, as well as, along with*). (*Remember:* The subject is never part of a prepositional phrase.)

<u>Friendship</u>, unlike relations with relatives, *reflects* personal choice.

<u>Kinship</u>, for better or worse, *is* a condition of birth that we have no choice in.

✎ EXERCISE 6   Subject-verb agreement: Guidelines 1 and 2

Underline the subjects in each sentence and circle the correct form of the verbs.

1. A friend accepts/accept our weaknesses, whereas relatives often pretends/pretend that we don't have any weaknesses.
2. Sharing confidences with friends and trusting them to be discreet is/are important requirements of friendship.
3. Loyalty, or an unspoken agreement to remain faithful and supportive, is/are more often expected in friendship than in kinship.
4. A cousin and a brother never stops/stop being relatives, but a friend sometimes does/do stop being a friend.
5. A friend, to deepen the friendly relations, shares/share his or her deepest feelings with you.
6. A relative, especially a close one, very likely knows/know how you are feeling without having to ask.

Follow-up   Write two original sentences illustrating Guideline 1 and two sentences illustrating Guideline 2. Write about the differences between friendship and kinship in your country.

Guideline 3 The subject usually comes before the verb but can come after it. (*Remember: There* is never the subject of a sentence.)

> Among the most important components of friendship *is* the ability to compromise.
>
> There *are* different categories of friend.

Guideline 4 In relative clauses, *who, which,* and *that* as subjects take their number from the word they refer to.

> Friends need to see our good side, of course, but also our flaws, which *are* just as much a part of who we are.
>
> To show your bad side to others, which *includes* telling your fears, disappointments, and negative feelings, can sometimes be hard. (*Note:* an infinitive phrase, like a gerund phrase, is singular by definition, so the relative pronoun that refers to it takes a singular verb.)

✎ EXERCISE 7 Subject-verb agreement: Guidelines 3 and 4

Underline the subject in each sentence and circle the correct forms of the verbs.

1. People who knows/know only your good side doesn't/don't know all of you.
2. Being honest about negative feelings, which includes/include saying that you have been hurt, lets/let a friend get to know you better.
3. There is/are a number of habits that can keep a friendship from growing.
4. Among the worst of these habits is/are the tendency to "keep score," which means/mean comparing what one gives to what one receives in a friendship.
5. Keeping score in friendships that is/are important to you may harm the relationships.
6. Related to keeping score is/are another problem, in which some individuals has/have difficulty accepting help from a friend.
7. Those who has/have trouble accepting others' generosity needs/need to remember how happy they are to help a friend.

Follow-up Write two original sentences illustrating Guideline 3 and two illustrating Guideline 4. Write about showing both your good and bad sides to a friend.

Guideline 5 With correlative conjunctions *either . . . or* and *neither . . . nor,* the verb agrees with the second subject.

When a break in a friendship occurs among Americans, either a betrayal or <u>differing views</u> on something important *are* often the cause.

When a break in a friendship occurs among Americans, either differing views on something important or a <u>betrayal</u> *is* often the cause.

Guideline 6   Most indefinite pronouns, though often plural in meaning, take a singular verb. (Singular indefinite pronouns include *each, either, neither, everyone, everybody, somebody, something, everything, anybody, nothing, no one,* and *nobody.*)

<u>Everyone</u> *needs* friends, so <u>no one</u> *is* completely happy without them.

Not <u>everything</u> that *has been said* about friendship necessarily *holds* true for kinship.

Notes on Guideline 6   *Neither* and *either* as pronouns take singular verbs. Do not confuse them with the correlative conjunctions *either . . . or* and *neither . . . nor,* whose grammar is different.

CORRELATIVE CONJUNCTION   Either my sister or my <u>parents</u> *plan* to watch my house while I'm gone.

INDEFINITE PRONOUN   <u>Neither</u> of my brothers *has* the time to help me.

Both, few, several, and *many* take plural verbs.

<u>Both</u> of my brothers *have* demanding jobs.

None, some, most, and *all* take a singular verb when used with non-count nouns and a plural verb when used with plural count nouns.

<u>Most</u> of Tim's time *is* spent watching television.

<u>Most</u> of my friends *have* children.

✎ EXERCISE 8   Subject-verb agreement: Guidelines 5 and 6

Underline the subject in each sentence and circle the correct forms of the verbs.

1. Neither France nor other European countries has/have the same friendship patterns as the United States.
2. In the United States, neither a person's intellect nor his or her interests plays/play as big a part in friendship as in France.
3. In France, a friend is someone who encourages/encourage one's best thinking.

4. Each of the friends develops/develop a clearer sense of politics, art, or sports, for example.
5. In Germany, on the other hand, most friendships is/are based on feeling.
6. Both devotion and loyalty is/are important in German friendships.
7. English friends are comfortable in a relationship in which everyone is/are able to anticipate how the others will react in any given situation.
8. Neither the French nor the English brings/bring friends into the family circle as often as Germans do.
9. All three groups is/are sometimes confused by the American tendency to treat a casual acquaintance like a friend.
10. No American has/have trouble distinguishing between a casual friend and a good one, but Americans' casual acceptance of strangers is/are often misunderstood by foreigners.

> (Based on "Different Lands, Different Friendships,"
> by Margaret Meade, in *Redbook*, Aug. 1966.)

Follow-up   On a separate sheet, write two sentences illustrating Guideline 5 and two illustrating Guideline 6. Write sentences about the difference between casual relationships and good friendships in your country.

Guideline 7   Group nouns have a plural meaning but usually take a singular verb in American English. (Group nouns include *family, class, committee, government, team, audience, band, group,* and *company*.)

My <u>family</u> *is* very large if I count all my cousins.

The gas <u>company</u> *employs* more people than any other company in town.

Guideline 8   Some nouns that end in *-s* appear to be plural but take singular verbs. (Nouns in this category include *physics, economics, mathematics, news,* and *politics*.)

<u>Mathematics</u> *was* my hardest subject at school.

No <u>news</u> *is* good news, they say.

✎ EXERCISE 9   Subject-verb agreement: Guidelines 7 and 8

Underline the subject and circle the correct form of the verb.

1. A young audience is/are often more enthusiastic than an older one.
2. He found that physics was/were more difficult for him than he had thought it would be.

3. From what they said on TV, the government is/are going to announce tax reforms soon.
4. Politics has/have never made much sense to me.
5. The news about the earthquakes was/were quite discouraging.

Follow-up Write two sentences illustrating Guideline 7 and two illustrating Guideline 8.

✎ EXERCISE 10   Editing for subject-verb agreement

This paragraph contains subject-verb agreement errors. Read through the paragraph and rewrite it to correct the errors.

> For me loyalty is an important part of friendship. A loyal friend is true and faithful to me. Loyalty do not mean that my friend should support me when I am wrong, however. Sometimes people supports friends who has lied or been dishonest to others. This kind of support is not loyalty. A loyal friend would support my decision to go away to school, even if it meant our separation. A loyal friend supports decisions and actions which honestly benefit you, even if the friend lose something in the process.

5 CORE WRITING ASSIGNMENT

A. Writing topics

Choose an essay topic from the list that follows. In the remaining sections of this chapter, you will be asked to develop an essay on this topic.

1. *Comparison/contrast* Compare or contrast friendship and kinship.
2. *Cause/effect* What causes a friendship to break apart?
3. *Definition* Write your own definition of friendship.
4. *Classification* How many different kinds of friends are there? Classify friends into all the categories that they fall into.
5. *Additional topics* If you and your teacher agree on one or more additional topics, list them here:

_____

_____

B. Generating ideas: Mind mapping

Generate ideas for your essay by drawing a map of your mind. A sample mind map for topic 1 in Section A, "Compare or contrast friendship and kinship," appears on the following page.

To start your mind map, think of one word or phrase that characterizes how you feel about your topic and which expresses your purpose in writing. Write that word in a box in the middle of the page. (In the sample mind map for topic 1, the student has written "friendship and kinship are different.")

Write more specific ideas on arms that lead out of the box, and on branches leading off of the arms. Draw as many arms and branches as you need. Try to get all of your ideas on paper.

When you finish the mind map, evaluate your ideas. Circle the ideas that you like best. Then draw lines to connect the circled ideas that go together logically. Concentrating on these better ideas, write three questions that you would like to explore with classmates.

C. Expanding your point of view: Group discussion

Get together with a small group of students in your class who have chosen the same writing topic. Take turns asking the questions each of you wrote in Section B. Discuss and listen to each other's ideas.

Follow-up Quickly write down at least three new ideas that came out in the discussion.

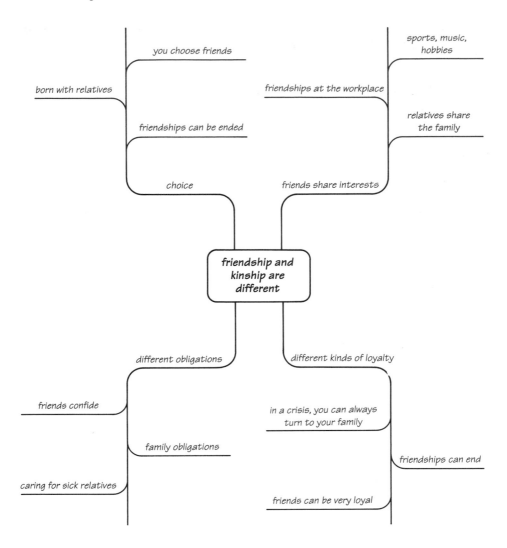

Sample mind map for Section B, "Generating ideas: Mind mapping."

D. Initial drafts

The standard academic essay has an introduction, body paragraphs, and a conclusion. In your paper, let what you have to say determine how many paragraphs there will be.

The essay topics in this chapter are labeled by pattern of organization: comparison/contrast, cause/effect, definition, and classification. These labels do not mean that every body paragraph must be a comparison if you chose topic 1. You can use examples and definitions to compare and contrast two ideas. Likewise, you can use a narrative paragraph to develop an essay defining friendship. The important thing to keep in mind is your *overall* purpose in writing – to compare, define, classify, or to analyze cause – and to use any patterns that serve your overall purpose.

GUIDELINES

Title Write a title for your composition. Make it short, relevant to your topic, and interesting.

Paragraph 1: Introduction Include a sentence that expresses your main idea, or thesis. You might want to write the introduction after you write the rest of your essay. However, decide on your thesis before writing the body to keep your purpose in writing in mind. Be sure your thesis statement makes a logical assertion.

The introduction does not need to be long, but it must be more than one sentence. Do not begin your introduction with a pronoun or refer to the title; the introduction, not the title, begins your composition.

Body paragraphs (Paragraphs 2, 3, etc.) Each paragraph should be complete and unified, with its own topic sentence that supports the thesis statement in the introduction. Make sure you keep body paragraphs distinct: Each one has its own main idea and does not repeat information from other body paragraphs.

Last paragraph: Conclusion This can be short, but it should be more than one sentence. Remind your readers of your thesis, or give them something related to think about.

REVISION 1: Adding specific details

Let your first draft sit for a while. Then revise it, with attention to *specific details*. To gain a clearer understanding of the form and function of specific details, read these two paragraphs and answer the questions that follow.

(1)   The story of the friendship of Phintias and his friend is a wonderful example of loyalty. Phintias was sentenced to death. However, because of family obligations, he got permission to return home before his execution. As a guarantee that he would return, his friend was held by the leader. Phintias was delayed but returned just before his friend was executed in his place. The leader was so impressed by their loyalty that he pardoned Phintias.

(2)   The story of the friendship of the two Greeks, Damon and Phintias, which goes back more than 2000 years, is a wonderful example of loyalty. For attempting to assassinate the leader, Dionysius I, Phintias was sentenced to death. Because he wanted to attend the marriage of his sister, however, he got permission to return home for three days before he was to be executed. As a guarantee that he would return for his sentence, his friend Damon was held by Dionysius. When returning from the wedding, Phintias was delayed, first by raging floods, then by a collapsed bridge, and finally by thieves. It seemed he would never return before Damon was crucified in his place. But just moments before Damon was nailed to the cross, Phintias arrived, in rags and gasping for breath. Dionysius was so impressed by Damon and Phintias's loyalty to each other that he not only pardoned Phintias but asked to be their friend.

1. It is easy to see which paragraph is longer. Which version will you probably remember better? Why?
2. Decide which item in each of the following pairs is more general and which is more specific:

   leader/Dionysius I   Damon/friend
   wedding/family obligations   executed/crucified

3. Both versions of the story of Phintias and his friend are narratives. Which version put "pictures" in your mind? When you think of that version, what pictures do you see in your mind?
4. Which paragraph is more effective – that is, which one better achieves its purpose of giving an example of loyalty?

(*Note:* Most people will find the second version of this story more effective because it offers specific details that create mental images, or pictures in the reader's mind.)

REVISION 2

For more direction in revising, study the criteria listed in the "Essay Assessment Guidelines" at the end of this chapter. Revise your paper with these guidelines in mind. Label this latest draft "Revision 2."

E. Review, revision, and assessment

PEER FEEDBACK

Get feedback on how clear and logical your thinking and writing are. Read your essay to a group of two or three classmates. Each member of the group will read his or her paper to the group. Follow the "Peer Feedback Guidelines" at the end of this chapter.

FURTHER REVISION

How well did your group receive your paper? Could they summarize it accurately? Did they understand your main points? Secondary points? How could your paper be clearer and/or more interesting to your audience? Make notes of changes you need to make.

If necessary, revise your paper using the feedback you got from your group. Edit your paper for subject-verb agreement. Submit all drafts to your teacher, with the last one marked "Revision 3" at the top.

If you choose not to revise, write a paragraph to your teacher summarizing the feedback you received and explaining why you decided not to revise.

TEACHER ASSESSMENT

Your teacher will assess your paper using the detailed set of essay assessment guidelines in Appendix B. Your teacher may grade the paper or allow you to make further revisions before assigning a grade.

PEER FEEDBACK GUIDELINES

Writers

- ☐ Read the paper clearly, a second time if necessary.
- ☐ Respond to listeners' comments and questions.
- ☐ Ask for suggestions if you want them.

Listeners

- ☐ Listen quietly until the writer finishes reading.
- ☐ Briefly summarize what you understood, orally.
- ☐ Pick out parts of the paper (words, expressions, or ideas) that stand out for you. Share these parts with the group.
- ☐ If you wish, share with the group how the writing makes you feel and ask questions about parts that are not clear.
- ☐ Do not make negative comments or tell the writer what changes to make.

ESSAY ASSESSMENT GUIDELINES

These are the criteria for a well-written paragraph. Use this checklist to critically examine your writing and determine how it can be improved. See Appendix B for the more detailed set of guidelines that your teacher will use to assess your final draft.

Content and ideas

- ☐ The writer has thought about the topic and has a clear thesis.
- ☐ The writer discusses each main point enough to give the reader a reason to believe it. The writer supports each main point, and no important point is left out.
- ☐ The writer's voice is clear because he or she writes in a sincere way, with the audience in mind.

Organization and form

- ☐ The paper has a clear beginning, middle, and end, with separate introductory, body, and concluding paragraphs. It moves logically in a straight line.
- ☐ The reader wants to continue reading and can understand the thesis and other main points fully after one reading.
- ☐ It is clear which are the main points and which are the secondary points.

Writing conventions

☐ The writer uses a variety of sentence types to add interest to the writing.

☐ The writer chooses vocabulary carefully to communicate clearly.

☐ The writer avoids problems of sentence structure including fragments, comma-splices, and run-together sentences.

☐ The writer uses English grammar effectively to convey the message. There are few problems of verb tense, subject-verb agreement, word order, count/noncount use, or word form.

☐ The writer follows rules for spelling, capitalization, and punctuation.

Human Nature and the Nature of Work

This drawing depicts two characters from a traditional fable,
"The Ant and The Grasshopper."
Where might the ant be going with the kernel of corn?
What do its actions suggest about its attitude toward work?

1 GETTING A GRIP ON THE TOPIC

A. Reflection

Aesop was a writer of fables who lived in Ancient Greece. A fable is a very short story that the author uses to teach a lesson. Read this Aesop's fable to answer the following question: Are you more like the ant or the grasshopper in this story?

VOCABULARY

plodding (line 2): moving along slowly without resting
scoffed (line 8): laughed, mocked
slaved away (line 14): worked very hard

The Ant and the Grasshopper
AN AESOP'S FABLE

A grasshopper was singing away one summer's day when an ant came plodding by, bent under the weight of a kernel of corn.

"Why work so hard in this fine warm weather?" the grasshopper
5 called to the ant. "Why not enjoy yourself, like me?"

"I'm storing up food for the winter," the ant replied. "And I suggest you do the same."

"Winter!" scoffed the grasshopper. "Who cares about winter! We have more food than we can eat."

10 The ant held his tongue and went about his business.

Then winter set in, and soon the grasshopper couldn't find so much as a grain of barley or wheat. He went to the ant to beg for some food, knowing the ant had plenty.

"Friend grasshopper," said the ant, "you sang while I slaved away
15 last summer, and laughed at me besides. Sing now and see what it will get you."

SAVE FOR THE FUTURE AND YOU WON'T BE WITHOUT.

B. Discussion

Reread the fable out loud in groups of three, and take parts: the narrator, the grasshopper, and the ant. (The narrator begins.) Then discuss these questions as a group and as a class.

1. During the summer months, which insect seems more content?
2. How does the situation change in the winter?
3. Do you think most people live according to the moral expressed in the last line of the fable? Do you?
4. In life, is industry (hard work) always rewarded and idleness punished?

C. Notes on the main reading

W. Somerset Maugham introduces this humorous variation on the Aesop's fable of the ant and the grasshopper with another version of the same fable, written by La Fontaine. Maugham recounts La Fontaine's fable in a rather stilted (literary, formal) style, but he quickly changes to a more conversational style to tell the story of the industrious George Ramsay (a fictional character), which you should have little trouble following. Notice that there is a flash-back; the writer uses the past to help us understand the present in the story. We learn from the flashback about George's younger brother, Tom, the *black sheep* in the family. Tom is the one who is different from other family members, less respectable, and a source of worry to George. George and Tom resemble the ant and the grasshopper in the fable.

VOCABULARY EXERCISE

Look over the following vocabulary with a partner. With what you already know about George and Tom, suggest how you think each word or expression might be used in the story. Check a dictionary for the meanings of unknown words.

charming   philander
promises of amendment   idle
blackmail (verb)   end in the gutter

GLOSSARY

Review the glossary before reading the selection, for help with some of the more difficult vocabulary.

giddiness (line 5): lack of seriousness
blade (line 9): leaf

larder (line 11): room where food is kept
saving your presence (line 14): without meaning to annoy you
gloom (line 18): sadness, hopelessness
in hilarious spirits (line 24): in a very good mood
chuck (line 28): give up on, discard
a sore trial (lines 30–31): an annoyance, a problem
wasn't suited for (line 36): didn't have the right qualities for
expostulations (line 37): friendly protests
unscrupulous (line 43): not extremely honest, unprincipled
insensible to such enticements (line 49): not persuaded by his brother's
    charm
qualm (line 55): doubt, hesitation
as if he had just stepped out of a bandbox (line 64–65): very well dressed
    and neat (Brit.)
grudged (line 69): was unwilling to give
levied on (line 69): collected (like a tax) from
scapegrace (line 74): good for nothing
unfaithful (line 78): having a sexual relationship with someone else
blameless (line 82): free from faults
infamous (line 92): wicked, shameful
thrift (line 100): careful use of money, without waste
gilt-edged securities (lines 100–101): safe investments
Providence (line 102): God's care
dissolute (lines 104–105): evil, immoral
workhouse (line 106): place for poor people to live
wrathful (line 116): angry
trifle (line 119): small amount
sovereign (line 120): an old British gold coin

D. Read for the main idea

Read the story quickly to decide whether the message in this modern story is
the same as, or different from, the one in the Aesop's fable.

The Ant and the Grasshopper
W. Somerset Maugham

When I was a very small boy I was made to learn by heart certain
of the fables of La Fontaine, and the moral of each was carefully
explained to me. Among those I learnt was *The Ant and the
Grasshopper,* which is devised to bring home to the young the useful

lesson that in an imperfect world industry is rewarded and giddiness   5
punished. In this admirable fable (I apologise for telling something
which everyone is politely, but inexactly, supposed to know) the ant
spends a laborious summer gathering its winter store, while the
grasshopper sits on a blade of grass singing to the sun. Winter comes
and the ant is comfortably provided for, but the grasshopper has an   10
empty larder: he goes to the ant and begs for a little food. Then the
ant gives him her classic answer:

'What were you doing in the summer time?'

'Saving your presence, I sang, I sang all day, all night.'

'You sang. Why, then go and dance.'   15

I could not help thinking of this fable when the other day I saw
George Ramsay lunching by himself in a restaurant. I never saw anyone wear an expression of such deep gloom. He was staring into
space. He looked as though the burden of the whole world sat on his
shoulders. I was sorry for him: I suspected at once that his unfortu-   20
nate brother had been causing trouble again. I went up to him and
held out my hand.

'How are you?' I asked.

'I'm not in hilarious spirits,' he answered.

'Is it Tom again?'   25

He sighed.

'Yes, it's Tom again.'

'Why don't you chuck him? You've done everything in the world
for him. You must know by now that he's quite hopeless.'

I suppose every family has a black sheep. Tom had been a sore   30
trial to his for twenty years. He had begun life decently enough: he
went into business, married, and had two children. The Ramsays
were perfectly respectable people and there was every reason to suppose that Tom Ramsay would have a useful and honourable career.
But one day, without warning, he announced that he didn't like work   35
and that he wasn't suited for marriage. He wanted to enjoy himself.
He would listen to no expostulations. He left his wife and his office.
He had a little money and he spent two happy years in the various
capitals of Europe. Rumours of his doings reached his relations from
time to time and they were profoundly shocked. He certainly had a   40
very good time. They shook their heads and asked what would hap-

pen when his money was spent. They soon found out: he borrowed.
He was charming and unscrupulous. I have never met anyone to
whom it was more difficult to refuse a loan. He made a steady income
from his friends and he made friends easily. But he always said that
the money you spent on necessities was boring; the money that was
amusing to spend was the money you spent on luxuries. For this he
depended on his brother George. He did not waste his charm on him.
George was a serious man and insensible to such enticements. George
was respectable. Once or twice he fell to Tom's promises of amendment and gave him considerable sums in order that he might make a
fresh start. On these Tom bought a motor-car and some very nice jew-
ellery. But when circumstances forced George to realize that his
brother would never settle down and he washed his hands of him,
Tom, without a qualm, began to blackmail him. It was not very nice
for a respectable lawyer to find his brother shaking cocktails behind
the bar of his favourite restaurant or to see him waiting on the box-
seat of a taxi outside his club. Tom said that to serve in a bar or to
drive a taxi was a perfectly decent occupation, but if George could
oblige him with a couple of hundred pounds he didn't mind for the
honour of the family giving it up. George paid.

For twenty years Tom raced and gambled, philandered with the
prettiest girls, danced, ate in the most expensive restaurants, and
dressed beautifully. He always looked as if he had just stepped out of
a bandbox. Though he was forty-six you would never have taken him
for more than thirty-five. He was a most amusing companion and
though you knew he was perfectly worthless you could not but enjoy
his society. He had high spirits, and unfailing gaiety, and incredible
charm. I never grudged the contributions he regularly levied on me
for the necessities of his existence. I never lent him fifty pounds without feeling that I was in his debt. Tom Ramsay knew everyone and
everyone knew Tom Ramsay. You could not approve of him, but you
could not help liking him.

Poor George, only a year older than his scapegrace brother,
looked sixty. He had never taken more than a fortnight's holiday in
the year for a quarter of a century. He was in his office every morning
at nine-thirty and never left it till six. He was honest, industrious, and
worthy. He had a good wife, to whom he had never been unfaithful
even in thought, and four daughters to whom he was the best of

fathers. He made a point of saving a third of his income and his plan   80
was to retire at fifty-five to a little house in the country where he proposed to cultivate his garden and play golf. His life was blameless. He
was glad that he was growing old because Tom was growing old too.
He rubbed his hands and said:

'It was all very well when Tom was young and good-looking, but   85
he's only a year younger than I am. In four years he'll be fifty. He
won't find life so easy then. I shall have thirty thousand pounds by
the time I'm fifty. For twenty-five years I've said that Tom would end
in the gutter. And we shall see how he likes that. We shall see if it
really pays best to work or be idle.'   90

Poor George! I sympathized with him. I wondered now as I sat
down beside him what infamous thing Tom had done. George was
evidently very much upset.

'Do you know what's happened now?' he asked me.

I was prepared for the worst. I wondered if Tom had got into the   95
hands of the police at last. George could hardly bring himself to
speak.

'You're not going to deny that all my life I've been hardworking,
decent, respectable, and straightforward. After a life of industry and
thrift I can look forward to retiring on a small income in gilt-edged   100
securities. I've always done my duty in that state of life in which it has
pleased Providence to place me.'

'True.'

'And you can't deny that Tom has been an idle, worthless, dissolute, and dishonourable rogue. If there were any justice he'd be in   105
the workhouse.'

'True.'

George grew red in the face.

'A few weeks ago he became engaged to a woman old enough to
be his mother. And now she's died and left him everything she had.   110
Half a million pounds, a yacht, a house in London, and a house in the
country.'

George Ramsay beat his clenched fist on the table.

'It's not fair, I tell you, it's not fair. Damn it, it's not fair.'

I could not help it. I burst into a shout of laughter as I looked at   115
George's wrathful face, I rolled in my chair, I very nearly fell on the
floor. George never forgave me. But Tom often asks me to excellent

dinners in his charming house in Mayfair, and if he occasionally borrows a trifle from me, that is merely from force of habit. It is never
120   more than a sovereign.

Follow-up The message in Maugham's story is (check one):

_____   the same as

_____   different from

the message in the Aesop's fable of the ant and the grasshopper.

E. Read for more detail

Read the story a second time. Use the questions to understand it better and to
bring your own experience to the reading.

1. What things didn't George Ramsay like about his brother Tom? Do you
   feel the same way about Tom?
2. How was it that Tom always had money if he didn't work regularly? Why
   did George give Tom money even after George had "washed his hands of
   him"?
3. In what ways was George like the ant and his brother like the grasshopper
   in the fables?
4. Why was George so upset by Tom's good fortune at the end of the story?
   Were you happy for Tom or disappointed?
5. How is the message in Maugham's story different from the message in the
   fables?
6. *Key words* Make a list of six words or expressions that you feel are
   important to the story. Be ready to explain why each word or phrase is
   important, and what it means, if necessary.

Follow-up Discuss your answers in small groups or as a class.

2   RESPONDING TO THE MAIN READING

A. Journals: A private audience

Choose two topics. Write at least 75 words on each in your journal notebook. Express yourself honestly. These journal entries are for your eyes only, so do not spend a lot of time using a dictionary or worrying about grammar.

1. Which insect from the fables, the ant or the grasshopper, do you resemble more in personality? How?
2. Which of the two brothers in the story do you admire more? Why?
3. Does either Tom or George remind you of someone you know? Who? In what ways?

B. Shared writing

Choose at least two topics and write for a total of 30 minutes. Your audience is your classmates, with whom you will share your writing. They will be interested not only in *what* you feel but also in *why* you feel that way. Therefore, you will want to express your views clearly and support them.

1. Which moral, or message, do you agree with, the one in the Aesop's fable or the one in Maugham's story? Why?
2. Do you dislike one of the brothers? Which one? Why? Imagine how he might defend his actions in the story.
3. Write a letter to Tom or George, giving him advice on how to improve his life. Explain the reasons for the advice you give.
4. Which "Ant and the Grasshopper" did you like better, the fable or the Maugham story? Why?

C. Feedback on your writing

Get feedback on how clear and logical your thinking and writing are. Select one of your writings from the previous section, "Shared Writing," and read it to a group of two or three classmates. Each member of the group will read one of his or her writings. Follow the procedure in "Peer Feedback Guidelines" at the end of this chapter.

Follow-up   In 5 minutes, evaluate in writing how well your audience received your paper. Could they summarize it accurately? Did they understand your points? How could you make your paper clearer? More interesting to your audience?

3 GOING MORE DEEPLY INTO THE TOPIC

These photographs, all taken in the United States, show
people working at three different kinds of jobs.
Do you think that these workers all have the same amount
of control over their work?

A. Preparing to read

In this article from the popular magazine *Psychology Today*, social researcher
Daniel Yankelovich discusses the American work ethic. A work ethic is a culture's attitude toward work. In the past, the United States had a very strong

work ethic. People worked hard out of a sense of obligation, expecting to work hard with little time for recreation and taking pride in their work and in doing their job well. Today many experts believe that the Protestant work ethic, as this attitude has been called, is not as strong as it once was. They see countries like Korea, Germany, Japan, and Taiwan threatening the U.S. standard of living by working harder than Americans are willing to work. Yankelovich investigates these judgments about the American work ethic today.

   Before you read, take a look at three conceptions of work. Which one best describes why people work, in your opinion? Would most people in your country agree with your answer?

1. People work only because they wouldn't be able to support themselves if they didn't.
2. People see work like a business deal: the more money they get, the harder they work; the less money they get, the less effort they give to the job.
3. There is a moral imperative (an obligation based on the principles of right and wrong) that workers must do their best at a job without thinking of the money they will get for the work.

Follow-up   Discuss your choices as a class.

GLOSSARY

Review the glossary before reading the selection, for help with some of the more difficult vocabulary.

embrace (line 15): accept
reconcile (line 23): make consistent
reveals a slackening effort (line 25–26): shows they are trying less hard
outpace us (line 28): leave us behind
deeply flawed reward system (line 30): a system offering too little pay and
   satisfaction
adequacy (line 45): being good enough to meet the requirements, only
acknowledged (line 49): agreed, admitted
benefit from (line 54): gain from

B. First reading

In an earlier part of this article, Yankelovich acknowledges a decline in U.S. workers' effort and productivity. However, he does not believe the American work ethic is weaker than before. Read the whole selection to answer this main idea question: *How does Yankelovich explain why U.S. workers have been working less than before?*

*The Work Ethic Is Underemployed**

Daniel Yankelovich

A 1982 pilot study for the nonprofit Public Agenda Foundation explores three conceptions of what might be called the "unwritten work contract" – the assumption that each individual makes about what he or she will give to the job and expects to get in return. The

5 first conception is one that historians recognize as the dominant attitude toward work throughout human history: the view that people labor only because they would not otherwise have the resources to sustain themselves. A second conception regards work as a straight economic transaction in which people relate effort to financial return:

10 The more money they get, the harder they work; the less money they receive, the less effort they give. The third conception views work as carrying a moral imperative to do one's best apart from practical necessity or financial remuneration.

Nearly four out of five people in the work force (78 percent)

15 embrace the third conception, aligning themselves with the statement: "I have an inner need to do the very best job I can regardless of pay." Fewer than one out of ten working Americans (7 percent) embrace the idea of work as a mere "business transaction" whereby one regulates one's effort according to the size of one's paycheck, and an addi-

20 tional 15 percent regard work as a necessary but disagreeable chore. ("Working for a living is one of life's necessities. I would not work if I did not have to.") . . .

How then, are we to reconcile these two sets of seemingly incompatible facts? Why do Americans endorse the ideal of giving one's

25 best to the job while their actual performance reveals a slackening effort? What forces have produced this self-defeating situation at the precise moment when economic competition from Japan, Taiwan, Germany, and other nations threatens to outpace us and drag down our standard of living?

30 The answer lies, I believe, in the deeply flawed reward system, both psychological and financial, that now rules the American workplace. To grasp this argument, we need to understand just what most

*REPRINTED WITH PERMISSION FROM *PSYCHOLOGY TODAY* MAGAZINE, Copyright ©
1982 (Sussex Publishers, Inc.).

work is like today. The Public Agenda survey asked people the amount of control they exercised over how hard they worked and over the quality of the products they made or services they performed. A huge majority (82 percent) stated that they had some degree of discretion and control over the effort they gave to their job, and an even larger majority (88 percent) said that they had control over the quality of the work or service they performed (72 percent, a great deal of control; 16 percent, moderate control). This finding illuminates a little-noted but important fact about the modern workplace: Most working Americans have it in their power to decide whether they will satisfy only the minimum requirements of their job or exert the extra effort that makes the difference between ordinariness and high quality, between adequacy and excellence.

When the Public Agenda survey asked people whether they were using this freedom of choice to fulfill their "inner need to do the very best job" they can, fewer than one out of five (16 percent) said they were. All others acknowledged that they could improve their effectiveness – if they really wanted to. And many claimed that they could be twice as effective as they are now.

Why aren't they? The answer could hardly be plainer. When Gallup's Chamber of Commerce study asked workers whom they thought would benefit from the improvements in their productivity, only 9 percent felt that they, the workers, would. Most assumed that the beneficiaries would be others – consumers or stockholders or management. This finding accords with the findings of Yankelovich, Skelly and White several years ago that a majority of college students no longer believe that working hard pays off. Some interpreted this finding to mean that the work ethic was eroding. It signifies, rather, the growing doubt that hard work will bring the rewards people have come to cherish. When Gallup's Chamber of Commerce study asked people whether they would work harder and do a better job if they were more involved in decisions relating to their work, an overwhelming 84 percent said they would. One need not take this finding literally to appreciate the vast sea of yearning that underlies it.

Follow-up　Answer the main idea question here: _____

C. Additional readings

Read the selection again. Mark any places in the text that are still unclear to you. Then read these passages once more to improve your understanding of them.

D. Negotiating the meaning

Write at least 75 words on this selection. Write on any or all of the following:

▶ whether you liked it or not and why
▶ whether you prefer it to the previous selection
▶ what you have trouble understanding

Follow-up   To a group of two or three, read what you have written. Read your reaction a second time if necessary.

   Each group member will respond with (1) a question, (2) a comment, and/or (3) clarification. Every group member should read what he or she has written. As a group, choose one response to share with the whole class.

E. Discussion: Critical thinking

Discuss these questions in pairs, small groups, or as a class.

1. Do Yankelovich's conclusions about workers' productivity apply only to the United States? Would his conclusions about involving workers in decision-making be valid for your country, too? Give evidence to support your answer.
2. In Maugham's story, George and Tom obviously have different work ethics. Does this difference explain why they don't get along? Is there a better explanation?
3. Summarize Yankelovich's distinction between work attitudes and work behaviors. Discuss other issues towards which attitudes and behaviors may differ in the same people, in politics or business, for example.
4. Can Yankelovich's ideas be applied to education? Where does your motivation to study come from – from your own desire to learn or from the promise of a better job?

4   IMPROVING WRITING SKILLS

A. Using another's writing: Summarizing a story

Summarizing another's writing helps you to fully absorb what the author is saying, as well as develop your own writing skills. In Exercise 1, you and a partner will be asked to summarize Maugham's "Ant and the Grasshopper" in 85 words or less. Start by stating the message of the story. Then briefly tell what happened in the story, keeping the message in mind to help you decide which details are important to include. Before you begin the exercise, read this summary of the Aesop's fable and answer the questions that follow.

> In "The Ant and the Grasshopper," Aesop tells us that hard work is rewarded later. The grasshopper played all summer long, while the industrious ant worked to collect food. When winter came, the grasshopper had no food, but the ant had plenty.

1. Is the first sentence more general or more specific than the others?
2. Did the writer use actual text from the fable or his own words, in his summary?
3. Did the writer probably work through the fable line by line as he wrote the summary? Or did he read and "digest" it completely and then begin writing? Why do you think so?
4. Did the writer express his opinions about the fable?

✎ EXERCISE 1   Collaborative summary of "The Ant and the Grasshopper"

Work with a partner and write a summary of Maugham's story in 85 words or less, beginning with these words:

> In "The Ant and the Grasshopper," Maugham . . .

Follow-up   Exchange summaries with at least one other pair of students. Find two things you like in other summaries, either ideas or the way they are expressed.

B. Meeting reader expectations: Introductions and conclusions

For the essay you will write in this chapter, your teacher will expect you to include a well-written introduction and conclusion. Look again at how

Maugham introduced and concluded his story (lines 1–15 and 115–120). Then answer these questions:

1. Does the introduction catch your interest and make you want to read further?
2. Does it give you an idea of what the story will be about?
3. Does the conclusion end the story effectively?
4. Does the conclusion let you know what the writer thinks of what has happened? Would the writer's message be complete without this particular conclusion?
5. How long are the introduction and conclusion in relation to the whole story?

INTRODUCTIONS

There are many ways to introduce an essay. Just as Maugham used a fable in his story, sometimes writers use:

▶ an anecdote (a very short story)
▶ a suitable quotation
▶ a question
▶ background necessary for the reader to understand their point

CONCLUSIONS

Conclusions are as varied as introductions. Conclusions leave the reader with some final thoughts (but not new ideas) on the main idea and the supporting points. In a conclusion a writer can:

▶ explain the significance of his points to his own life
▶ discuss how the reader might use his information
▶ briefly list the main points of support again for the reader to keep in mind, especially in a very long composition

Conclusions, like introductions, are typically more general than body paragraphs because they move away from the specific topic and shift toward the reader's or the writer's life. The flow in a typical essay is from *general* (introduction) to *specific* (the body) and back to *general* (the conclusion).

✎ EXERCISE 2   Student essay

Read this student essay on a topic from this chapter. Answer the questions that follow by yourself; then compare your answers in pairs or as a class.

WORK AND LABOR

There are many opinions about the question, "Why don't people work?" Aesop's famous fable clearly illustrates what the result of not working is. The ant and grasshopper are opposites in that one of them doesn't want to work. People of many genera- tions have accepted the moral of Aesop's fable as the rule. According to Aesop's moral, the ant was right, and the grasshopper was not because it did not work during the summer. It was singing and dancing all the time and didn't anticipate what would happen in the winter. That is a simple moral. It is also too idealistic. For Aesop, the world is divided into two groups - the ants and the grass- hoppers. However, people in real life are more var- ied and complex than the ant and the grasshopper. Maugham tried to depict the world in more realistic colors. He showed two brothers, one of whom didn't work but was still rewarded. It is the way life is. So, Aesop defined a rule and Maugham showed that people don't always want to live by the rules. Why? Life is more complicated than Aesop's fable because there is a big difference between labor and work.

Most people consider labor as a way to exist, to provide themselves with the necessities of life. They work in order to live - even if they hate their jobs - and they would not work if they could manage not to. A work ethic and moral rules have been created by society. Political orientation does not matter; in any case, society will create condi- tions which require people to work hard. Daniel Yankelovich considered three conceptions of work: first, as a way to exist; second, as a way to improve one's level of life; and third, as a moral necessity. Some people accept these rules. They work hard and consider this way of living as the only right one. They believe that their labor will eventually be rewarded. They are obvious characters of Aesop's fable. They are ants. And they do labor, not work.

There is another reason that people work. It doesn't fit into any of Yankelovich's definitions of work. There are some people who work not for money, not for the best possible material life, not because of a moral necessity or society's rules - but because they cannot live without working. For them, work is a natural necessity which has nothing to do with either morals or money.

There are three good examples of people who illustrate that work is different from labor. A good example of someone who could not live without working was Wolfgang Amadeus Mozart, the great Viennese musician and composer. He could not accept life without making music. To live without creating music was meaningless to him. Jack London, a great American writer, spent his entire life in an effort to describe people with strong personalities and will power, people who were trying to realize the truth about life. Roald Amundsen, the great Norwegian explorer, sacrificed his life for the work of exploration. He was the first person to reach the South Pole.

The people I have been talking about lived in order to work. They considered work something very interesting. It made existence more exciting; it gave meaning to their lives. Life and work were the same for them. However, they don't fit into the character of Aesop's ant or Yankelovich's workers. The three of them spent long periods of time without working. These were times of terrible depression, stress, and even the threat of madness. Mozart was under a depression after his mother's death. The last years of his life, he drank heavily, and he died in poverty. Jack London wasn't more successful: alcoholism and financial problems led him to commit suicide at the age of 40. Roald Amundsen was killed during the air search for an Italian explorer, Umberto Nobile. It would be very simple to say that these people didn't do any real work because they were lazy or because they could not handle problems due to a weak will. However, like a glowworm, which does nothing at all, they made a beautiful light through their work. The light they made illuminated whole generations.

   I believe that the difference between work and labor can explain a lot of things. Sometimes it is difficult to recognize the difference between them, but it is important to do so. Since man became human, he has created. His creativity has brought the greatest advances and inventions into the world. Uncreative work, or labor, leaves no trace in history. The majestic pyramids of Egypt, built through the labor of thousands of slaves but the work of only a few architects, still stand today as a monument to creative work. They are a combination of work and labor. So, why are we trying to differentiate the two terms? First, it is important to understand the difference between work and labor. Second, it is important to work rather than labor in order to create rather than merely produce.

                    (Igor Shchegolev, Azerbaijan)

1. Does the introduction grab your attention? If so, what stands out for you?
2. Which of the four ways to introduce an essay did Mr. Shchegolev use?
3. Did you want to continue reading after you finished the introduction?
4. What is the writer's thesis? Does it appear in a thesis statement? If so, underline it.
5. How effectively does Mr. Shchegolev develop his thesis? How does he explain the difference between *work* and *labor*?

6. Are you convinced by his explanation?
7. Which of the ways to conclude an essay did Mr. Shchegolev use? Is his conclusion effective?
8. How long are the introduction and conclusion in relation to the body of the essay? The right length? Too long? Too short?

C. Language conventions: Adding coherence

Writing is easier to follow if the writer helps the reader stay on track by making the logic as clear on paper as it is in the writer's mind. Making the logic clear means making the relationships between the events and ideas clear. Writing in which these relationships are clear is said to have *coherence*.

Take a look at this paragraph, which has little coherence and is therefore hard to understand:

(1)   There were only 10 minutes left in the class. The teacher rushed to put all the rules and examples on the board. The students took out their notebooks to copy the rules down. They were a little upset. The students had an assignment with the present perfect tense. They weren't sure they would be able to do the assignment correctly. They didn't have enough oral practice with the present perfect tense.

Although the language is perfect and the sentences are short and simple, this paragraph is challenging for a reader because it lacks coherence. Each action is clear in itself, but the relationship between the different sentences is not clear. The reader has to use a lot of imagination and still may not get the writer's full message.

Now read the revised paragraph. The *logic* of the paragraph is clearer because of the addition of *cohesive devices*, or words and phrases that make the relationships between the events clear to you. As you read the paragraph, underline the cohesive devices.

(2)   [1]There were only 10 minutes left in the class, so the teacher rushed to put all the rules and examples for the present perfect tense on the board. [2]The students took out their notebooks to copy the rules down. [3]However, they were a little upset because they had an assignment with the present perfect for the next day, and they weren't sure they would be able to do it correctly. [4]In addition, they were upset because they hadn't had enough oral practice with the present perfect.

A good reader might unlock the logic of paragraph 1, but only after several readings and a lot of thinking. Paragraph 2, with its attention to cohesive devices, is clearer and easier to read.

COHESIVE DEVICES

There are many devices that can be used to add coherence in writing. What they have in common is that they help you, the writer, to make explicit the relationships between the ideas and events you wish to describe. As you read the list of devices below, look for examples of them in paragraph 2 in the sentences specified.

1. *Pronouns* that refer back to a clear antecedent: See sentence 3, *it.*
2. *Coordinating conjunctions:* See sentence 1, *so;* sentence 3, *and.*
3. *Subordinating conjunctions:* See sentence 3, *because;* sentence 4, *because.* (Combining sentences with this subordinating conjunction introduced some logic that was missing in paragraph 1.)
4. *Transition words:* See sentence 3, *however;* sentence 4, *in addition.* (These transition words make clear how these sentences relate to the previous sentences.)
5. *Repetition* of an important word: See sentence 4, *upset.* (The significance of "not enough practice" is not clear until the writer points out that the students were upset about it.)
6. *Verb tenses*: See sentence 4, *hadn't had.* (The change to past perfect helps the reader see that not practicing enough caused the students to be upset.)

✏️ EXERCISE 3   Adding coherence to a paragraph

Read the paragraph and circle the best cohesive device for each numbered position from the list of choices given on the following page. Rewrite the paragraph, inserting your choices and making any necessary changes in capitalization and punctuation.

> Yankelovich helps explain the dilemma of American workers. Most want to do their best. [1] They do not work as hard as they could. [2] They feel that others receive the benefits of their hard work. [3] Yankelovich doesn't see this attitude as a sign of a weak work ethic. [4] He feels the attitude would change if workers made more of the decisions that affect their work. There is a message for managers in Yankelovich's findings. Managers need to allow workers to express their needs. [5] They need to listen to what workers say.

1. a. However,
   b. For example,
   c. Therefore,

2. a. because
   b. even though
   c. whereas

3. a. First,
   b. Unfortunately,
   c. (no cohesive device needed)

4. a. Rather,
   b. However,
   c. (no cohesive device needed)

5. a. and
   b. but
   c. or

✎ EXERCISE 4   More practice adding coherence to paragraphs

Read the paragraph and circle the best cohesive device for each numbered
position from the list of choices given. Rewrite the paragraph, inserting your
choices and making any necessary changes in capitalization and punctuation.

Some companies do actually try to address their workers' needs
and suggestions. [1] A few companies offer day-care facilities for
workers' children. [2] Workers can have more contact with their
children during the day. The workers' minds are freed from worries
about their children. [3] They work better. [4] Some other companies
offer workers flexible working hours. Workers can begin and finish
work at times they choose. [5] They have to put in the required number of hours. [6] If they begin work late, they have to stay late. Other
companies are listening to workers' suggestions about improving
efficiency in the factory or office. [7] _____ managers make
the final decisions, they consider the workers' input when making
those decisions.

1. a. On the whole,
   b. For instance,
   c. At the beginning,

2. a. On the contrary,
   b. (no cohesive device needed)
   c. That way,

3. a. and, for example,
   b. so, theoretically,
   c. however,

4. a. (no cohesive device needed)
   b. For example,
   c. Finally,

5. a. because
   b. Besides,
   c. Of course,

6. a. Therefore,
   b. However,
   c. Moreover,

7. a. Since
   b. Even though
   c. Precisely because

✎ EXERCISE 5   Editing for coherence

Edit this paragraph for coherence. Read it carefully, and insert cohesive devices where they are needed. Then rewrite the paragraph.

English, and undoubtedly other languages, has conflicting sayings about important matters like love, friendship, and work. In English we say, "Never put off till tomorrow what you can do today." The implication is that one can and should always work more – at least until all the work is done. In English we also have this proverb: "All work and no play makes Jack a dull boy." The advice is not to work too much because life without recreation makes one an uninteresting person. How is it that the same culture has produced two sayings that give opposite messages? We can assume that work is important to Americans. They respect it a lot – perhaps too much. The second saying may be a kind of safety valve. It warns people against going too far in following the advice of the first saying.

5 CORE WRITING ASSIGNMENT

A. Writing topics

So that you can think at length about what you will write, look at the following essay topics now. Choose the one that interests you the most.

1. *Cause/effect* Why do people work? Think about the readings and your own knowledge of human nature.
2. *Classification* For what different reasons do people work? Think of as many reasons as you can and then organize them into three or four general categories that cover all the possibilities.
3. *Comparison/contrast* Compare the work ethic in your country to that in the United States. Use Yankelovich's description of the American work ethic. Be sure to compare/contrast the same points for each country.
4. Yankelovich advocates that workers be more involved in decisions that affect them. Do you think students should be more involved in decisions that affect their education? Which decisions? How should students be involved?
5. Does your language have a fable like "The Ant and the Grasshopper," a fable that encourages people to work hard? How does your culture look at the division of work and recreation?
6. *Student-generated topics* If you and your teacher agree on one or more additional topics, list them here:

_____

_____

B. Generating ideas: Looping

1. With your topic and purpose in mind, write freely for 5 minutes. Keep writing without stopping and without worrying about grammar and vocabulary. Concentrate on *ideas*. After 5 minutes, read what you have written. What main idea do you see in your writing? Skip a line and write that main idea in one sentence.
2. Begin with the main idea sentence, and write for 5 more minutes. Then stop writing and read what you have written. What main idea do you see in your writing now? Skip a line and write that new main idea in one sentence.
3. Write for 5 more minutes on the new main idea sentence. When you finish, read what you have written. Once again, write the new main idea in one sentence.

Follow-up   After looping three times, you will probably have a clear idea of your thesis and of some secondary ideas to support it. If not, you may want to continue looping until a good thesis for your essay emerges.

C. Expanding your point of view: Interview

All five writing topics in this chapter can be informed by outside input. Choose someone outside your class to interview about your topic. Select your informant according to the topic you have chosen: For topics 1 and 2, choose someone who works. For topics 3 and 5, talk to someone from your country. For topic 4, speak to a student or administrator.

Interview questions   Work with other students who have chosen the same topic. Together, write six or eight interview questions that you will ask your informants. Make sure the questions relate directly to your topic and purpose in writing.

Interview procedure   Introduce yourself and explain the purpose of your interview. Use the questions your group decided on. Listen attentively to your informant's answers. Ask additional questions if you don't understand fully and summarize what the informant says to show your interest and understanding. Write down your informant's exact words if possible.

D. Initial drafts

FIRST DRAFT

Write an essay on your topic that includes an introduction, body paragraphs, and a conclusion. Keep balance in mind: A good introduction might be about 20 percent of your total paper, *but no longer*. The conclusion is often shorter, but not so short that it seems abrupt or as if the writer is in a hurry to finish. For your introduction, you may want to incorporate the summary you wrote of the Maugham story. Or you may want to paraphrase some of Yankelovich's ideas or those of the people you interviewed if they are appropriate.

If it is easier, write the body of the essay first and then the introduction and conclusion. You already have a lot of ideas from the looping and interview you did for the previous sections. If you write the body before the introduction and conclusion, keep in mind the thesis statement that emerged from the looping exercise to help direct your thinking and writing. Taking the interview into account, do you need to adjust your thesis? Support your thesis statement with your own ideas and/or those from the readings and interviews. Then set your paper aside for a while.

REVISION

Look at your paper through your teacher's eyes. Measure your paper against the criteria listed in the "Essay Assessment Guidelines" at the end of this chapter. Revise your paper with these criteria in mind. Mark this revised draft "Revision 1."

E. Review, revision, and assessment

PEER FEEDBACK

Get feedback on how clear and logical your thinking and writing are. Read your essay to a group of two or three classmates. Each member of the group will read his or her paper to the group. Follow the "Peer Feedback Guidelines" at the end of this chapter.

FURTHER REVISION

How well did your group receive your paper? Could they summarize it accurately? Did they understand your main points? Secondary points? How could your paper be clearer and/or more interesting to your audience? Make notes of changes you need to make.

If necessary, revise your paper using the feedback you got from the group. Edit your paper for coherence. Submit all drafts to your teacher, with the last one marked "Revision 2" at the top.

If you choose not to revise, write a paragraph to your teacher summarizing the feedback you received and explaining why you decided not to revise.

TEACHER ASSESSMENT

Your teacher will assess your paper using the detailed set of essay assessment guidelines in Appendix B. Your teacher may give you a grade on the essay or allow you to make further revisions before assigning a grade.

PEER FEEDBACK GUIDELINES

Writers

- ☐ Read the paper clearly, a second time if necessary.
- ☐ Respond to listeners' comments and questions.
- ☐ Ask for suggestions if you want them.

Listeners

- ☐ Listen quietly until the writer finishes reading.
- ☐ Briefly summarize what you understood, orally.
- ☐ Pick out parts of the paper (words, expressions, or ideas) that stand out for you. Share these parts with the group.
- ☐ If you wish, share with the group how the writing makes you feel and ask questions about parts that are not clear.
- ☐ Do not make negative comments or tell the writer what changes to make.

ESSAY ASSESSMENT GUIDELINES

These are the criteria for a well-written essay. Use this checklist to critically examine your writing and determine how it can be improved. See Appendix B for the more detailed set of guidelines that your teacher will use to assess your work.

Content and ideas

- ☐ The writer has thought about the topic and has a clear thesis.
- ☐ The writer discusses each main point enough to give the reader a reason to believe it. The writer supports each main point, and no important point is left out.
- ☐ The writer's voice is clear because he or she writes in a sincere way, with the audience in mind.

Organization and form

- ☐ The paper has a clear beginning, middle, and end, with separate introductory, body, and concluding paragraphs. It moves logically in a straight line.
- ☐ The reader wants to continue reading and can understand the thesis and other main points fully after one reading.
- ☐ It is clear which are the main points and which are the secondary points.

Writing conventions

☐ The writer uses a variety of sentence types to add interest to the writing.

☐ The writer chooses vocabulary carefully to communicate clearly.

☐ The writer uses cohesive devices to make the relationships between the ideas clear.

☐ The writer avoids problems of sentence structure including fragments, comma-splices, and run-together sentences.

☐ The writer uses English grammar effectively to convey the message. There are few problems of verb tense, subject-verb agreement, word order, count/noncount use, or word form.

☐ The writer follows rules for spelling, capitalization, and punctuation.

5

Manners
How we behave with others

What kind of manners do these students have?
What does their behavior tell you about their attitude towards
their teacher? Towards other people in general?

1 GETTING A GRIP ON THE TOPIC

A. Reflection

Read the following list of possible college student behaviors. Imagine that you are a teacher in your country. Which behaviors would you disapprove of? Mark them with a *D*. Which behaviors would seem acceptable to you? Mark them with an *A*.

_____ 1. Student A regularly comes to your class late but enters quietly and takes her seat without disrupting the class.

_____ 2. Student B makes himself very comfortable in class, to the extent of resting his chin on his desk while listening to your lecture.

_____ 3. Student C stands in the hall outside class listening to a walkman radio until class has begun.

_____ 4. Student D often raises her hand in the middle of your lecture to ask a question and occasionally to say that she disagrees with you.

_____ 5. Student E is having trouble with your class, so you ask her to see you the next day in your office. She agrees to the appointment but does not show up.

_____ 6. Student F brings his breakfast coffee to class, where he sits and finishes it.

_____ 7. Just before class, student G says, "Are we doing anything important in class today? I need to pick up a friend at the airport."

_____ 8. Before class, you overhear students H and J discussing a private matter and using profanity.

Follow-up Compare lists with a classmate, if possible someone from another country.

B. Discussion

Discuss these questions in small groups or as a class.

1. Consider the behaviors you disapproved of above. Which do you find the most discourteous, or rude? What principle of your culture do they violate?
2. Are good manners defined independently by each culture, or is there a universal definition that applies to all cultures? If so, what is that definition?
3. If you asked many Americans for the most important rule governing relations between people, most would probably say, "Do unto others as you would have them do unto you." This saying is referred to as *the golden rule*. It is known, if not followed, by every American.

▶ What does the saying mean?

▶ Do you agree with its advice?

▶ Does your language have the same golden rule? A similar one?

4. Another well-known saying is, "When in Rome, do as the Romans do." It applies to people living in a new country.

▶ What does the saying mean?

▶ Do you agree with it?

▶ To what extent should one "do as the Romans do," in your opinion?

Notes on Section A, "Reflection"   Many if not most U.S. college teachers would probably not even notice, much less disapprove of, the behaviors of students B, C, D, and F. Some would probably disapprove of students H and J. Most U.S. college teachers would be bothered by students A, E, and G. Their behavior would be seen as disrespectful to the teacher. Student A's behavior implies that her time is more important than the teacher's. Student E shows the same lack of respect; moreover, she does not keep her word.

Student G, in the roundabout way he goes about asking to be excused, makes it clear that often he does not find the class to be worthwhile. This would be an insult to most U.S. teachers.

C. Notes on the main reading

Dr. Norman Vincent Peale, a minister and writer, is known in the United States for his inspirational writing on a variety of topics. This article of his, "Courtesy: Key to a Happier World," appeared in a well-known magazine, *The Saturday Evening Post*.

In the first half of the article, Dr. Peale classifies the components of courtesy. In the second half, he gives three pieces of advice on how to improve one's manners. Although his topic is a serious one, Dr. Peale writes about it simply, with down-to-earth examples to illustrate his points; he keeps his large, public audience in mind.

VOCABULARY EXERCISE

To preview the article and practice guessing word meanings from context, find the following words in the text, in the lines indicated in parentheses. Write down what you think each word or expression means from its context. If you are very doubtful after making a guess, check your guess in a dictionary. (For expressions, look up the word in italics.)

1. wreck (line 33) _____

2. *fair* play (line 39) _____

3. *spare* the feelings (line 87) _____

4. goad (line 124) _____

5. displace (line 159) _____

6. with no *strings* attached (lines 184–185) _____

GLOSSARY

Review the glossary before reading the selection, for help with some of the more difficult vocabulary.

conviction (line 4): strong belief
grim-faced (line 18): unhappy-looking
sullen surliness (lines 22–23): a silent, angry mood
justice (lines 36–37): rightness or fairness
endured (line 53): suffered, put up with
innate (line 57): natural, that which you are born with
minimize (line 64): make it less
crippled (line 71): weakened, damaged
busboy (line 73): waiter's helper
feigned (line 79): pretended
impelled (line 85): caused, drove
worthy (line 96): deserving
monitor yourself sternly (lines 116–117): observe yourself very carefully
retaliating in kind (lines 124–125): returning the same kind of bad treatment
dim (line 129): turn down
tangle with (line 138): fight with
considerate (line 150): thoughtful
blow over (line 174): pass, end
rejoice (line 178): be very happy
suspicious of (lines 179–180): not trustful of
ulterior motive (line 182): unseen or hidden reason
trials (line 198): problems
beatitude (lines 203–204): pronouncement on how to attain bliss (happiness)
blessed (line 205): fortunate

D. Read for the main idea

Read the article quickly to answer this main idea question: *Does Dr. Peale feel good manners are more a matter of (1) how we look at ourselves or (2) how we look at other people?*

COURTESY: KEY TO A HAPPIER WORLD

Dr. Norman Vincent Peale

Many years ago trying to help people with every kind of trouble left me with one sure conviction: In case after case the difficulty could have been overcome – or might never have arisen – if the people involved had just treated one another with common courtesy.

Courtesy, politeness, good manners – call it what you will, the supply never seems to equal the demand. "It's not so much what my husband says," a tearful wife confides, "as the way he says it. Why does he have to yell at me?" "I hate my boss," a grim-faced office worker mutters. "He never shows appreciation for anything." "All we get from our teenagers," a harassed parent says, "is a sullen surliness."

Such complaints are not limited to people who sit in my study. Human beings everywhere hunger for courtesy. "Good manners," said Ralph Waldo Emerson, "are the happy way of doing things." And the reverse is equally true. Bad manners can ruin a day – or wreck a friendship.

What are the basic ingredients of good manners?

Certainly a strong sense of justice is one; courtesy is often nothing more than a highly developed sense of fair play. A friend once told me of driving along a one-lane, unpaved mountain road. Ahead was another car that produced clouds of choking dust, and it was a long way to the nearest paved highway. Suddenly, at a wider place, the car ahead pulled off the road. Thinking that its owner might have engine trouble, my friend stopped and asked if anything was wrong. "No," said the other driver. "But you've endured my dust this far; I'll put up with yours the rest of the way." There was a man with manners, and an innate sense of fair play.

Another ingredient of courtesy is empathy, a quality that enables a person to see into the mind or heart of someone else, to understand the pain or unhappiness there and to do something to minimize it. Recently in a book about a famous restaurant chain I came across such an episode.

A man dining alone was trying to unscrew the cap of a bottle of catsup but his fingers

were so badly crippled by arthritis that he couldn't do it. He asked a young busboy to help him. The boy took the bot-
75 tle, turned his back momentarily and loosened the cap without difficulty. Then he tightened it again. Turning back to the man, he feigned a great effort
80 to open the bottle without success. Finally he took it into the kitchen and returned shortly, saying that he had managed to loosen it – but only with a pair
85 of pliers. What impelled the boy to take so much trouble to spare the feelings of a stranger? Courtesy, compassionate courtesy.

90 Yet another component of politeness is the capacity to treat all people alike, regardless of all status or importance. Even when you have doubts about
95 some people, act as if they are worthy of your best manners. You may also be astonished to find out that they really are.

I truly believe that anyone
100 can improve his or her manners by doing three things. First, by practicing courtesy. All skills require constant repetition to become second nature; good
105 manners are no exception.

One simple way is to concentrate on your performance in a specific area for about a week. Telephone manners, for exam-
110 ple. How often do you talk too

long, speak abruptly, fail to identify yourself, keep people waiting, display impatience with the operator or fail to
115 return a call? Or driving a car, why not monitor yourself sternly for aggressive driving, unnecessary horn-blowing, following too closely, failing to
120 yield the right-of-way?

One difficult but essential thing to remember is to refuse to let other people's bad manners goad you into retaliating in
125 kind. I recall a story told by a young man who was in a car with his father one night when a driver in an oncoming vehicle failed to dim his lights. "Give
130 him the brights, Dad!" the young man urged in exasperation. "Son," replied the father, "that driver is certainly discourteous and probably stupid. But
135 if I give him the brights he'll be discourteous, stupid and *blind* – and that's a combination I don't want to tangle with!"

The second requirement for
140 improving your manners is to think in a courteous way. In the long run, the kind of person you are is the result of what you've been thinking over the
145 past twenty or thirty years. If your thoughts are predominantly self-directed, a discourteous person is what you will be. If on the other hand you train
150 yourself to be considerate of

others, if you can acquire the habit of identifying with their problems and hopes and fears, good manners will follow
155 almost automatically.

Nowhere is thinking courtesy more important than in marriage. In the intimacy of the home it is easy to displace dis-
160 appointment or frustration or anger onto the nearest person, and that person is often a husband or wife.

"When you feel your anger
165 getting out of control," I have often said to married couples, "force yourself for the next ten minutes to treat your married partner as if he or she were a
170 guest in your home." I knew that if they could impose just ten minutes of good manners on themselves, the worst of the storm would blow over.
175 Finally, to have good manners you must be able to accept courtesy, receive it gladly, rejoice when it comes your way.

Strangely, some people are sus-
180 picious of gracious treatment. They suspect the other person of having some ulterior motive.

But some of the most precious gifts in life come with no
185 strings attached. You can't achieve a beautiful day through any effort on your part. You can't buy a sunset or even the scent of a rose. Those are the
190 world's courtesies to us, offered with love and no thought of reward or return. Good manners are, or should be, like that.

In the end, it all comes down
195 to how you regard people – not just people in general, but individuals. Life is full of minor irritations and trials and injustices. The only constant, daily, effec-
200 tive solution is politeness – which is the golden rule in action. I think that if I were allowed to add one small beatitude as a footnote to the other it
205 might be: Blessed are the courteous.

Follow-up Answer the main idea question here: _____

_____

_____

E. Read for more detail

Read the article a second time. Use the questions to read for more detail and to bring your experience to the work.

1. Which of the three "basic ingredients" of courtesy makes the most sense to you?

2. What do people in your country consider to be the main ingredients of good manners?
3. Which of Dr. Peale's ways of improving manners would you find the most difficult to follow? Why?
4. What examples or points stand out for you in this article?
5. *Key words*   Make a list of six words that you feel are important to the article. Be ready to explain why each word is important, and what it means, if necessary.

Follow-up   Discuss your answers in small groups or as a class.

2 RESPONDING TO THE READING

A. Journals: A private audience

Choose two of the following topics. Write at least 75 words on each of them in your journal notebook. These journal entries are for your eyes only, so do not spend a lot of time using a dictionary or worrying about grammar.

1. Think of an incident in which someone was very rude to you. What did that person do? How did you feel? What did you do in return?
2. Do you feel that you have good manners? Do people think of you as a polite person? Explain.
3. What is the rudest thing you have ever done to another person? Why did you do it?
4. What impression do you have of Dr. Peale from this article? What kind of person do you think he is? Likeable? Kind? Somewhat naive?

B. Shared writing

Choose at least two topics and write for a total of 30 minutes. Your audience is your classmates, with whom you will share your writing. They will be interested not only in *what* you feel but also in *why* you feel that way. Express your views clearly and support them.

1. Does your culture have its own golden rule that people try to live by? What is it? How do people apply it?
2. Are there universal good manners that all cultures recognize? Or are good manners defined by each culture?
3. Dr. Peale wrote this article primarily for an American audience. Do you think people outside the United States would find the article interesting? Helpful? Why?
4. Do you agree with Dr. Peale that our lives would be happier if we all had better manners? Explain.

C. Feedback on your writing

Get feedback on how clear and logical your thinking and writing are. Select one of your writings from the previous section, "Shared Writing," and read it to a group of two or three classmates. Each member of the group will read one of his or her writings. Follow the instructions in "Peer Feedback Guidelines" at the end of this chapter.

Follow-up In 5 minutes, evaluate in writing how well your audience received your paper. Could they summarize it accurately? Did they understand your points? How could you make your paper clearer? More interesting to your audience?

3   GOING MORE DEEPLY INTO THE TOPIC

This cartoon shows a boy being questioned by his father about
a broken window. Do you think the boy is telling his father the truth?
Would you? Why or why not?

A. Preparing to read

In her book, *Lies, Deception and Truth*, Ann E. Weiss discusses the ethics of
lying. Ethics deals with moral questions of right and wrong. The ethics, or
morality, of lying is a topic that has interested philosophers for ages. In fact,
Weiss cites the writing of a seventeenth-century playwright and a seventeenth-
century English philosopher, as well as that of St. Augustine, a religious
thinker and writer from sixteen centuries ago!

Because we are interested here in manners and how people get along, we
will look only at what Weiss has to say about *white lies*. White lies are social
lies, lies we tell to spare someone's feelings. White lies are lies we tell when
we feel the truth would be harmful or damaging to others. Considered unim-
portant by most people, white lies fall into a category called *fibs*, which are
less serious lies. However, St. Augustine felt that even white lies were *deceptions*, acts intended to make others believe something false, and he was against
them. He was in favor of absolute frankness.

Before reading Weiss's discussion of white lies, consider the situations below. In which cases would you tell a white lie? What would you say in each case?

1. Your friend has bought a new coat, which you think is unattractive. Your friend asks your opinion of the coat.
2. A five-year-old child asks when you are going to die.
3. You miss class because you preferred to visit with an old friend whom you ran into. Your teacher later asks you why you missed class.
4. Your boss tells you of a fight he had with a co-worker of yours. You feel that the boss was wrong and the co-worker was right. The boss asks whether you agree with her or with your co-worker.
5. You've been very upset and sad for a number of days because of a family problem. You meet a friend, who asks, "How are you?"

Follow-up Discuss your decisions in small groups.

B. First reading

Read this selection from *Lies, Deception and Truth* the first time to answer this main idea question: *What is Weiss's final opinion about telling white lies? Is she* for *or* against *them?* (Be careful to distinguish Weiss's views from those of the other thinkers.)

Lies, Deception and Truth
Ann E. Weiss

St. Augustine [considered] the matter of white lies, lies put forth for the purpose of sparing the feelings of someone who might be hurt in some way if he or she was forced to hear the truth. He proposed this situation: a desperately ill man, unaware that his beloved only son has died, asks how the boy is. If the father learns the truth, it may   5
kill him.

Naturally, it would be wrong to assure the father that his son is well or to say "I don't know how he is." Augustine made plain his belief that the only right course would be absolute frankness. But [the father's] feelings as a man also had to be considered. "Often . . .   10
human sympathy overcomes me," Augustine confessed. For such painful truth telling, he wondered, "who is sufficient?" Yet we ought

to make ourselves sufficient, he was convinced, because the habit of
lying has a way of growing. Bit by bit, well-meant little white lies can
15 add up to a mountain of big serious deceptions. Therefore, he concluded, "it is not true that sometimes we ought to lie." Inevitably,
however, we sometimes will, and ranking lies on a scale of moral seriousness was the way Augustine chose to help fallible human beings
cope with that reality.

20   Rating lies according to their consequences seems an excellent
idea, and not just for lies in public life. Looking at *what happens*
when a child is deceived in a specific instance sheds new light on the
ethics of that particular deception.

For example, lying to a five-year-old about death has the effect of
25 protecting that child from a reality she is not yet equipped to handle.
Isn't that what makes the lie seem right? Telling a fearful child that a
doctor's shot won't hurt may also seem to have a beneficial result. But
will the consequences of the lie end there? What will the child do
when he finds that the shot does hurt? What about the next time he
30 needs an innoculation? How will he react to finding that grown-ups –
his own mother among them – are not to be trusted?

In a few cases, the good effects clearly outweigh the bad ones. A
mother's lie to a child about a dying relative may be an example of
such a deception. Another example is recounted by Harvard
35 University ethicist Sissela Bok in her book *Lying: Moral Choice in
Public and Private Life.** According to Bok, a young woman was
traveling in a remote part of Africa when she came upon a village.
The villagers invited her to a feast and – mark of special honor –
asked her to partake of the tribal delicacy: baby mice dipped in
40 melted butter and swallowed live. As her hosts eyed her expectantly,
the woman thought quickly and grasped at a lie. Her religion, she
announced regretfully, specifically forbade the eating of live baby
mice.

How could anyone condemn such a fib? And how, many ask,
45 could anyone condemn the other white lies that all of us hear – and
tell – under far less drastic circumstances every day of our lives? The
petty insincerities of unmeant compliments and phony excuses are far
too trivial to be counted as unethical, they say. They may even be nec-

*Random House, 1989.

essary, serving to make life easier and more agreeable for everyone.
"A mixture of a lie doth ever add pleasure," Sir Francis Bacon wrote.   50
He was thinking not just of flattery, but of the "deceptions" of fiction
and poetry. Others, like the seventeenth-century French playwright
Jean-Baptiste Molière, have agreed that white lies are essential among
civilized people. "Wouldn't the social fabric come undone," one of
Molière's characters asks, "if we were wholly frank with everyone?"   55
   Many think so, and social lies abound. But are all of them really
as harmless as people like to think they are? St. Augustine would not
have said so. The most innocent-seeming of white lies can grow to "a
plague . . . [of] huge proportions through small additions," he
warned. The plague of consequences can affect both the liar and the   60
lied-to, Augustine might have continued. Making a practice of solicit-
ing or accepting insincerities leaves a person vulnerable to a rude
awakening when reality intrudes – as it is sure to do eventually.
Making a practice of uttering them can have the effect of turning an
honest person into a hypocrite.   65

Follow-up   Answer the main idea question here: _____

C. Additional readings

Read the selection again. Mark any places in the text that are still unclear to
you. Then read these passages once more to improve your understanding of
them.

D. Negotiating the meaning

Write at least 75 words on this selection. Write on any or all of the following:

▶ whether you liked it or not and why
▶ whether you prefer it to the previous selection
▶ what you have trouble understanding

Follow-up   To a group of two or three, read what you have written. Read your
reaction a second time if necessary.
   Each group member will respond with (1) a question, (2) a comment,
and/or (3) clarification. Every group member should read what he or she has
written. As a group, choose one response to share with the whole class.

E. Discussion: Critical thinking

Discuss these questions in pairs, small groups, or as a class.

1. Are there times when a person must lie in order to be polite? Give examples.
2. Should doctors lie to patients about serious life-threatening diseases? Should doctors lie to the patient's family? Why or why not?
3. Imagine that you were turned down for a job that you wanted very badly. Would you rather hear the truth about why you were rejected or a tactful lie?
4. Letters of recommendation for job applicants and students are conventionally positive, to the point of being false, or at least misleading. (One study showed that 60 percent of a graduating college class was described as "in the top 10 percent" in letters of recommendation for jobs and graduate school.) Is it ethical for a teacher to tell white lies in a letter of recommendation? If everyone else does it, can a teacher not tell white lies in good conscience?
5. How would Weiss look at Peale's examples of courteous behavior? Would she approve or disapprove of the busboy and the angry spouse who treats his or her partner like a guest?

4 IMPROVING WRITING SKILLS

A. Using another's writing: Summarizing an article

Students often want to use portions of an author's writing in their essays to support their thesis with strong ideas. This is a good idea, but only if students do so honestly and effectively. You can use another's writing honestly and effectively if you (1) mention the author's name and (2) put many words into a few by summarizing.

✎ EXERCISE 1   Summarizing Peale's main points

Summarize the main points of the two major parts of Peale's article in 45 words or less (two or three sentences). Use Peale's vocabulary but your own sentences to summarize the three ingredients of courtesy and the three ways to improve one's manners. Revise your first try to make your summary clear, concise, and grammatical.

Follow-up Exchange summaries in small groups. Find something you like in each of the other summaries.

B. Meeting reader expectations: Outlining

We have no way of knowing whether Peale outlined his writing before starting, but a close look at his article shows it is logically organized. Not all writers use an outline, but no one will deny that outlining before writing helps organize one's thinking by giving ideas order and priority. If the order and priority of the ideas in one's writing are clear, it will be clear to readers which ideas are main points and which are secondary points.

In Exercise 2 on the next page, you will be asked to complete the missing parts of an outline of Peale's article, "Courtesy: Key to a Happier World." As you review the outline, keep in mind that:

▶ Ideas with Roman numerals (I, II, etc.) are the most general. Roman numerals II and III express the main points of Peale's article.
▶ Ideas with capital letters (A, B, etc.) are more specific and support the ideas with Roman numerals directly above them. Letters A, B, and C in the outline express *secondary* points of support.
▶ Ideas with Arabic numerals (1, 2, etc.) are even more specific and support the more general ideas directly above them.

✎ **EXERCISE 2   Completing an outline**

Complete the outline using information from the reading. As you work on the outline, notice that the points in the introduction are not included, but the writer's thesis is expressed.

Outline of "Courtesy: Key to a Happier World"

 I. Introduction
    Thesis: Life's difficulties would be minimized if people were more courteous to each other.

 II. Basic ingredients of good manners

    A. Justice

    B. _____

    C. _____

 III. Three ways to improve one's manners

    A. Practice courtesy

       1. _____

       2. Don't let other's bad manners make you rude

    B. _____

    C. Be able to accept courtesy

 IV. Conclusion: Politeness is the golden rule in action.

✎ **EXERCISE 3   Outlining a student essay**

Practice this skill further by outlining part of this student essay. Start by reading the essay carefully. Then answer the questions that follow.

TEACHING THE GOLDEN RULE

(1)   The behavior of individuals is very complicated;
    it is influenced by heredity, environment, and cul-
    ture. Culture includes rules of how an individual
    is expected to behave in a particular society.
    Sometimes rules for behavior differ from one cul-
    ture to another, and sometimes the rules are simi-
    lar. The English and Mexican golden rules are very

similar, if not in words, in sentiment. The English golden rule, "Do unto others as you would have them do unto you," instructs people how to behave with others inside and outside the home. The Mexican golden rule, "Between individuals, as between nations, respect for other people's rights means peace," likewise instructs people how to behave with others. Perhaps because all cultures are equally concerned about their children's manners, we find many more similarities than differences in the way Mexicans and Americans teach children the golden rule.

(2)   Children in both cultures first learn the golden rule of their country inside the home. Inside the family is where children learn their culture and where they learn to behave. In both the United States and Mexico, parents teach their children how to respect other people and, as a consequence, to receive respect from others. At home, siblings are taught to take care of each other's belongings. Furthermore, they are taught not to call each other names or hurt each other's feelings. They are also taught to trust each other and their parents by always telling the truth. Parents teach the golden rule to avoid quarrels and misunderstandings among the members of the family. Children learn how to treat others by learning how to apply the golden rule with family members.

(3)   When children get older, they go to school, and the parents have to teach them how to get along with other children and adults at school. Mothers in both cultures worry about this adjustment and think of ways to apply the golden rule. They expect their children to make friends at school, so they may tell their children to respect others by not taking their belongings. They will tell their children to be good students and follow the teacher's

instructions. Mothers also remind children that, like at home, they should not call other children names or hurt anyone's feelings. Finally, if other children do not treat them with respect, or cause them trouble, children are told to avoid fights by going to the teacher and telling the truth.

(4) As part of their upbringing, children are also taught to respect neighbors, but the golden rule as it applies to neighbors is different in Mexico from in the United States. Among Mexican families, it is very common to offer help when a new family comes to live in the neighborhood. Mexicans offer their help in moving or by lending equipment like ladders or tools. If it is needed, some people will even offer food to their new neighbors. However, American families apply the golden rule by not getting in anyone's way. They do try to make friends with the neighbors and offer support, but they will be careful about interfering in the beginning, perhaps because they are more independent and expect others to be or perhaps because people move more often in the United States. This difference in relations between neighbors, which children learn by example from their parents, may explain why neighbors in Mexico are more likely to become friends than they are in the United States.

(5) In the case of strangers, the golden rule is applied similarly and differently in the two countries. In American culture, the family emphasizes independence and teaches children how to take care of themselves. This lesson often includes a warning that they can't trust everyone and should be careful with strangers. Children are taught what to do, how to use the phone, and whom to call for help in case of emergency or trouble with a stranger, for example. Although Mexicans are not as wary of strangers, they also tell their children to be careful of them and to tell an adult if help is

needed. Mexicans may not need to warn their children about strangers quite as much as Americans do simply because children, who are more dependent in Mexico, are with their parents most of the time. Possibly because independence is not as big a cultural value in Mexico as in the United States, people give and accept help more readily. Children, then, are taught to help elderly people and pregnant women, for example, by helping them to cross the street or to carry a parcel.

(6)   In both the Mexican and the American cultures, parents want their children to have good manners. Parents teach the golden rule in order to have peace at home, to guide children's behavior in school, and to teach children to respect the neighbors and how to deal with strangers. The similarities in teaching the golden rule in both cultures exist because of the common concern of parents to teach good manners. The differences are not as relevant but stand out because of the differences between the two cultures.

(Adanari Navarro, Mexico)

1. What is Ms. Navarro's thesis? Which sentence expresses this thesis?
2. How many main points of support does she give?
3. Is the paper logically organized? Does each paragraph support the thesis? Are the paragraphs in a logical order? Is it clear which ideas are main ideas, which are secondary ideas, and which are details? Explain.
4. Outline paragraph 4, beginning with the main idea (topic sentence) as shown:

    I. The golden rule as it applies to neighbors is different in Mexico from in the United States.

C. Language conventions: Sentence variety

A teacher who always teaches a class in the same way gets to be boring. Likewise, a writer who uses the same kind of sentence over and over produces boring writing. Using diverse sentence types adds interest and variety to writing. Writers achieve variety by using all three sentence types: simple, compound, and complex.

SIMPLE SENTENCES

A simple sentence has one independent clause and no dependent clauses:

> The student yawned.

Although a simple sentence cannot have a dependent clause, it can have modifiers:

> The tall student sitting in the back in my algebra class yawned loudly.

A simple sentence contains only one independent clause, but it can have more than one subject or verb:

> TWO SUBJECTS   The student and his friend yawned.
> TWO VERBS   The student yawned and fell asleep.

A sentence with all these elements will be long, but it is still simple because it contains only one independent clause:

> The tall student sitting in the back in my algebra class and his friend yawned loudly and fell asleep.

✎ EXERCISE 4   Expanding a simple sentence

Expand this simple sentence by adding a second subject, a second verb, a prepositional phrase (e.g., *in my algebra class*), an adjective (e.g., *tall*), and an adverb (e.g., *loudly*), according to the steps listed. (The items above in italics are only examples and are not to be used in this exercise.)

> A young man did something rude.

1. Add another subject with *and*.
2. Add another verb with *and*.
3. Add a prepositional phrase.
4. Add an adjective and an adverb.
5. Combine all the elements above, making sure they all work together to form a good simple sentence.

✎ EXERCISE 5   Expanding another simple sentence

Expand this simple sentence by adding a second subject, an adverb of frequency (e.g., *sometimes*), a prepositional phrase (e.g., *in my algebra class*), and a second verb, as directed. (The items above in italics are only examples and are not to be used in the exercise.)

White lies hurt others.

1. Add a subject with *and*.
2. Add an adverb of frequency before the verb.
3. Add a prepositional phrase.
4. Add a verb with *and*.
5. Combine all the elements above, making sure they all work together to form a good simple sentence.

COMPOUND SENTENCES

A compound sentence has two or more independent clauses joined by a coordinating conjunction:

Henry got a new job, so he has to move.

I have a lot of homework, but I'm not going to study tonight.

Notice the difference between a simple sentence with a compound verb and a compound sentence with two clauses:

SIMPLE   My house guests returned from a long day of shopping and went straight to bed.

COMPOUND   My house guests returned home from a long day of shopping, and we decided to stay at home instead of going out.

In the simple sentence, what is the subject of the second verb? Is it expressed or understood? What is the subject of each verb in the compound sentence?

✎ EXERCISE 6   Distinguishing compound from simple sentences

In the blanks, write *C* for a compound sentence and *S* for a simple sentence.

_____ 1. John didn't show up for his test or inform the teacher.

_____ 2. The teacher was quite upset with John, but she allowed him to take a make-up test two days later.

_____ 3. With extra time to study, John did better on the test than most of the other students.

_____ 4. One student with a low grade found out John's grade and complained to the teacher.

_____ 5. At first, the teacher wasn't sure how to handle the situation, but a solution soon occurred to her.

_____ 6. She took ten points away from John for taking the test late.

_____ 7. John was disappointed, but the other students felt better.

COMPOUND SENTENCES WITH COORDINATING CONJUNCTIONS

Most compound sentences are formed with a coordinating conjunction: *and, or, but, so, for, nor, yet.* The last three occur almost exclusively in writing, so they add a level of formality:

> Fred is quite good-looking, *yet* he doesn't think so.
> (As a coordinating conjunction, *yet* is similar to *but* in meaning. Don't confuse this use with its meaning in *I'm not ready yet.*)

> The students were unhappy with their professor, *for* he often wasted their time in class.
> (*For* means *because* in this usage.)

> I'm not going to the party, *nor* do I plan to inform the hostess.

> I didn't offer to show my driver's license to the police, *nor* did they ask for it.
> (*Nor* continues the negative meaning from the previous clause. Word order after *nor* is inverted.)

✏️ **EXERCISE 7   Writing compound sentences**

Make these partial sentences compound by adding a suitable independent clause (with a subject and verb).

1. Did you go out last night, or . . . ?
2. Cynthia always gets good grades, for . . .
3. I want very badly to take a vacation, yet . . .
4. . . . , nor does it matter to me.
5. . . . , so they sent him to prison.
6. . . . , but he has quite a bit of money.
7. . . . , and they probably won't tell him.
8. . . . , nor will I ever be able to.
9. The exam was unbelievably difficult, so . . .
10. . . . , for chess is a rather difficult game.
11. . . . , yet he always greets me in a friendly way.

Follow-up Write four compound sentences about telling lies. Use *so, or, yet, for.* Use a comma before the coordinating conjunction to separate the two clauses, as in the examples in the exercise.

COMPLEX SENTENCES

A complex sentence has an independent clause with one or more dependent clauses (independent clauses are in italics):

Since we got to the concert late, *we had to make our way to our seats in the dark.*

We left class early so that we could attend a special lecture.
(The subordinator *so that* is different from the coordinating conjunction *so*; *so that* communicates purpose and usually occurs with *can* or *could*.)

Her car is different from mine in that her sports car needs more expensive repairs and more fuel.

Complex sentences should be punctuated like this:

▶ INDEPENDENT CLAUSE dependent clause (no comma)
▶ dependent clause, INDEPENDENT CLAUSE (comma)

Which examples above illustrate the first rule? The second one?

EXERCISE 8   Writing complex sentences

Add a clause (subject and verb) to each example to make a good complex sentence. Keep the meaning of the subordinators (in italics) in mind to preserve the logic of the sentences.

1. *Even though* that corporation has a lot of employees, . . .
2. *Whatever* you decide to do, . . .
3. *Whenever* it rains a lot here, . . .
4. *Ever since* Jason graduated from high school, . . .
5. . . . *whose* book was never found.
6. . . . *because* I have a problem with my schedule.
7. . . . *so that* we can save money for a new car.
8. *Although* she went to a prestigious university, . . .
9. *Even if* he loses his job, . . .
10. . . . *in that* Jason has larger eyes and a beard.
11. *While* I was looking for a book in the library, . . .
12. They probably won't pass the exam *unless* . . .
13. Don't take the cake out of the oven *before* . . .
14. *After* he realized his mistake, . . .

COMPARING COMPOUND AND COMPLEX SENTENCES

Combining ideas in compound and complex sentences is a good way to give interest, variety, and coherence to writing. The use of these sentences adds coherence by making clear the relationship between different ideas. Keep in mind, however, that compound sentences differ from complex sentences in one important way: In a compound sentence, both clauses have equal importance; in a complex sentence, the independent clause is more important. Compare these sentences:

COMPOUND   John was tired, but he finished his homework.
COMPLEX   Although John was tired, he finished his homework.

In the first sentence, the writer is communicating that both clauses are equally important. In the second sentence, the writer is saying that the subordinate clause ("John was tired") is less important than the independent clause ("he finished his homework").

EXERCISE 9   Distinguishing simple, compound, and complex sentences

In the blanks, write *S* for a simple sentence, *CD* for a compound sentence, and *CX* for a complex sentence.

_____   1. Joe is not going to take a vacation during spring break because of an assignment to earn extra credit in his economics class.
_____   2. He has to write two long papers, which will take him the whole spring holiday.
_____   3. The library has reduced hours during break, so Joe will have to work at home.
_____   4. With little knowledge of the topics, he will have to do a lot of research.
_____   5. The library's computerized indexing system will make his research much easier.
_____   6. He will try to finish his research by the middle of the week; then he can spend the rest of the week writing the papers.
_____   7. A friend who knows word processing well has volunteered to type the paper if it's finished by Saturday.
_____   8. Joe will do all he can to finish by Saturday so that he can take advantage of his friend's help.
_____   9. He has to finish on time, or he'll have to type the paper himself.
_____ 10. Joe has promised himself that he will never miss another vacation because of school work.

Follow-up   In all the sentences you have marked *CX,* circle the subordinators and underline the dependent clauses.

LONG RAMBLING SENTENCES

Writing that has too many strings of independent clauses joined by coordinating conjunctions can be tiresome and frustrating for the reader. These long rambling sentences leave the reader out of breath and wondering which information is important. Long rambling sentences are also perceived as informal because they duplicate spoken language. Compare these versions of the same paragraph:

(1)   I went home, but my roommate wasn't there, so I started to cook dinner, but my roommate came in and saw me trying to cook his favorite recipe, but I didn't really know how to make it well, and he got really angry, so I stopped cooking, and he made dinner for us, and then everything was all right.

(2)   When I went home, my roommate wasn't there, so I started to cook dinner. Then, my roommate came in and saw me trying to cook his favorite recipe even though I didn't know how to make it well. I stopped cooking because he got really angry. In the end, he made dinner for us, and everything was all right.

The compound structure of version 1 is easier to write, perhaps, but not very satisfying to read. Version 2 has more coherence and interest because the writer took the time to think and make decisions about the importance of each clause and its relationship to the others.

✎ EXERCISE 10   Editing for sentence variety

Rewrite each long rambling sentence into several shorter, more coherent and interesting ones. Use subordinators, transition words, and simple sentences to achieve variety in sentence type.

(1)   Statistics is one of the most difficult classes, but most university students have to take it, so I recommend they take Professor Williams's statistics class because he's a good teacher, and hard-working students are rewarded, but lazy ones fail, so students should make an honest effort to learn.

(2)   I always got good grades in English before, but now my grades are low, but I work rather hard, so I think my teacher doesn't like me, or maybe I don't always do the homework on time, but in the future I will try to be a better student, and I won't make excuses for my bad grades, or perhaps I should talk to my teacher, and then I'll know how to improve my grades.

(3)   I think the food in my country is very good, and there is a big variety of things to eat, so a person doesn't get bored, but, of

course, home-cooked food is better than restaurant food, so visitors shouldn't judge our cuisine by restaurants, but they should try to visit a family, and they will probably enjoy the food.

(4)   People need to get along, so it's difficult to avoid telling white lies sometimes, but we can all try to be truthful without hurting other people's feelings, and that is difficult, but if we try to be tactful and truthful, we can spare feelings without saying things which are complete deceptions, so I think we should try to avoid white lies with acquaintances as well as friends.

5 CORE WRITING ASSIGNMENT

A. Writing topics

Choose a topic for an essay from the following list:

1. *Comparison/contrast*   Compare your culture's golden rule to the English one: "Do unto others as you would have them do unto you."
2. *Cause/effect*   Explore the causes that lie behind white lies. Why do we tell them?
3. Are there universal good manners? In other words, is there a core of good manners that polite people of all countries recognize? Or are good manners different for each individual culture?
4. *Definition*   In the first half of his article, Peale defines courtesy and lists its "ingredients." Do you have a different definition of courtesy? If so, explain it.
5. *Student-generated topics*   If you and your teacher agree on one or more additional topics, list them here:

_____

_____

B. Generating ideas: Free writing

On a separate sheet, write freely on your topic for 20 minutes. Then read what you have written. Write down three questions about the topic that you would like to explore with classmates.

Follow-up   Meet in a small group with other students who have chosen the same topic. Share your questions with each other. Then compose a list of six interview questions to ask an informant outside your class.

C. Expanding your point of view: Interview/research

INTERVIEW

Conduct an interview with an informant outside your class. Let your topic help you choose the informant for your interview.

Use the interview questions your group wrote in the previous section, "Generating Ideas: Free Writing." Explain your purpose in interviewing, listen attentively, and summarize orally what your informant says. Ask additional questions if you are not sure you understand what your informant has said.

Take notes during the interview, but also try to maintain eye contact with your informant.

Take down the informant's name and other relevant personal data that you might use in your essay.

RESEARCH

If your teacher wishes, go to the library and find a suitable article in a book, magazine, or journal. The article should relate to your topic. Read the article carefully. Summarize useful parts or the whole piece if it is relevant to your essay. Note the page numbers for all the information you take down. Write down *bibliographic* information in this form:

MAGAZINE OR JOURNAL ARTICLE	Peale, Norman Vincent. 1975. "Courtesy: Key to a Happier World." *The Saturday Evening Post.* May/June.
BOOK	Weiss, Ann E. 1988. *Lies, Deception and Truth.* Houghton Mifflin Company. pp. 29, 30, 66–69.

D. Initial drafts

OUTLINE

In Parts 1–3 of this chapter on manners, you thought, read, discussed, and wrote as a way to develop ideas on the topic. In Part 5, you have done additional free writing and conducted an interview to help you think about your particular essay topic. You most likely have more ideas in your head now than you can use effectively in your essay. To help select the best ideas and organize your thoughts, prepare an outline similar to the one in Part 4, Exercise 2. First form a thesis statement to help you choose the best ideas to use for support. Then decide on three main points of support, which will become the topic sentences for your body paragraphs. Think through each body paragraph and include in your outline the ideas you will use to support each main point. If an idea comes to you for a conclusion, add it to your outline.

FIRST DRAFT

Write the first draft from your outline. Give your writing your voice, your mark. Do this by using a true personal anecdote in the introduction, for example. Use real examples from your experience in the body paragraphs; choose examples that will also appeal to your audience. If you use another author's ideas, connect them to your own experience. When the writer's voice is clear and true, the writing is more genuine and interesting to the reader.

REVISION

Look at your first draft through your teacher's eyes. Measure your paper against the criteria listed in the "Essay Assessment Guidelines" at the end of this chapter. Revise your paper with these criteria in mind.

If you got ideas from outside research, list the bibliographic information under "References" at the end of your paper. If you use the ideas of interview informants, identify the informants in your essay. Label your revised draft "Revision 1."

E. Review, revision, and assessment

PEER FEEDBACK

Get feedback on how clear and logical your thinking and writing are. Read your essay to a group of two or three classmates. Each member of the group will read his or her paper to the group. Follow the "Peer Feedback Guidelines" at the end of this chapter.

FURTHER REVISION

How well did your group receive your paper? Could they summarize it accurately? Did they understand your main points? Secondary points? How could your paper be clearer and/or more interesting to your audience? Make notes of changes you need to make.

If necessary, revise your paper using the feedback you got from the group. Edit your paper for sentence variety. Submit all drafts to your teacher, with the last one marked "Revision 2" at the top.

If you choose not to revise, write a paragraph to your teacher summarizing the feedback you received and explaining why you decided not to revise.

TEACHER ASSESSMENT

Your teacher will assess your paper using the detailed set of essay assessment guidelines in Appendix B. Your teacher may give you a grade on the essay or allow you to make further revisions before assigning a grade.

PEER FEEDBACK GUIDELINES

Writers

☐ Read the paper clearly, a second time if necessary.

☐ Respond to listeners' comments and questions.

☐ Ask for suggestions if you want them.

Listeners

☐ Listen quietly until the writer finishes reading.

☐ Briefly summarize what you understood, orally.

☐ Pick out parts of the paper (words, expressions, or ideas) that stand out for you. Share these parts with the group.

☐ If you wish, share with the group how the writing makes you feel and ask questions about parts that are not clear.

☐ Do not make negative comments or tell the writer what changes to make.

ESSAY ASSESSMENT GUIDELINES

These are the criteria for a well-written essay. Use this checklist to critically examine your writing and determine how it can be improved. See Appendix B for the more detailed set of guidelines that your teacher will use to assess your work.

Content and ideas

☐ The writer has thought about the topic and has a clear thesis.

☐ The writer discusses each main point enough to give the reader a reason to believe it. The writer supports each main point, and no important point is left out.

☐ The writer's voice is clear because he or she writes in a sincere way, with the audience in mind.

Organization and form

☐ The paper has a clear beginning, middle, and end, with separate introductory, body, and concluding paragraphs. It moves logically in a straight line.

☐ The reader wants to continue reading and can understand the thesis and other main points fully after one reading.

☐ It is clear which are the main points and which are the secondary points.

Writing conventions

- ☐ The writer uses a variety of sentence lengths and types to add interest to the writing.
- ☐ The writer chooses vocabulary carefully to communicate clearly.
- ☐ The writer uses cohesive devices to make the relationships between the ideas clear.
- ☐ The writer avoids problems of sentence structure including fragments, comma-splices, and run-together sentences.
- ☐ The writer uses English grammar effectively to convey the message. There are few problems of verb tense, subject-verb agreement, word order, count/noncount use, or word form.
- ☐ The writer follows rules for spelling, capitalization, and punctuation.

6

Courtship
Choosing the best mate for the best marriage

Scene from an American wedding

In your country, do couples go out on dates before they get married?
How do young men and women find marriage partners?

1 GETTING A GRIP ON THE TOPIC

A. Reflection

Read these proverbs about marriage and answer the questions that follow.

    (a) Marriages are made in heaven. (English)
    (b) Marry in haste, repent at leisure. (English)
    (c) Love and blindness are twin sisters. (Russian)
    (d) Love does not choose the blade of grass on which it falls. (Zulu)*
    (e) Better to choose the worst than to settle for second best. (Icelandic)
    (f) A go-between needs a thousand pairs of sandals. (Japanese)

1. Which proverb do you like the best? Why?
2. Which proverbs would seem strange to people in your country? Why?

Follow-up Compare answers with a classmate or as a class.

B. Discussion

Read these descriptions of courting practices from around the world. In the column marked *United States*, write *C* next to practices you think are *currently* in use in the United States and write *P* next to practices that you believe were common in the *past*. (For practices in common use in the past as well as the present, write both letters.) Next to customs that have never been part of American courtship practices, write *N*.

    Then fill in the blanks in the column marked *Your Country*, using the same letters (*C, P,* and *N*) to indicate current and past practices and those that have never been in widespread use in your country.

United States	*Your Country*	
_____	_____	1. Young men and women usually meet at a community or church social activity or through relatives.
_____	_____	2. Many young couples meet on their own at school or at the workplace.
_____	_____	3. A young man can visit a young woman at her home, but only in the company of her family.

*The Prentice-Hall Encyclopedia of World Proverbs. W. Mieder. Prentice-Hall, 1986.

United States	Your Country	
_____	_____	4. Young couples socialize by dating, or going out for an evening alone together. Usually they go to a public place, like a restaurant or movie theater.
_____	_____	5. Couples who go out together for an evening are chaperoned, or accompanied by an older relative.
_____	_____	6. Dating functions as a part of the process of selecting a future husband or wife.
_____	_____	7. Sexual intimacy and sometimes cohabitation by the couple are often part of the process of selecting a husband or wife.
_____	_____	8. Marriage partners are selected for young people by an older relative or family friend.

Follow-up Read the notes in the next paragraph and discuss how similar courtship in the United States was and is to courtship in your country.

Notes on Section B, "Discussion": Most Americans would probably describe items 1 and 3 as past practices *(P);* items 2, 4, 6, and 7 as current *(C);* and items 5 and 8 as "never in use" *(N).*

C. Notes on the main reading

Sociologist Martin King Whyte's journal article, "Choosing Mates – The American Way," is formal but not too technical. The organization, in which the introduction is followed by "Study and Conclusions" and "Future Trends," is logical and easy to follow.

According to Whyte, in choosing a spouse, or mate, Americans follow one of two approaches: one based on love, and the other based on the *marketplace learning viewpoint.* A technical term, *marketplace learning viewpoint* refers to an approach to marriage in which a person "shops" for a spouse with certain qualities in mind. Unlike the approach based on love, the marketplace learning viewpoint sees selecting a mate as a rational process. The person dates different people in an attempt to find the one with all the qualities that he or she is looking for in a husband or wife. The process necessarily includes dating different people and often leads to sexual intimacy. The marketplace learning viewpoint treats choosing a mate something like shopping for a car or breakfast cereal, hence the word *marketplace* in the name.

Whyte cites another sociologist, Waller. Like Whyte, Waller is critical of dating as a means of mate selection. His views may not always be the same as Whyte's, however, so do not confuse the two.

VOCABULARY EXERCISE

To preview the text and practice guessing word meaning from context, find the following words in the text, in the lines indicated in parentheses. Write down what you think each word or expression means from its context. If you are very doubtful after making a guess, check your guess in a dictionary. (For phrases, look up the word in italics.)

1. yearning (line 4) _____

2. compatible (line 6)_____

3. *premarital* experiences (line 34) _____

4. virgins (line 61) _____

5. takes the *initiative* (line 85) _____

6. promote (line 94) _____

7. doomed (line 98) _____

GLOSSARY

Review the glossary before reading the selection, for help with some of the more difficult vocabulary.

soaring (line 1): going very high
anxieties (line 1): fear and uncertainty
drive you to distraction (line 5): make you crazy
pave the way (line 23): prepare
misguided (line 43): based on information or beliefs that are wrong, mistaken
pregnancy (line 45): carrying an unborn, developing baby
cohabited (line 52): lived together
alternatives (line 57): other choices, i.e., other men
analogy (lines 65–66): comparison
facilitate (line 69): help lead to
realms (line 72): areas
crap-shoot (line 73): a game of chance
arranged marriages (line 75): marriages in which the partners are chosen by relatives or others
double standard (line 86): code giving men more freedom than women
pooling (line 95): combining
mutual (line 96): shared

D. Read for the main idea

Read the article through once to answer this main idea question: *Which seems to be a better predictor of success in marriage: how well the man and woman know each other or how much they love each other at the time of marriage?*

Choosing Mates – The American Way
Martin King Whyte

As America's divorce rate has been soaring, popular anxieties about marriage have multiplied. Is it still possible to "live happily ever after" and if so, how can this be accomplished? How can you tell whether a partner who leaves you breathless with yearning will, as your spouse, drive you to distraction? Does "living together" prior to   5
marriage provide a realistic assessment of how compatible you and your partner might be as husband and wife? Questions such as these suggest a need to examine our American way of mate choice. How do we go about selecting the person we marry, and is there something wrong with the entire process?   10

For most twentieth-century Americans choosing a mate is the culmination of a process of dating. Examination of how we go about selecting mates thus requires us to consider the American dating culture. Dating is a curious institution. By definition it is an activity that is supposed to be separate from selecting a spouse. Yet, dating is   15
expected to provide valuable experience that will help in making a "wise" choice of a marital partner. Does this combination work?

How well dating "works" may be considered in a number of senses of this term. Is it easy or difficult to find somebody to go out with? Do dates mostly lead to enjoyable or painful evenings?   20
However, these are not the aspects of dating I wish to consider. The issue here is whether dating works in the sense of providing useful experience that helps pave the way for a successful marriage.

Study and Conclusions

My desire to know whether dating experiences affected marriage was the basis for my 1984 survey in the Detroit area. A representa-   25

tive sample of 459 women was interviewed in three counties in the
Detroit metropolitan area (a diverse, multi-racial and multi-ethnic
area of city and suburbs containing about 4 million people in 1980).
The women ranged in ages from 18 to 75, and all had been married
30   at least once. (I was unable to interview their husbands, so unfortunately marriages in this study are viewed only through the eyes of
women.) The interviewees had first married over a sixty year span of
time, between 1925 and 1984. They were asked to recall a variety of
things about their dating and premarital experiences. They were also
35   asked a range of questions about their marital histories and (if currently married) about the positive and negative features of their relations with their husbands. The questionnaire enabled us to test
whether premarital experiences of various types were related to marital success, a concept which in turn was measured in several different
40   ways. (Measures of divorce and of both positive and negative qualities in intact marriages were used.)

The conclusions were a surprise. It appears that dating does not
work and that the "marketplace learning viewpoint" is misguided.
Marrying very young tended to produce unsuccessful marriages.
45   Premarital pregnancy was [also] associated with problems in marriage. However, none of the other measures – dating variety, length of
dating, length of courtship or engagement, or degree of premarital
intimacy with the future husband or others – was clearly related to
measures of marital success. A few weak tendencies in the results
50   were contrary to predictions drawn from the marketplace learning
viewpoint. Women who had dated more partners or who had engaged in premarital sex or cohabited were slightly less likely to have
successful marriages. This might be seen as evidence of quite a different logic.

55   Women who had married their first sweethearts were just as likely
to have enduring and satisfying marriages as women who had married only after considering many alternatives. Similarly, women who
had married after only a brief acquaintance were no more (nor less)
likely to have a successful marriage than those who knew their hus-
60   bands-to-be for years. And there was no clear difference between the
marriages of women who were virgins at marriage and those who

had had a variety of sexual partners and who had lived together with their husbands before the wedding.

Dating obviously does not provide useful learning that promotes marital success. Although our dating culture is based upon an analogy with consumer purchases in the marketplace, it is clear that in real life selecting a spouse is quite different from buying a car or a breakfast cereal.

Dating experience might facilitate marital success if deciding whom to marry was like deciding what to eat for breakfast (although even in the latter regard tastes change, and toast and black coffee may replace bacon and eggs). But these realms are quite different, and mate selection looks more like a crap-shoot than a rational choice.

Is there a better way? Traditionalists in some societies would argue that arranged marriages are preferable. However, in addition to the improbability that America's young people will leave this decision to their parents, there is the problem of evidence.

Future Trends

Perhaps dating is evolving into new patterns in which premarital experience will contribute to marital success. Critics from Waller onward have claimed that dating promotes artificiality, rather than realistic assessment of compatibility. Some observers suggest that the sort of superficial dating Waller and others wrote about has become less common of late. Dating certainly has changed significantly since the pre-Second World War era. Many of the rigid rules of dating have broken down. The male no longer always takes the initiative; neither does he always pay. The sexual double standard has also weakened substantially, so that increasingly Americans feel that whatever a man can do a woman should be able to do. Some writers even suggest that dating is going out of style, replaced by informal pairing off in larger groups, often without the prearrangement of "asking someone out."

While these conclusions are for the most part quite negative, my study leads to two more positive observations. First, marital success is not totally unpredictable. A wide range of features of how couples structure their day-to-day marital relations promote success – sharing in power and decision-making, pooling incomes, enjoying similar

leisure time activities, having similar values, having mutual friends and an active social life, and other related qualities. Couples are not "doomed" by their past histories, including their dating histories, and they can increase their mutual happiness through the way they struc-
100 ture their marriages.

Second, there is something else about premarital experience besides dating history that may promote marital success. We have in America not one, but two widely shared, but quite contradictory, theories about how individuals should select a spouse: one based on the
105 marketplace learning viewpoint and another based on love. One viewpoint sees selecting a spouse as a rational process, perhaps even with lists of criteria by which various prospects can be judged. The other, as songwriters tell us, is based on the view that love conquers all and that "all you need is love." Love is a matter of the heart (per-
110 haps with some help from the hormonal system) and not the head, and love may blossom unpredictably, on short notice or more gradually. Might it not be the case, then, that those couples who are most deeply in love at the time of their weddings will have the most successful marriages? We have centuries of poetry and novels, as well as
115 love songs, that tell us that this is the case.

Follow-up   Answer the main idea question here: _____

_____

E. Read for more detail

Read the article a second time. Use the questions to understand it better and to bring your own experience to the reading.

1. Why did Whyte undertake his survey of marital success?
2. Does the survey seem valid to you? Consider the number of women interviewed, their ages, races, and the kinds of questions that the women were asked.
3. Why do you think the author was surprised by the results of the survey? Which results do you find surprising? Why?
4. Which of the following conditions clearly affected the success of the marriages negatively in the study?

    a. marrying one's first sweetheart   d. not being a virgin at marriage
    b. marrying at a young age   e. premarital pregnancy
    c. marrying after a short courtship

5. What features do successful American marriages have in common? Are these features characteristic of successful marriages in your country too?
6. What final conclusions does the writer suggest about courtship and marital success in the United States? Do you agree?
7. *Key words* Make a list of six words that you feel are important to the article. Be ready to say why each word is important, and what it means, if necessary.

Follow-up Discuss your answers in small groups or as a class.

2 RESPONDING TO THE MAIN READING

A. Journals: A private audience

Choose two of the following topics. Write at least 75 words on each of them in your journal notebook. Express your opinions and feelings honestly. These journal entries are for your eyes only, so do not spend a lot of time using a dictionary or worrying about grammar.

1. Write a letter to Martin King Whyte telling him your reactions to his article.
2. Do you approve of dating as a way of selecting a spouse? Why or why not?
3. If a couple is not compatible, should they stay married or get divorced?
4. How important do you consider love as a reason for a couple to get married?

B. Shared writing

Choose at least two topics and write for a total of 30 minutes. Your audience is your classmates, with whom you will share your writing. They will be interested not only in *what* you feel but also in *why* you feel that way. Express your views clearly and support them.

1. Do spouses select each other in your country? How do they meet? Do families or matchmakers play a part?
2. What role does love play when one is deciding on a spouse in your country? What other criteria are used when one is selecting a mate?
3. Whyte reports elsewhere that arranged marriages did not result in greater marital success in a Chinese survey and suggests that arranged marriages are not a good alternative for Americans. Do arranged marriages suit your culture? Why or why not?
4. Whyte concludes that dating and the marketplace learning viewpoint do not contribute to marital success in the United States. However, dating is not the cause of failure, either. What might explain the high rate of divorce in the United States?

C. Feedback on your writing

Get feedback on how clear and logical your thinking and writing are. Select one of your writings from the previous section, "Shared Writing," and read it to a group of two or three classmates. Each member of the group will read one of his or her writings. Follow the instructions in "Peer Feedback Guidelines" at the end of this chapter.

Follow-up In 5 minutes, evaluate in writing how well your audience received your paper. Could they summarize it accurately? Did they understand your points? How could you make your paper clearer? More interesting to your audience?

3 GOING MORE DEEPLY INTO THE TOPIC

Scene from a modern Egyptian wedding

A. Preparing to read

In arranged marriages, unlike love marriages, spouses are generally chosen on
the basis of what may be a complicated series of rational criteria. In this
excerpt from *Family in Contemporary Egypt*, anthropologist Andrea B. Rugh
discusses the process of mate selection in Egypt, where arranged marriages
were once common and are still found in certain segments of the population.

Interestingly, most societies where arranged marriages are the norm have
far lower divorce rates than societies that do not. Of course, other factors
influence divorce rates, and lack of divorce may not mean happier marriages.
Nevertheless, it will be informative to read about arranged marriages in Egypt
to judge whether such marriages have a more solid basis for success than love
marriages.

Look at the characteristics listed on the next page. Rank them from most
important (1) to least important (9) in a prospective spouse.

The prospective spouse . . .

_____ a. is well educated.

_____ b. has a temperament that seems compatible with your own.

_____ c. has good employment potential.

_____ d. has a strong moral character.

_____ e. is of the same social class as your family.

_____ f. is about the same age as you.

_____ g. is physically attractive.

_____ h. is a blood relative (e.g., cousin).

_____ i. comes from a family with a good reputation.

Follow-up   Compare your rankings in small groups.

B. First reading

Read the selection the first time to answer this main idea question: *In what ways do arranged marriages look at marriage more realistically than love marriages do?*

BEFORE YOU READ

As you read the selection, keep in mind that, as Rugh states later on in her book, while "most parents feel an obligation to help their children find suitable marriages," arranged marriage is now only "one of several options available" for selecting marriage partners in Egypt, and the practice has fallen out of use among upper class and university-educated men and women, who have other means of meeting prospective mates.

Marriage: Practice
Andrea B. Rugh

Most parents are genuinely interested in providing the best matches for their children. Good matches reflect well on the whole family, increasing the possibility that later matches for younger children will also be good ones. A good match is financially and emotionally stable and happy. In general, parents and children believe this state of marital bliss comes about more as a result of carefully matching the characteristics of the couple than it does in finding out   5

whether the couple are temperamentally suited to each other or even
currently in love. Some of the relevant characteristics are income,
beauty and other physical characteristics, social status, moral factors,
educational level, employment potential, and temperament.

The more positive the attributes of the candidate the better,
though it is generally recognized that to marry someone much above
or below one's own level in such characteristics as wealth is to court
trouble. Certain characteristics also have much greater value attached
to them than others. Moral behavior is one that is ranked high.
Others may vary in their degree or regard depending on the sex of the
individual. A woman of great beauty may be excused a number of
other faults. A man who earns a good income not only can ask for
more in a wife but is excused less agreeable physical or personality
traits. Among the middle classes, a strong value placed on women
now is their ability to earn an income at a job that has a prestige compatible with her husband's position – that is, not higher than his job
but not significantly lower either.

In general, among all the classes there is a strong preoccupation
with matching characteristics between potential mates as closely as
possible. Evidence of this preoccupation is found in television serial
shows, which spend a great deal of time debating the issue – in dra-
matic form – of whether young people should marry suitors wealthier
or poorer, older or younger, better or less well-educated than themselves. The common tragic theme in these melodramas is always one
of a couple in love who believe they cannot marry because a parent or
society feels there is some flaw in how their characteristics match.

[Moreover,] the tragedy of unsatisfactory qualifications is not
confined to television drama. It is found frequently in real-life experiences.

Nowal is the fourth in a middle-class family of five sisters. As a
child she was a cheerful relaxed girl whom everyone liked but
who did not take her studies seriously. As a consequence she
failed her intermediate school exam and after repeated attempts
to succeed finally left school. She was fortunate, without formal
qualifications, to find a job that satisfied her family's middle-class
requirements – as a teacher in a literacy handicraft program at a

welfare center. As the years passed her sisters graduated from the university and the three eldest married three brothers. Nowal did not marry and her father refused to allow the youngest daughter to marry before Nowal, out of concern that his children marry in birth order. It was not that Nowal did not have suitors, but all those who were interested in her possessed less than university degrees and thus her father considered them not appropriate to the family's social level. Those with university degrees were not interested in her because of her low educational level. Nowal is in her late twenties now, a time considered late in Egypt for a girl to marry. Her younger sister feels frustrated that her own marriage has been delayed.

Nowal's father was particularly rigid about her marriage prospects. Most parents in the same circumstances would be willing to make trade-offs, exchanging one weak characteristic in one area for a stronger one in some other area.

The idealized system does not break down completely even when children openly choose their own mates. The children themselves are aware of the critical criteria by which marriage partners are chosen and usually monitor their own behavior from this knowledge. The importance of family ties in a child's future constrains him or her from breaking with other family members. Children obtain their information about mate selection not only from their life's experiences but also from watching the barrage of television programs – dramatizations and advice shows that focus on the subject of mate selection and family life. From sheer weight of time spent on a single subject, marriage emerges on television as the clear winner above all other social issues. Most programs individually depict a clear-cut "right way" to select a mate, but overall there is variety, even sometimes contradiction in the answers they provide. In several programs for example, parents were implicitly criticized for choices they made which, though adhering to the structural principles that should guarantee a happy marriage, did not result in such a marriage because they did not weigh carefully enough the "irrational" factors of love and attraction. In other serials, however, the converse was true, and marriages turned out poorly because children did not heed the advice of their parents – they were consumed by irrational motivations. The

lack of a clear-cut stand reflects better than anything the present conflicts over how the process of mate selection should proceed. The goal
– a stable and happy family life – remains the same; only the means
by which the goal is achieved is subject to debate.

Follow-up Answer the main idea question here: _____

_____

C. Additional readings

Read the selection again. Mark any places in the text that are still unclear to
you. Then read these passages once more to improve your understanding of
them.

D. Negotiating the meaning

Write for 15 minutes on this selection. Write on any or all of the following:

▶ whether you liked it or not, and why
▶ whether you prefer it to the previous selection
▶ what you have trouble understanding

Follow-up To a group of two or three, read what you have written. Read your
reaction a second time if necessary.
    Each group member will respond with (1) a question, (2) a comment,
and/or (3) clarification. Every group member should read what he or she has
written. As a group, choose one response to share with the whole class.

E. Discussion: Critical thinking

Discuss these questions in pairs, small groups, or as a class.

1. Both the dating process based on the marketplace learning viewpoint and
   the tradition of arranged marriage are rational approaches to mate selection.
   However, arranged marriages are far less likely to end in divorce. Suggest
   reasons why this is so.
2. Many cultures have strong taboos about marriages between blood relatives,
   whereas other cultures see cousins as an ideal match. Which pattern does
   your country follow? Can you explain why your culture has rejected the
   other pattern?
3. Despite the relatively lower rates of divorce among arranged marriages,
   many young people in Egypt prefer not to follow the traditional methods of
   mate selection. What might account for the change?

4 IMPROVING WRITING SKILLS

A. Using another's writing: Summarizing a newspaper column

Ann Landers is one of the most widely read advice columnists in the United States. Millions of people read her advice column in newspapers across the country every day. Many consider her an expert in human relationships. Therefore, the advice she gives on choosing a spouse in "How to Make an Intelligent Decision" would be good support in an essay on this topic. The column is far too long to quote in an essay, however, so you would need to summarize it in your own words. Practice summarizing Ann Landers's column in the exercise that follows.

✎ EXERCISE 1   Summarizing Ann Landers's advice

Read Ann Landers's six pieces of advice several times to be sure that you understand them thoroughly. Then work with a partner to summarize her advice in 65 words or less. In your summary, group Landers's positive statements (1, 5, 6) together and her negative statements (2, 3, 4) together for economy of expression.

How to Make an Intelligent Decision

(1) The more you have in common with the one you choose, the better your chances for a successful marriage. This means religious training, cultural, social and financial background. The old saying "opposites attract" may be true in the field of electromagnetics, but it seldom works out in choosing a lifetime partner.

(2) Don't marry on the spur of the moment. If love is real, it will last. The tired line "marry in haste, repent in leisure" may be a cliché, but it still makes good sense.

(3) Don't marry a person whose chief attraction is sexual. A marriage based on sex will fall apart when the passions cool, and they'll cool a whole lot faster than you thought.

(4) Don't marry with the intention of changing your beloved to meet your specifications. It won't work. If during courtship a person is unfaithful, a heavy drinker, a gambler or abusive, marriage

will not provide the magic cure. In fact, he'll undoubtedly get worse as time goes on.

(5) Choose someone who wants the same things from life that you want. Discuss in detail your aims, goals and objectives. Marriage should mean companionship and building a life together.

(6) Approach marriage as a permanent relationship and not as an experiment which can be tossed aside if it doesn't work. Remember, a good marriage is not a gift – it's an achievement. It takes working at. You must repeatedly compromise. Forgive and forget. And then be smart enough to *forget* what you forgave. Often the difference between a successful marriage and a mediocre one is leaving four or five things a day – unsaid.

Documentation

At the end of your summary, add the parenthetical reference *(Landers, 1978)* to give Landers credit for her ideas. If you use this summary in your essay, list her book as a reference at the end of your paper. Follow this format:

Landers, Ann. 1978. *The Ann Landers Encyclopedia: A to Z.* Doubleday & Company, Inc. Garden City, New York. pp. 716–17.

Follow-up   Exchange summaries with at least one other pair of classmates. Find something you like in each of the other summaries.

B. Meeting reader expectations: Persuasive essays

In Chapter 3, we discussed the informative and persuasive nature of academic writing. In Chapters 3, 4, and 5, you wrote informative essays intended to prove a logical assertion that you formulated in a thesis statement.

Although persuasive essays may also be informative, they are different from informative essays because in a persuasive essay the writer expresses an opinion on a controversial issue and tries to argue convincingly in support of that opinion. The issue might be whether or not to teach sex education in schools or whether an arranged marriage is a better form of mate selection than dating, among others.

To support your position in a persuasive essay, remember that people seldom accept others' opinions just as they are. An intelligent listener or reader wants evidence that supports a stated opinion. Do not limit yourself here; in addition to your own logical arguments, there are many persuasive forms of support:

1. *Expert opinion*   The ideas of an author or someone else who is recognized as knowing a lot about your topic can be good support. Make sure you agree with the expert so that your writing keeps your voice.
2. *Facts, statistics*   Facts may not be more interesting than opinions, but they are more convincing because they are difficult to reject. You will have to do research to present honest, accurate facts. Do not make up your own statistics.
3. *Examples*   These will be better support if they are real examples, that is, ones from your own experience rather than hypothetical ones from your imagination.
4. *Personal anecdote*   This is a short narrative. A personal anecdote can be a very effective argument if it supports the main idea closely.
5. *Description*   A well-written description that appeals to the senses (sight, hearing, touch) is effective if the description is relevant to the point of the essay.

✎ EXERCISE 2   Student model of a persuasive essay

Read this essay a first time to see if you agree with the writer's position on arranged marriage. Read it a second time to answer the questions that follow it.

SUCCESS IN MARRIAGE

There are two main ways of selecting a spouse in Japan: by dating and by using a matchmaker for an arranged marriage. Traditionally, people in the United States meet future spouses through dating. Unfamiliar with arranged marriages, most Americans reject them without knowing what they are really like. In an arranged marriage, prospective spouses meet each other through a matchmaker, and they have the opportunity to meet many different possible mates. At the same time, they can refuse any of the matches proposed by the matchmaker, which means they are not obligated to marry anyone the matchmaker introduces to them. Marriage is a serious matter everywhere: It is not merely for playing house, nor is it just for fun. When people make a mature decision to get married and resolve that their first marriage will be their last one, it is time to get married. Comparing dating and arranged marriage as ways to find the right mate, I am sure that arranged marriages result in more successful marriages.

In an arranged marriage, both prospective spouses are committed and have a very clear objective: marriage. They are both serious about getting married and have a mature attitude toward marriage. This point becomes very clear when we consider that the average age of Japanese seeking an arranged marriage is higher than the average marrying age. In arranged marriages, the average is 28 for women and 32 for men. With a clear objective in mind and a mature outlook, one is more likely to choose a mate who will help build a long, successful marriage. On the other hand, marriages which are the result of dating are not always approached with the same commitment. Although a woman may want to continue working instead of getting married, very often her fiance will pressure her to quit working and get married. Moreover, many young couples get married because they are curious about married life, which they think will make them seem older and more sophisticated. If only one partner wants to marry, or if one marries merely to seem older, there is not a full commitment to marriage.

People choosing an arranged marriage follow more mature criteria when selecting a mate than people who marry after dating. Seventy-eight percent of Japanese women seeking an arranged marriage put a strong earning potential as the first requirement for the prospective husband. This does not mean that he must have a lot of money but rather that he should have a stable job, which will contribute greatly to the success of the marriage. Financial problems are always painful, and in marriage they can be destructive. The criteria which men follow usually stress the social status of the woman's

family. Women from good families make good wives.
Women from good families are also often traditional
wives who are obedient, respectful, and content to
stay home. On the other hand, young people who are
dating follow different criteria in choosing dates,
and predictably, spouses. They are primarily interested in the appearance of the other person and in
having fun. They are also interested in gaining
experience by having relationships with different
kinds of people. The criteria they follow are not
as mature as the ones couples in an arranged marriage follow. And divorce statistics suggest that
the criteria young people follow in entering a love
marriage in both the United States and Japan do not
lead to success. Over 40 percent of Americans get
divorced, and one out of five Japanese marriages
ends in divorce.

The matchmaker, or go-between, in an arranged
marriage also plays a role in ensuring the marriage's success. First, the matchmaker will look
for someone of similar background and temperament.
When people apply for an arranged marriage, they
give the matchmaker a list of their personal
qualifications to let the matchmaker know their
background: educational level, work experience,
family background, hobbies, and even salaries. The
matchmaker will concentrate on finding someone who
is similar. Even though many people claim not to
care about the educational level of their spouse,
for example, a discrepancy in how well each partner
is educated can cause a couple to be at each
other's throats when they are married. Second, the
matchmaker will screen many potential candidates
and propose only ones that he/she can put a seal of
approval on, ones that are found to be totally
suitable. Since the matchmaker is usually someone
older and wiser as well as a friend or relative of
at least one of the people seeking marriage, he/she
can be trusted to make the best possible match.

Last, the matchmaker has an interest in seeing that
the marriage succeeds. If there are problems later
in the marriage, the matchmaker will attempt to
help the couple iron out the problems.

A successful marriage needs the support and commitment of both the husband and wife. In order to
have success in marriage, a young man or woman
needs to find a suitable mate because an unsuitable
one will not make a successful marriage. A suitable
mate is not only a partner that one gets along well
with. A couple is suited to each other when they
look at life in the same way and understand each
other. A person must be mature to choose a suitable
mate, but, to tell the truth, this is difficult for
young people to do by themselves. Fortunately,
there are matchmakers who can lead young people
along the right way to choosing a spouse. Arranged
marriages will create more success in marriage.

(Yumiko Asano, Japan)

1. Does Ms. Asano give you enough background on Japanese arranged marriages in the introduction for you to understand her argument?
2. In what sentence does she state her thesis? Do you agree with her position
   on arranged marriages?
3. How many paragraphs does she use to support her point? What is the topic
   sentence of each one?
4. Do you think that the criteria used to select a spouse in an arranged marriage are mature ones?
5. Which aspect of the matchmaker's role do you think contributes most to a
   successful marriage?
6. Do you find the essay persuasive? Explain. What would you change if you
   wrote an essay on the same topic?

C. Language conventions: Consistency in tense, person, number, and tone

SHIFTS IN TENSE

The logic of your writing determines the verb tenses you use. Sometimes a
shift in tenses is necessary and therefore logically consistent:

I *remember* that he *put on* the parking break before he *turned off* the engine. (*remember:* present tense; *put on, turned off:* past tense)

A logically inconsistent shift in tense, however, is confusing to the reader:

WRONG   I *cleaned* the ice from the window while the car *is running*.

He *thought* his sister *was* busy and *cannot see* him.

Since all the verbs in the two examples above describe actions in the past, they should all be in the past tense:

CORRECT   I *cleaned* the ice from the windshield while the car *was running*.

I *cleaned* the ice from the windshield *with the car running*. (Notice that the participle in the prepositional phrase *with the car running* takes its tense from *cleaned*.)

He *thought* his sister *was* busy and *could not see* him.

He *thought* his sister *was* busy and *unable to see* him. (The adjective phrase *unable to see him* takes its tense from *was*.)

Consistent use of tenses makes your writing easier to read and more effective.

✎ EXERCISE 3   Correcting tense shifts

Decide which verbs are logically inconsistent in tense, and correct them. Consider the logic of the whole passage in making your decisions.

Our teacher let us out of class early so that we can go to a lecture on campus. The lecture began late, so we have to wait. I am usually impatient, so I become upset when we had to wait 15 minutes for the talk to begin. Since I know a lot about geology, I was able to follow the lecture, but many of my classmates can't. I noticed that one of my classmates, Mario, is sleeping. Fortunately, our teacher wasn't there because I think she will be angry with him.

SHIFTS IN PERSON AND NUMBER

Pronouns refer to the first person (*I* or *we*), second person (*you*), and third person (*he, she, it, they*). An illogical or unnecessary shift in person or number is distracting to readers, as in the following examples:

WRONG   *One* has to be careful when *you* buy a used car. (There's a shift from third person [*one*] to second person [*you*] for no reason.)

WRONG   *I* often buy clothes on sale because *we* can save a lot of
money that way.
(There's a shift from singular to plural first person that is not
called for by the context.)
The *students* didn't find the exam difficult, but *you* couldn't
finish it in two hours.
(There's an unnecessary shift from third person to second
person.)

In these revised examples, the inconsistencies in person and number have been
corrected:

CORRECT   *You* have to be careful when *you* buy a used car. (informal)

One has to be careful when *one* buys a new car. (formal)

I often buy clothes on sale because *I* can save a lot of money
that way.

The *students* didn't find the exam difficult, but *they* couldn't
finish it in two hours.

✎ EXERCISE 4   Correcting shifts in person and number

Rewrite the sentences, correcting the shifts in person and number. Verbs and
possessive pronouns may need to change to agree with new subjects.

1. Anyone can learn a foreign language if you study.
2. Everyone has the ability to learn, so one should never give up when it
   seems difficult to you.
3. You also need to keep in mind that one might be better at oral skills than at
   reading and writing.
4. Students should be proud of their strengths, but at the same time you need
   to work on your weaknesses.
5. Students often focus on vocabulary, but you need to realize that vocabulary
   is only one part of a language.
6. A language learner should remember that they can't communicate without
   knowing the structure and phonology of a language.

THE INFORMAL *YOU*

When you are speaking with someone, the antecedent for *you* is obvious. Your
roommate might say this to you:

INFORMAL   You need to get to registration early to avoid long lines.

The same sentence does not work as well in writing, however. *You* probably
does not refer to your audience as it usually does in speaking, so its use is

imprecise in this sentence. (Your probable audience, the teacher, is most likely not registering for classes).

Less formal writing often uses *you* in a conversational, general way to be closer to the reader. This informal use is usually not appropriate in academic writing, however. The third person is more precise and formal.

INFORMAL   *You* need to heat the solution to 120 Celsius.

You could see how much pain the patient was in.

If *you* live in Miami, *you* must have air-conditioning.

Notice how these three sentences become more formal when third person constructions are substituted for *you.*

FORMAL   The solution needs to be heated to 120 degrees Celsius.

It was evident how much pain the patient was in. (or)
A person could see how much pain the patient was in.

To live in Miami, one must have air-conditioning.

EXERCISE 5   Avoiding the informal *you*

Rewrite these sentences, replacing *you* to produce more precise, formal sentences. Make any other necessary structural changes as well.

1. During the afternoon, when it's very hot in my country, you need to dress in cooler clothes.
2. You should try to avoid wearing dark colors.
3. You can't wear shorts in public in my country, however.
4. People consider shorts indecent, and they would stare at you.
5. At home, of course, you can wear whatever you want.
6. If you receive company, though, you should make sure you look presentable.

SHIFTS IN TONE

Colloquial language and slang should also be avoided in academic writing because such language conflicts with the formal tone that is usually appropriate. Notice the shifts from formal to informal tone in the following examples:

The university president addressed the faculty at length on issues including tenure, salary, the importance of research, and *hanging out with students.*

The faculty reported that raises of less than a thousand *bucks* per year would be unacceptable.

The same sentences with a consistent formal tone follow:

The university president addressed the faculty at length on issues including tenure, salary, the importance of research, and *faculty-student relationships.*

The faculty reported that raises of less than a thousand *dollars* per year would be unacceptable.

✎ EXERCISE 6   Correcting shifts in tone

Change the words and expressions in italics to maintain a formal tone.

1. John *blew off* his math class to prepare for his history exam.
2. It was difficult to give the accident victim the necessary medical attention because he was *screaming his head off.*
3. Two *guys* approached the managing editor's office to see what the commotion was all about.
4. A family with lots of *kids* will find making ends meet more difficult.
5. Marcella remarked that John's new sunglasses were *pretty cool.*
6. Smaller children often refuse to eat vegetables, which they find *yucky.*
7. Archibald will probably have trouble selling his car for a good price because it is *an old junk.*
8. The students reported that they had had an *awesome* time on their spring break holiday.

✎ EXERCISE 7   Editing for shifts in tense, person, number, and tone

Read the paragraph, underlining any shifts in tense, person, number, and tone. Then rewrite the paragraph, correcting the shifts.

There is a basic difference between societies that prefer arranged marriages and those that did not. That difference lies in how much you value the opinion of elders. In societies preferring arranged marriages, young people defer to the judgment of older relatives. Societies that think arranged marriages are not cool trust the judgment of young people to choose their own mates. When young men and women get married in such a society, he/she feels they know better than their parents. This belief may come from the high value the society placed on individualism, which says that each person is the best judge of what is good for you.

5   CORE WRITING ASSIGNMENT

A. Writing Topics

For your writing assignment in this chapter, you will be developing arguments for, and then writing a persuasive essay on this topic: *Are you* for *or* against *arranged marriages?*

If this topic does not appeal to you, you may write a persuasive essay on the following alternative topic: *In order to have a successful marriage, is it important to marry someone with whom you have many things in common, such as level of education, interests, and socioeconomic background?* If you and your teacher agree on other topics related to marriage that lead to persuasive essays, you may choose to write on one of them.

B. Generating ideas: Panel discussion

Follow these steps to conduct a panel discussion on arranged marriages.

1. Form two panels, or groups, of three students each, one of which is for arranged marriages and one of which is against them.
2. Divide the blackboard into two areas: *for* and *against.* The rest of the students, after determining their opinions on the issue, should write one-sentence arguments supporting their positions on the appropriate side of the board. As students write their arguments on the board, they should check to make sure they are not repeating someone else. All students not on the panels should have a chance to write an argument. The panels then have 5 minutes to discuss how they will refute the arguments on the opposing side.
3. The three students on the panel *for* arranged marriages attempt to refute the first point on the list *against* arranged marriages.
4. The three students on the panel *against* arranged marriages attempt to refute the first point on the list *for* arranged marriages.
5. The two panels take turns discussing points until all points have been addressed.

Follow-up   All students should spend a few minutes taking notes on the best arguments in favor of their position.

C. Expanding your point of view: Research

To make your argument a strong one, you will probably want to use facts and possibly an expert opinion to support your position. The readings in this chapter may provide the support you need. If not, the best source of both facts and expert opinion is the library. Look up subjects that are relevant to the topic you chose in Section A, "Writing Topics." If you have decided to write an essay on the topic of arranged marriages, these subjects will include:

courtship   dating
marriage, arranged   mate selection

Take down bibliographical information, including page numbers, on all sources that you may wish to use in your essay. Take notes by paraphrasing or summarizing points that you think will help you.

D. Initial drafts

FIRST DRAFT

Since you already know your position on the issue you have chosen, it will be easy to formulate your thesis statement. Write an introduction that catches the interest of your readers and leads naturally to your thesis statement.

Choose support for your position carefully. Remember that your opinion by itself is not persuasive. Your opinion backed up by facts, expert opinion, real examples, and relevant description and narrative is persuasive.

Take either an inductive or deductive approach to writing, whichever you are more comfortable with. If you choose the inductive approach, write freely for 15 or 20 minutes. Then read what you have written and find at least three good main points of support for paragraphs. If you choose the deductive approach, outline your paper before writing the first draft.

REVISION

Ask a roommate or someone outside your class to read your first draft. Ask the reader to summarize your position and argument to make sure they are understood. Find out what questions remain in the reader's mind after reading your draft.

With your reader's reaction in mind, evaluate your paper using the criteria listed in the "Essay Assessment Guidelines" at the end of this chapter. Revise your first draft, and mark it "Revision 1."

E. Review, revision, and assessment

PEER FEEDBACK

Get feedback on how clear and logical your thinking and writing are. Read your paragraph to a group of two or three classmates. Each member of the group will read his or her paper to the group. Follow the "Peer Feedback Guidelines" at the end of this chapter.

FURTHER REVISION

How well did your group receive your paper? Could they summarize it accurately? Did they understand your main points? Secondary points? How could your paper be clearer and/or more interesting to your audience? Make notes of changes you need to make.

If necessary, revise your paper using the feedback you got from the group. Edit your paper for shifts in tense, person, number, and tone. Submit all drafts to your teacher, with the last one marked "Revision 2" at the top.

If you choose not to revise, write a paragraph to your teacher summarizing the feedback you received and explaining why you decided not to revise.

TEACHER ASSESSMENT

Your teacher will assess your paper using the detailed set of essay assessment guidelines in Appendix B. Your teacher may give you a grade on the essay or allow you to make further revisions before assigning a grade.

PEER FEEDBACK GUIDELINES

Writers

- [ ] Read the paper clearly, a second time if necessary.
- [ ] Respond to listeners' comments and questions.
- [ ] Ask for suggestions if you want them.

Listeners

- [ ] Listen quietly until the writer finishes reading.
- [ ] Briefly summarize what you understood, orally.
- [ ] Pick out parts of the paper (words, expressions, or ideas) that stand out for you. Share these parts with the group.
- [ ] If you wish, share with the group how the writing makes you feel and ask questions about parts that are not clear.
- [ ] Do not make negative comments or tell the writer what changes to make.

ESSAY ASSESSMENT GUIDELINES

These are the criteria for a well-written essay. Use this checklist to critically examine your writing and determine how it can be improved. See Appendix B for the more detailed set of guidelines that your teacher will use to assess your work.

Content and ideas

- [ ] The writer has thought about the topic and has a clear thesis.
- [ ] The writer discusses each main point enough to give the reader a reason to believe it. The writer supports each main point, and no important point is left out.
- [ ] The writer's voice is clear because he or she writes in a sincere way, with the audience in mind.

Organization and form

- [ ] The paper has a clear beginning, middle, and end, with separate introductory, body, and concluding paragraphs. It moves logically in a straight line.
- [ ] The reader wants to continue reading and can understand the thesis and other main points fully after one reading.
- [ ] It is clear which are the main points and which are the secondary points.

Writing conventions

- ☐ The writer uses a variety of sentence lengths and types to add interest to the writing.
- ☐ The writer chooses vocabulary carefully to communicate clearly.
- ☐ The writer uses cohesive devices to make the relationships between the ideas clear.
- ☐ The writer avoids problems of sentence structure including fragments, comma-splices, and run-together sentences.
- ☐ There are no illogical shifts in tense, person, or number, and the tone is consistently formal.
- ☐ The writer uses English grammar effectively to convey the message. There are few problems of verb tense, subject-verb agreement, word order, count/noncount use, or word form.
- ☐ The writer follows rules for spelling, capitalization, and punctuation.

A Better Quality of Life
Through modernization or tradition?

An American supermarket

A market in Indonesia

Compare these two very different markets.
In which one would you prefer to shop? Why?

1 GETTING A GRIP ON THE TOPIC

A. Reflection

The title of the main reading in this chapter, "Nothing Is Black, Nothing Is White," is a variation of an often-heard saying in English: "Nothing is ever just black and white." What do you think this saying means? How might this expression apply to development, the process of raising the standard of living and production levels of a nation or geographical area?

B. Discussion

Imagine that you must decide where you are going to live for the rest of your life. You may choose between two countries, A and B, but once you have made your choice, you cannot change your mind. Read the lists of advantages and disadvantages of life in these two countries and decide whether you would rather live in country A or country B.

COUNTRY A

Advantages

1. People there seem happy and content with their lives.
2. People there lead lives that are close to nature and to other people.

Disadvantages

3. Few of the comforts of modern life are available there.
4. People there have limited communication with the outside world.
5. There is a high illiteracy rate.
6. Infant mortality is high and life expectancy is short.

COUNTRY B

Advantages

1. People there enjoy all the comforts and conveniences of modern technology.
2. Its people receive excellent health care.
3. There is good communication with the outside world, and many foreign products are imported.

Disadvantages

4. Crime, inflation, and unemployment are serious social problems.
5. People's independence makes them less connected to other people.
6. Many people are discontent with their lives.
7. People there sometimes use the environment (nature) in ways that are not sustainable, i.e., in ways that cannot continue without harming nature.

Which country would you choose to live in for the rest of your life, country A or country B? Why?

Follow-up   Explain your choice to a partner and then discuss it with the whole class. *Note:* In your class discussion, talk about the difference between life in a developing country (a poorer one making progress towards a higher standard of living) and a developed country (a richer one with a high standard of living). Is country A developing or developed? Country B?

C. Notes on the main reading

Helena Norberg-Hodge has spent many years living and observing changes in the primarily Buddhist district of Ladakh, a region in the Himalaya Mountains between India and Pakistan. She saw the very traditional Ladakh as it was before development and has watched it become more modern over the years. This excerpt from Norberg-Hodge's book, *Ancient Futures: Learning from Ladakh,* is written in the form of an argument: First she describes the advantages and disadvantages of both traditional life and modernization, and then she reconciles the two by making a final decision about modernization in Ladakh. Keep this organization in mind as you read, to help you understand her writing more easily.

VOCABULARY EXERCISE

Predict what the author will say about development in Ladakh by imagining how she might use the following expressions. Work with a partner or in small groups; suggest how each item might be used in the reading. Check a dictionary for the meanings of unknown words.

seen through rose-tinted glasses
using Western yardsticks
a higher position on the social ladder
two thousand years of trial and error
interconnectedness of all phenomena

GLOSSARY

Review the glossary before reading the selection, for help with some of the more difficult vocabulary.

alienation (line 4): feeling like a stranger, unconnected to others
far from ideal (lines 13–14): very unsatisfactory
misleading (line 20): giving a wrong impression
intimate (line 20): very close
perplexed (line 31): confused
on the periphery (line 36): on the edge, far from the center of activity
longevity (line 52): long life
hardships (line 63): difficulties, suffering
advent (line 65): (the) coming, arrival
seductive (line 76): attractive and persuasive
bonds (lines 76 and 99): connections and obligations
burden (line 100): something difficult to bear
prerequisite (line 101): something required beforehand

D. Read for the main idea

Read the selection a first time to answer this main idea question: *Does Norberg-Hodge think Ladakhis were more content with their lives before or after modernization?*

Nothing Is Black, Nothing Is White
Helena Norberg-Hodge

In the preceding pages I have tried to give an overview of both the traditional way of life in Ladakh and the forces of change in the modern sector. In talking about happiness, cooperation, and balance with the land in the old Ladakh and contrasting it with alienation, social
5 breakdown, and pollution in the modern sector, my description might well seem exaggerated, as though I have seen the traditional life through rose-tinted lenses and painted the modern [life] much too black. But while it is true that much of what I have described in the old Ladakh is positive and most of my description of the new looks at
10 negative changes, this is because I have primarily dealt with relation-

ships and connections. I have tried to describe the shape and feel of two contrasting ways of life rather than focusing on isolated factors.

Many individual aspects of the traditional culture were far from ideal: there was a lack of what we would consider basic comforts, like heating in the freezing winter temperatures. Communication with the outside world was limited. Illiteracy rates were high; infant mortality was higher and life expectancy lower than in the West. All of these are serious problems. But they are not quite as they appear when viewed from an outside perspective. Using Western yardsticks can be very misleading. Over the years, through intimate contact with Ladakhi society, I have come to see these limitations in a rather different light.

Traditional Ladakhi villagers did not consider it a hardship, as we would, to have to fetch water every day from a stream or to cook their food on a dung fire. Nor did they feel the cold to the same extent that we do. Once while I was hiking in late autumn with a nun from Hemis village, we crossed a stream that was so cold I screamed out in pain. My feet had turned bright red, and it took me fifteen minutes to recover. She, meanwhile, casually waded through the water, even pausing for a minute to look at something upstream, and looked quite perplexed when I asked her if she was not cold.

The limited nature of communication in Ladakh has also taken on a different meaning for me. The incredible vitality and joy that I experienced in the villages was almost certainly connected to the fact that the excitement in life was here and now, with you and in you. People did not feel that they were on the periphery; the center was where they were. Having the rest of the world through TV in your living room may not be as enriching as we tend to think. It may have just the opposite effect, in fact.

I certainly do not want to find myself in the position of defending illiteracy. There is no doubt that the Ladakhis now need to be able to read. In our society, being illiterate in effect means being powerless. We have become utterly dependent on the written word. However, in the traditional culture, the scale was such that if you could speak, you were in a position to influence decisions. Even if you were illiterate your power to decide matters affecting your own life was actually greater than that of the average citizen in the West. Illiteracy in the traditional context was not what the term implies in the modern world.

50 Of all the factors that influence people's thinking about modern versus traditional society, none is more important than health and longevity. In traditional Ladakh people die from diseases for which Western medicine has found a cure, and infant mortality has been estimated to be as high as fifteen percent. Reducing disease and

55 improving health are unquestionably important goals.

When one examines the reality of Western-style medical care in the Third World, however, things are not so clear. Surely it cannot be sensible to discard the traditional knowledge about local diseases and cures that has evolved over more than a thousand years. Nor can it

60 make sense to introduce a poor imitation of a Western system that offers inadequate health care to the majority and cannot be sustained economically.

Just as there were considerable hardships in the traditional society, so development has brought real improvements. Obviously both

65 the introduction of money and technology and the advent of modern medicine bring with them substantial benefits. Many Ladakhis are now much more comfortable than before. In addition, people enjoy being able to travel and to buy a wider range of material goods from outside. For example, rice and sugar, once luxuries, have become the

70 food of every day.

Education is providing some with new and exciting opportunities, and for those who were socially disadvantaged traditionally, like blacksmiths, modernization promises the possibility of a higher position on the new social ladder. For young men in particular, the free-

75 dom and mobility that the modern world seems to offer are extremely seductive. The new ideals release them from bonds to other people and to place. It is no longer necessary for them to listen to their neighbors, parents, or grandparents. In fact, the modern ideal is the strong independent male.

80 Despite the very real problems in the traditional society and the equally real improvements brought about by development, things look different when one examines the important relationships: to the land, to one another, and to oneself. Viewed from this broader perspective, the differences between the old and the new become stark

85 and disturbing – almost, but of course not quite, black and white. It

becomes clear that the traditional nature-based society, with all its flaws and limitations, was more sustainable, both socially and environmentally. It was the result of a dialogue between human beings and their surroundings, a continuing dialogue that meant that, over two thousand years of trial and error, the culture kept changing. The traditional Buddhist world view emphasized change, but change within a framework of compassion and a profound understanding of the interconnectedness of all phenomena.

The old culture reflected fundamental human needs while respecting natural limits. And it worked. It worked for nature, and it worked for people. The various connecting relationships in the traditional system were mutually reinforcing, encouraging harmony and stability. Most importantly of all, having seen my friends change over the last sixteen years, I have no doubt that the bonds and responsibilities of the traditional society, far from being a burden, offered a profound sense of security, which seems to be a prerequisite for inner peace and contentedness. I am convinced that people were significantly happier before development than they are today.

Follow-up Answer the main idea question here: _____

_____

_____

E. Read for more detail

Read the selection a second time. Use the questions to understand it better and to bring your own experience to the reading.

1. What negative effects has development had on life in Ladakh?
2. What disadvantages did Ladakh's traditional culture have?
3. How does the author make these disadvantages seem less important? Do you agree with her logic?
4. What advantages has development brought to Ladakh? Which is the most important in your opinion?
5. Is Norberg-Hodge in favor of the traditional culture or of modernization? Why? Do you agree or disagree with her?
6. *Key words* Pick out six words that you feel are important to the reading. Be ready to explain why you chose each one, and what it means, if necessary.

2 RESPONDING TO THE MAIN READING

A. Journals: A private audience

Choose two topics below. Write at least 75 words on each one in your journal notebook. Express yourself honestly. These journal entries are for your eyes only, so do not spend time using a dictionary or worrying about grammar.

1. Do you still feel the same way about the choice you made (country A or country B) in Section B, "Discussion," in Part 1? What would your current choice be?
2. How does the Norberg-Hodge reading on Ladakh make you feel about the future of developing countries – optimistic or pessimistic?
3. Would you like to visit Ladakh? Why or why not?
4. If you had the opportunity to speak with Helena Norberg-Hodge, what would you say to her?

B. Shared writing

Choose at least two topics and write for a total of 30 minutes. Your audience is your classmates, with whom you will share your writing. They will be interested not only in *what* you feel but also in *why* you feel that way. Therefore, you will want to express your views clearly and support them.

1. Which aspects of modernization are absolutely essential for a developing country, in your opinion?
2. Is it practical for countries to approach the twenty-first century without improving their level of technology?
3. If you have lived in both developed and less developed countries, which do you prefer? Which offers a better quality of life, speaking not only materially but spiritually?
4. Can a country keep its traditional way of life and develop? Or does development necessarily mean a change in traditions?

C. Feedback on your writing

Get feedback on how clear and logical your thinking and writing are. Read one of your writings from the previous section, "Shared Writing," to a group of two or three classmates. Each member of the group will read one of his or her writings. Follow the "Peer Feedback Guidelines" at the end of this chapter.

Follow-up In 5 minutes, evaluate in writing how well your audience received your paper. Could they summarize it accurately? Did they understand your points? How could you make your paper clearer? More interesting to your audience?

3 GOING MORE DEEPLY INTO THE TOPIC

Chinese technicians in Shanghai

What do these Chinese technicians appear to be doing?
How might technological change affect life in China?
Is new technology always beneficial to a country? Why?

A. Preparing to read

Engineer, businessman, and adviser to the Indian government Satyan Pitroda was born and educated in India. He did graduate studies in the United States, where he later worked on digital telephone switches, devices that allow telephone calls to travel from phone to phone without mechanical switches, which require constant maintenance. After much success, he turned his eye on his homeland, India, which he wanted to help by improving telephone service. In this article, Pitroda discusses the role of technology in developing countries. His views are quite different from Norberg-Hodge's.

Before you read, try to clarify your position on the use of technology in developing countries. Read each statement. If you agree, write *A;* if you disagree, write *D*.

_____ 1. The unsophisticated rural poor should be helped to get technology appropriate to their needs: immunization against disease, wells that provide clean water, electrification, and sanitation.

_____ 2. Higher technology like advanced telecommunications (e.g., electronic mail, fax, and telex systems) is probably not appropriate for the developing, or "Third World," nations.

_____ 3. Telecommunications play an essential role in spreading important information and knowledge in both developed and developing nations.

_____ 4. Increasing citizens' access to information can have profound social and political effects on a country.

_____ 5. International aid agencies like the World Bank are right to provide only the technology that agency experts feel is appropriate to the developing nations they assist.

Follow-up Discuss your responses in small groups or as a class.

B. First reading

Read the article the first time to answer this main idea question: _Why does the author think advanced technology is as appropriate to developing countries as it is to developed ones?_

Development, Democracy, and the Village Telephone*
SAM (SATYAN) PITRODA

I was born in 1942 and raised in a poor village in one of the poorest areas of rural India, a place with kerosene lamps and no running water. In 1980, at 38, I was a U.S. citizen and a self-made telecommunications millionaire. By 1990, I was 47 years old and
5 nearing the end of nearly a decade back in India as leader of a controversial but largely successful effort to build an Indian information industry and begin the immense task of extending digital telecommunications to every corner of my native country, even to villages like the one where I was born.
10 That effort persists today at an increased pace, but it remains controversial. Some of the controversy has centered on me and my

*Reprinted by permission of _Harvard Business Review_. Excerpted from "Development, Democracy, and the Village Telephone" by S. Pitroda, Nov./Dec. 1993. Copyrighted 1993 by the President and Fellows of Harvard College, all rights reserved.

methods. Most of it focuses on the efficacy and logic of bringing information technology to people who are in global terms the poorest of the poor.

Common sense and accepted thinking about economic develop- 15 ment have long held it ridiculous to supply Third-World villages with state-of-the-art technology. What subsistence farmers need is not high-tech science and complex systems, the argument goes, but immunizations, basic literacy, disease- and drought-resistant cereals and oilseeds, simple pumps, deep-drop toilets, two-phase electrifica- 20 tion – all the "appropriate" technologies that the unsophisticated rural poor can use and understand.

I agree with this argument as far as it goes. Third-World farming villages need water, hygiene, health, and power, and the need is usually great. But the argument falls short in its definition of "appropri- 25 ate." It ignores technology's profound social implications. And it comes dangerously close to consigning the Third-World poor to a life of third-rate capacities and opportunity. The policies of development agencies like the World Bank too often limit "appropriate technology" to the two-dimensional, twopenny solutions that bring the poor 30 to the doorway of the modern world but not actually across the threshold.

For me, three facts about Third-World development stand out with great force. First, high technology is already an essential element in effective water sourcing, sanitation, construction, agriculture, and 35 other development activities. Geohydrologic surveys are carried out from satellites. Bioengineering has revolutionized crop production. Appropriate technology has moved well beyond the water screw and the inclined plane.

Second, modern telecommunications and electronic information 40 systems are thoroughly appropriate technologies even in those regions of the world that still lack adequate water, food, and power. The reason is simply that modern telecommunications is an indispensable aid in meeting basic needs. If a U.S. community needed, say, widespread immunizations or replacement of a power grid, would the 45 telephone seem a vital or an irrelevant tool in getting the job done? Would the telephone seem more or less critical if the job were tied to a natural calamity such as flood or drought and required the mobilization of diverse resources over a broad area?

50   Third, as a great social leveler, information technology ranks second only to death. It can raze cultural barriers, overwhelm economic inequalities, even compensate for intellectual disparities. In short, high technology can put unequal human beings on an equal footing, and that makes it the most potent democratizing tool ever

55   devised. . . .

(Here Pitroda describes his work in India in detail, including: the creation of the Centre for Development of Telematics, or C-DOT; the installation of digital phone equipment partly manufactured in India; the installation of new telephone lines; and other

60   *improvements to the rural telephone system.)*

C-DOT [ran] a test in Karnataka state with hugely encouraging results. In one town of 5,000 people with almost no previous telephone service, business activity rose many times following installation of an automatic digital exchange for 100 lines. Suddenly, it was

65   possible for a truck owner to chase his drivers, line up goods and labor by telephone, and monitor the movement of his vehicles. Local farmers could call nearby cities and get real prices for their produce. Artisans could speak to customers, machine operators could arrange for service and repairs, shopkeepers could order goods – all by phone

70   and in real time. In the six months after the introduction of service, total bank deposits in the town rose by an impressive 80%.

There were also social benefits. The townspeople could call doctors and ambulances, order pumps and textbooks, call newspapers, speak to politicians, share experiences with colleagues, and organize

75   community ceremonies and functions. One villager told me that when his father died seven years earlier, he'd had to send 20 messengers on trains and buses to inform relatives in nearby villages. More recently when his mother followed, the villager went to the local tea shop and phoned all 20 villages – instant, certain, and far less

80   expensive.

By the turn of the century or very shortly after, almost all of India's 600,000 villages will [have telephone service]. Once in place, the village telephone becomes as critical as water, food, shelter, and health services. Once exposed, people in rural areas want a village

85   telephone more than they want any other community service.

Of nearly equal importance for me, the community phone becomes an instrument of social change, fundamental to the process of democratization. With telecommunications networks now spreading across the Second and Third Worlds, I believe that no amount of effort can put information back in the hands of the few, to be iso- **90** lated, concentrated, and controlled.

Follow-up   Answer the main idea question here: _____

_____

C. Additional readings

Read the selection again. Mark any places in the text that are still unclear to you. Then read these passages once more to improve your understanding of them.

D. Negotiating the meaning

Write for about 15 minutes on this selection. Write on any or all of the following:

▶   whether you like it or not, and why
▶   whether you prefer it to the previous selection
▶   what you have trouble understanding

Follow-up   To a group of two or three, read what you have written. Read your reaction a second time if necessary.
   Each group member will respond with (1) a question, (2) a comment, and/or (3) clarification. Every group member should read what he or she has written. As a group, choose one response to share with the whole class.

E. Discussion: Critical thinking

Discuss these questions in pairs, small groups, or as a class.

1. Contrast Norberg-Hodge's and Pitroda's views on introducing technology into developing countries. Which author do you agree with?
2. Norberg-Hodge and Pitroda not only have different views on development, they also write with different voices. Norberg-Hodge is from a highly developed country, and Pitroda is from a less developed one. How do the authors' origins affect their attitudes towards development?
3. Which of the two authors would you rather have a conversation with? What questions would you ask Norberg-Hodge or Pitroda? What do you think their answers might be?

4 IMPROVING WRITING SKILLS

A. Using another's writing: Summarizing the conclusions

The last two paragraphs of the reading by Helena Norberg-Hodge express her views on the advantages of traditional life over modernization in Ladakh. Her conclusions might be useful in the argument paper you will write in this chapter. Of course, to use her ideas effectively, you will need to summarize them. Prepare your summaries in advance by doing Exercise 1.

✎**EXERCISE 1**   **Summarizing Norberg-Hodge's conclusions**

Summarize each of the last two paragraphs of "Nothing Is Black, Nothing Is White" (beginning on line 80: "Despite the very real problems . . ." and line 94: "The old culture . . .") by following these steps:

1. Read each paragraph several times to understand it fully.
2. Concentrate on identifying the main ideas; take down key words as notes.
3. Then close your book and write a two- to three-sentence summary of each paragraph.

Follow-up   Exchange summaries with at least one classmate. Did you choose the same main ideas in your summaries?

B. Meeting reader expectations: Avoiding logical fallacies

Logical fallacies, or the use of faulty logic, occurs in writing as well as speech. There are three good reasons to avoid logical fallacies in your writing. First, they are wrong and, simply put, dishonest if you use them knowingly. Second, they take away from the strength of your argument. Finally, the use of logical fallacies can make your readers feel that you do not consider them very intelligent.

✎**EXERCISE 2**   **Recognizing logical fallacies**

Read the descriptions of the different kinds of logical fallacies in Part A. Then read each statement in Part B, and decide which kind of logical fallacy it contains. Label it with the appropriate letter. Use each letter once.

Part A: Kinds of logical fallacies

a. *False cause* Most problems are too complicated to have one simple cause. A sequence of events (one following another) does not prove that one event caused another; logical evidence does.

b. *Sweeping generalization* The writer asserts a general truth by implying that it is supported by authority. The implication is that there are no differences of opinion among the authorities.

c. *Circular argument* The assertion is not supported; it is simply repeated.

d. *Begging the question* Instead of proving that something is true, the writer simply asserts that it is true. Statements such as "It is common knowledge that . . ." are typical of this kind of fallacy.

e. *Faulty analogy* The analogy (comparison) is not a good one because there are more differences than similarities between the two items being compared.

f. *Genetic fallacy* The writer assumes that we can know what a person or thing is like from its origins.

g. *Either/or (black/white) fallacy* The writer tries to force us to choose between one of two very different alternatives, implying that there are no other choices.

h. *Emotional appeal* The writer appeals to deep biases many people have for certain things (country, family) or against others (homosexuality, abortion). The fallacy excites people's emotions; it does not deal with the issues.

Part B: Logical fallacies

_____ 1. Those people can't be trusted because everything they do proves they're dishonest.

_____ 2. Space exploration is as important as Columbus' voyage to the new world was.

_____ 3. The increase in cancer in our community must be the result of the nuclear reactor recently built nearby.

_____ 4. Everyone knows that national health care has failed in Canada.

_____ 5. How can we elect as governor a woman who admittedly does not believe in God?

_____ 6. If we build more factories, a dirtier environment is the only possible result.

_____ 7. This must be a good car; it was made in Germany.

_____ 8. Scientific research has proven that global warming will destroy our planet.

Follow-up Have you heard or read similar logical fallacies? Work with your class and list as many examples as you can.

✎ EXERCISE 3 Fixing logical fallacies

There is no help for some of the fallacies in Part B of Exercise 2 because they are based on false assumptions or premises. Others, with some thought and

editing, can be transformed into logical arguments. Rewrite the statements
indicated to improve the logic employed.

1. Rewrite sentence 3 to make clear that the nuclear reactor could be one of
   several factors leading to the increased cancer rate.
2. Rewrite sentence 6 to make clear that pollution-control devices and gov-
   ernmental restrictions could be used to help control the effects of factories
   on the environment.
3. Rewrite sentence 7 to consider specific aspects of car quality, such as the
   repair record, safety features, and owner satisfaction.
4. Rewrite sentence 8 so that it is clear that only some (and not all) authorities
   support the assertion.

EXERCISE 4   Identifying and correcting logical fallacies

With a partner, read these statements on the topic of this chapter. Which ones
contain logical fallacies? Mark statements containing fallacies with an ✗.
What makes each one a fallacy? How could you correct the fallacy?

_____ 1. Developing countries must industrialize, or they will never
develop.
_____ 2. Every sensible person knows that a little more pollution is the price
we have to pay for material progress.
_____ 3. International aid is essential to developing nations because they
cannot modernize without outside help.
_____ 4. It is obvious to any intelligent person that political problems are far
more important than economic problems in today's world.
_____ 5. Politicians cannot be trusted to do the right thing because they are
all corrupt.
_____ 6. Since developed countries caused the inequality among nations,
they have an obligation to solve the problem.
_____ 7. Experts agree that education is the key to developing a country.

Follow-up   Share your answers with another pair of partners or the class.

EXERCISE 5   Student model of an argument essay

This student essay is an example of an argument essay, the kind of essay you
will write later in this chapter. Read the paper the first time to answer these
questions: *(1) Has Mr. Orozco convinced you of his thesis? (2) Did he avoid
logical fallacies in his paper?*

Then read the paper a second time to answer the questions that follow it.

WHAT IS QUALITY OF LIFE?

When people have the great experience of living
in other countries, they can perceive how different
the inhabitants' values and lives are from those in
their own countries. In some countries, people base
their quality of life on the amount of material
goods they have. Most individuals in these countries base their welfare on the accumulation of
money, goods, and services. To be sure, infrastructure, technology, and material progress have
brought to these people a higher standard of living. In other countries, material factors play a
smaller role in the quality of life. People in
these countries judge that their traditions and
folklore, education, and social relations are the
most important qualities in their lives. Development is inevitable in every country, but as we
develop, we must remember that the quality of life
of individuals has two sides. When we talk about
improving a country's quality of life, we should
consider individuals living comfortably and fulfilling both material and spiritual needs. It is a
mistake to look only at the material side and to
ignore the spiritual side when considering quality
of life.

On the spiritual side, quality of life means
that people enjoy life the best way possible while
having spare time for their families and friends. A
country which stresses spiritual matters as quality
of life has the advantage of creating a peaceful,
secure environment for people to live in. People
have enough time to share with others and learn
about art, music, and traditions. They also find
themselves useful to others and do the things they
like without feeling the necessity to make more
money than they need. A country that emphasizes
non-material factors may also have disadvantages

such as slower progress and poor development. There is sometimes not enough money to build and create the infrastructure that inhabitants need.

In other countries, where a higher standard of living is the primary goal, it seems that everything around people ends up in monetary transactions. Personal economic growth seems to be an important issue for most people. On the positive side, a higher standard of living brings through our doors new technologies like TVs, VCRs, computers, fax machines, kitchen appliances, and so on. We also have social and medical services that make our lives more comfortable. On the other hand, a higher standard of living can bring us a number of bothersome consequences like unemployment, inflation, and a rising crime rate, all of which are evidence that a developed country is not 100 percent secure. In addition, social relations are often poor because people don't have time to talk and listen to their neighbors.

An experience of mine in southern Mexico has helped me to understand that quality of life consists of more than modern material goods. It was interesting to observe how spiritual matters were more significant than anything else in this small town. I looked at people in the streets talking to each other about their experiences and life. I saw handicrafts made by people who inherited the crafts from their ancestors. I heard musicians playing in the streets, and in the market I saw people trading what they didn't need for things they really did need. All the people had smiles on their faces and the time to talk to each other without stress or any rush. Mothers had time to attend to their children and teach them what had been passed down from generation to generation. Education was important for them too. In fact, one mother's priority each

day was to send her children off to school and to
supervise their homework. It was interesting to see
how happily the people in this town lived despite
their material poverty. Their reliance on a traditional life resulted for them in a more stable
society than any governed by money and goods.

  When we talk about development, we talk about
human progress with its positive and negative consequences. We should not forget that development
does not start with goods. Rather, as Schumacher
points out, it starts with people and their education, with organization, and with discipline
(Schumacher 1973). All three require time and
effort to succeed. However, even more important
than development is the quality of life of the people and the strong social structure it provides. A
good quality of life and a strong social structure,
which depend as much on the spiritual as on the
material, provide social welfare, the goal of every
society. At the same time they provide the foundation on which to build as the society develops and
prospers.

Reference
Schumacher, E.F. 1973. *Small Is Beautiful.* Harper,
p. 168.

                    (Francisco Orozco, Mexico)

1. What is Mr. Orozco's argument, or thesis? Which sentence expresses this
    thesis?
2. Does he present both sides of the argument? Where?
3. Does he make clear which side of the argument he prefers? If so, in which
    paragraph?
4. Does the introduction catch your interest and make you want to read on?
5. What point does he make in the conclusion? Does the conclusion leave you
    thinking about his thesis?
6. Which paragraph shows the writer's voice the most strongly?

C. Language conventions: Parallelism

Look at the examples marked *wrong.* Although the meaning of these examples can be guessed at, they are hard to read and understand because they contain grammatical forms that do not match. Ideas in the same grammatical form, i.e., ideas that are *parallel,* are easier to read and understand.

(1)	WRONG	He would rather swim than to jog for exercise.
	CORRECT	He would rather swim than jog for exercise.

(2) WRONG   Early to bed, early to rise,
                          makes a man healthy, wealthy,
                          and gives him wisdom.

         CORRECT   Early to bed, early to rise,
                          makes a man healthy, wealthy,
                          and wise.

(3) WRONG   A lot of students attend Pima College because of its low tuition, small class size, and the instructors all have professional status.

         CORRECT   A lot of students attend Pima College because of the low tuition, small class size, and professional status of the instructors.

✎ EXERCISE 6   Making segments parallel

Underline segments that are not parallel to the rest of the sentence. Then rewrite the sentence, revising for parallelism. (There is more than one solution for some examples; choose the solution that gives the shortest, clearest sentence.)

1. Ladakh, one of the highest regions in the world, is made up of high plains and it has deep valleys, too.
2. Agriculture is difficult for two reasons: a cold, dry climate and the growing season is short.
3. Depending on elevation, the weather permits inhabitants either to keep animals or they can grow crops.
4. In the higher regions, people are mainly shepherds because of the cold weather and agriculture is difficult.
5. At lower elevations, people grow crops because the temperatures are higher and a longer growing season.
6. Principal crops include wheat, barley, and millet, and peas and beans are very important, too.

7. With the cold climate and vegetation is scarce, firewood is a valuable resource.
8. Ladakh is divided between India and Pakistan, and China also controls a part of it.

✎ EXERCISE 7   More practice in making sentences parallel

Underline segments that are not parallel in form to the rest of the sentence. Then rewrite the sentence, revising for parallelism. (There is more than one solution in most sentences; choose the solution that gives a shorter, clearer sentence.)

1. India is the seventh largest country in the world in area but second in terms of how many people live there.
2. India's population is distributed unevenly, with four-fifths living in villages and the rest live in towns and cities.
3. India exports engineering products like machinery, transportation equipment, and electrical goods, and textile goods are also exported.
4. According to a recent census, more than 65 percent of the work force was employed in agriculture, 19 percent were factory workers, and the rest in trade and services.
5. The work force numbers 278 million people, but this figure does not include the unemployed, and secondary workers are not counted in this figure either.
6. Secondary workers, who do not receive their main support from their work activities, include people involved in household industry, and cultivation is another category of secondary workers.
7. In recent decades, India has experienced a "brain drain" of educated and trained Indians to other countries because of unemployment, and underemployment is also a factor in the brain drain.

✎ EXERCISE 8   Editing for parallelism

Read through this paragraph and mark segments that are not parallel in structure. Then rewrite the paragraph, correcting the mistakes in parallelism.

In his discussion of developing countries, Schumacher says that dual economies create political problems and tensions arise in society, too. Every country has poor people and those that are very rich. However, in a dual economy, the difference between the two groups is so great that a cultural gap develops between the two groups. The rich, a small percentage, typically live in the capital or are inhabitants of the second largest city. The poor live in the country or are town dwellers. The problem is that most development efforts go to the big cities and help the rich. The gap between the poor and people with money increases as the rich benefit from the changes and the poor do not.

(Adapted from *Small Is Beautiful: Economics as if People Mattered*, by E. F. Schumacher, Harper, 1973.)

5 CORE WRITING ASSIGNMENT

A. Writing topics

In this chapter you will be asked to write an argument essay – an essay in which the writer presents both sides of an issue, in the process of taking a position on one side or the other. Choose a topic for an argument essay from the following list. Decide on your position on the issue named in each topic.

1. Poorer countries should emphasize/de-emphasize technology as they move toward the future.
2. A country's quality of life is more/less important than its gross national product.
3. New technology and traditional elements of a culture can/cannot exist together.
4. *Additional topics* If you and your teacher agree on one or more additional topics, list them here. Phrase each one in terms of an argument that you can be for or against, as in the examples above.

_____

_____

B. Generating ideas: A debate

Consider this proposition: *Modernization is more important for a country than preserving its traditions.*

To debate this proposition, you need two small groups of students. Each group should choose a captain. The first group will argue the *pro* position (for the proposition). The other group will argue the *con* position (against the proposition). The remaining students will act as judges of the debate.

PREPARATION FOR THE DEBATE

The pro and con teams should meet separately to discuss their arguments, making sure to avoid logical fallacies. Each team member should construct a different one-to-two-minute argument to present to the class.

DEBATE

1. The captain of the pro team presents his or her argument to the class in 2 minutes or less. The con team then has 2 minutes to ask questions intended to show weaknesses in the argument or fallacies in the logic.

2. The captain of the con team presents his or her argument and the pro team members have 2 minutes to ask questions.
3. Pro and con team members continue to take turns speaking until all team members have spoken.
4. At the end, both teams have 5 minutes to prepare summaries of their arguments. The captain of each team will deliver the summary in 2 minutes or less.

DECISION

Classmates not participating in the debate vote to decide which team presented the strongest, most logical arguments. Students should vote for the team that showed the strongest debating skills, not for the side they agree with.

Follow-up   All students should take 5 minutes to make lists of the best arguments for and against the proposition. These lists will be useful in writing an argument essay later.

C. Expanding your point of view: Group discussion

Go over the list of arguments you wrote down after the debate. Circle the arguments that relate to your writing topic, both *for* and *against.*

Get together with other students in your class who have chosen the same topic. Share your arguments orally. Your purpose is not to reach a consensus but to share your points of view. At the end of the discussion, make any adjustments you would like to the *for* or *against* lists of arguments you have prepared for your topic.

D. Initial drafts

FIRST DRAFT

Once you are sure what position you are going to take on the issue you have chosen to write about, formulate the thesis statement for your essay. Remember that you are writing an argument paper. As with the persuasive essay you wrote in Chapter 6, you will want to use logical evidence to support your position. However, in the argument paper you will also present the arguments against your position. In the final body paragraph, you will bring the two sides together, showing why your position is the more logical and better one. In other words, the body of your essay should include your *thesis,* the *antithesis,* and finally a *synthesis* of the two. Your purpose is not merely to persuade but to refute the opposing view. (Reread the student essay in Part 4, Section B for an example of this structure.)

You may choose to prepare an outline or write your first draft freely. Use whichever approach works best for you. Keep a balance among the body paragraphs: Avoid having one paragraph very long (your position, for example) and the next very short (the opposing side). This looks and is unfair to the other side. Avoid logical fallacies.

REVISION

Let a friend (not a classmate) read your paper to see if you have expressed your position clearly, explained the opposing view, and then shown why your position is stronger. Ask your reader to summarize these parts of your paper to make sure they are clear.

You may choose to rewrite portions of the essay depending on your friend's comments. Revise your first draft following the "Essay Assessment Guidelines" at the end of this chapter; label this draft "Revision 1."

E. Review, revision, and assessment

PEER FEEDBACK

Get feedback on how clear and logical your thinking and writing are. Read your paragraph to a group of two or three classmates. Each member of the group will read his or her paper to the group. Follow the "Peer Feedback Guidelines" at the end of this chapter.

FURTHER REVISION

How well did your group receive your paper? Could they summarize it accurately? Did they understand your main points? Secondary points? How could your paper be clearer and/or more interesting to your audience? Make notes of changes you need to make.

If necessary, revise your paper using the feedback you got from the group. Edit your paper for logical fallacies and for parallelism. Submit all drafts to your teacher, with the last one marked "Revision 2" at the top.

If you choose not to revise, write a paragraph to your teacher summarizing the feedback you received and explaining why you decided not to revise.

TEACHER ASSESSMENT

Your teacher will assess your paper using the detailed set of essay assessment guidelines in Appendix B. Your teacher may give you a grade on the essay or allow you to make further revisions before assigning a grade.

PEER FEEDBACK GUIDELINES

Writers
- ☐ Read the paper clearly, a second time if necessary.
- ☐ Respond to listeners' comments and questions.
- ☐ Ask for suggestions if you want them.

Listeners
- ☐ Listen quietly until the writer finishes reading.
- ☐ Briefly summarize what you understood, orally.
- ☐ Pick out parts of the paper (words, expressions, or ideas) that stand out for you. Share these parts with the group.
- ☐ If you wish, share with the group how the writing makes you feel and ask questions about parts that are not clear.
- ☐ Do not make negative comments or tell the writer what changes to make.

ESSAY ASSESSMENT GUIDELINES

These are the criteria for a well-written essay. Use this checklist to critically examine your writing and determine how it can be improved. See Appendix B for the more detailed set of guidelines that your teacher will use to assess your work.

Content and ideas
- ☐ The writer has thought about the topic and has a clear thesis.
- ☐ The writer discusses each main point enough to give the reader a reason to believe it. The writer supports each main point, and no important point is left out.
- ☐ The writer's voice is clear because he or she writes in a sincere way, with the audience in mind.
- ☐ There are no logical fallacies used to support the writer's thesis.

Organization and form
- ☐ The paper has a clear beginning, middle, and end, with separate introductory, body, and concluding paragraphs. It moves logically in a straight line.
- ☐ The reader wants to continue reading and can understand the thesis and other main points fully after one reading.

☐ It is clear which are the main points and which are the secondary points.

Writing conventions

☐ The writer uses a variety of sentence lengths and types to add interest to the writing.

☐ The writer chooses vocabulary carefully to communicate clearly.

☐ The writer uses cohesive devices to make the relationships between the ideas clear.

☐ The writer avoids problems of sentence structure including fragments, comma-splices, run-together sentences, and lack of parallel structure.

☐ There are no illogical shifts in tense, person, or number, and the tone is consistently formal.

☐ The writer uses English grammar effectively to convey the message. There are few problems of verb tense, subject-verb agreement, word order, count/noncount use, or word form.

☐ The writer follows rules for spelling, capitalization, and punctuation.

8

Our Planet
Problems and solutions

*Clean-up of Exxon
Valdez oil spill*

An urban landscape

*Busy street
in Hong Kong*

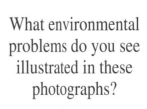

What environmental
problems do you see
illustrated in these
photographs?

Whose responsibility do
you think it is to solve each
of these problems?

1 GETTING A GRIP ON THE TOPIC

A. Reflection

With a partner, make a list of the three most serious global problems today.
Name problems that affect much of the world, not just a few countries.
Consider social, economic, and environmental problems.

Follow-up 1 Compare lists with at least one other pair of students. Revise
your list as desired. With your original partner, think of solutions to the three
problems on your revised list.

Follow-up 2 Compare problems and solutions as a class.

B. Discussion

Read the following statements. Mark each one *A* if you agree or *D* if you disagree.

_____ 1. Environmental problems like air pollution are global problems, so
solving them requires a concerted effort by all countries.

_____ 2. Richer countries do not have the right to lecture poorer countries
about birth control in an effort to reduce overpopulation.

_____ 3. Most pollution is caused by industrialized nations, who should be
responsible for reducing it.

_____ 4. There would not be a shortage of natural resources if richer, industrialized nations were not greedy for them.

_____ 5. Social problems caused by unemployment and poverty are more
serious than environmental problems.

_____ 6. Global environmental problems like depletion of the ozone layer in
the atmosphere can only be solved by a centralized international
organization.

_____ 7. Human beings are the highest form of creation; they should be free
to use nature as they wish.

_____ 8. A large centralized international organization is more efficient at
solving global environmental problems than many individual
countries working separately.

_____ 9. It is more important to look at population density than total population figures when considering overpopulation.

Follow-up Discuss your choices in pairs and then as a class.

C. Notes on the main reading

Ecologist Garrett Hardin writes about complicated subjects for the nonexpert audience. In this selection from his book, *Filters Against Folly,* he uses a hypothetical anecdote to make a point about global problems. Using the example of *potholes,* holes in streets caused by weather or traffic, as a metaphor for serious problems, Hardin makes a distinction between a *global* problem, one requiring the world's attention, and a *ubiquitous* problem, or one that simply occurs everywhere. Although Hardin's point is a serious one, he deals with it humorously. He makes fun of a number of practices and institutions.

    Language notes: If we *commonize* the expenses of something, like repairing potholes, we all contribute what we can afford. The rich contribute more money, the poor less. Hardin calls the phrase *global problem* a prescriptive term, meaning that its use directs the listener to respond to the problem in a specific way: by commonizing costs.

VOCABULARY EXERCISE

To preview the text and practice guessing the word meaning from context, find the following words in the text, in the lines indicated. Write down what you think each word or expression means from its context. If you are very doubtful after making a guess, check your guess in a dictionary. (For phrases, look up the word in italics.)

1. monstrous (line 6) _____

2. financing (line 22) _____

3. got *behind* the proposal (line 33) _____

4. *reproductive* force (lines 55–56)_____

5. evade (line 68) _____

6. mitigation (line 92) _____

GLOSSARY

Review the glossary before reading the selection, for help with some of the more difficult vocabulary.

slogan (line 3): phrase or motto
Genius (line 9): person of very great intelligence
requisitions (line 20): requests
Your Honor (line 26): a respectful form of address for a mayor

image (line 27): reputation
parochialism, provincialism (line 29): a narrow, limited concern for oneself
   or one's group
bigotry (line 29): intolerance for those who are different
ills (line 49): problems
breeding (line 54): reproducing
unitary (line 55): one, united
bickering (line 56): arguing over small matters
in the ascendant (line 58): becoming widely used
folly (line 60): foolishness
delegating (line 65): assigning tasks to others
monitor (line 69): supervisor
counterproductive (line 77): having bad effects
internalized (line 82): understood and learned
feasible (lines 93–94): reasonable, practical

D. Read for the main idea

Read the selection once quickly to answer this main idea question: *Why does Hardin advise finding local solutions for local problems?*

The Global Pothole Problem
GARRETT HARDIN

Once upon a time there was a city whose streets suffered an [epidemic] of potholes. Plainly more tax money was needed to fix the streets, but people marched to the slogan of "No unfair taxes!" Since every new tax is unfair to somebody, the mayor could not find the
5   money needed to fill the potholes. Things went from bad to worse, until finally the holes became so monstrous that they broke the springs of the mayor's limousine and he had henceforth to come to City Hall in a three-ton truck. The mayor decided things had gone far enough. He asked the local Genius for advice.
10   "The answer is simple," said the Genius (after spending six months and seven hundred thousand dollars on a study). "I have made a survey of all the nations and have found potholes everywhere. Clearly we are confronted with a Global Pothole Problem. Everything is connected to everything else. Global problems call for
15   global solutions. If we want to get our potholes filled, we must establish a Global Pothole Authority [GPA]."

"The GPA will be responsible for surveying and studying the pothole problem, following which it will resurvey and restudy it. At some point in time it will undertake to fill in the potholes. For uniformity and fairness, all requisitions for this work, from whatever part of the world, must be processed by the central office of the GPA in Geneva. Approval will be based on need. Financing will be by taxes based on national ability to pay. This means that for many years to come all of the potholes filled will be in the poor countries, while the taxes will be levied only against the rich. This is only fair.

"Let me emphasize to Your Honor that this is a great opportunity for polishing up your image as a citizen of the world. By taking the larger view, the global view, you can strike another blow against parochialism, provincialism, bigotry, and selfishness. Global thinking is the mark of the truly civilized man. Under your inspired leadership, our city can make the future happen."

The regional Council of Churches and the local chapter of the United Nations Association got behind the proposal, and the Global Pothole Authority was born. The future began to happen.

Unfortunately the city's potholes remained unfilled. The Genius took his fee and bought a cottage in a fashionable lakeside community; he wasn't going to let the potholes bother him. The Mayor continued to ride to City Hall in a truck.

Why "Global"?

The word "global" indicates a desire on the part of the speaker to commonize regional expenses over the whole globe. Since the regions that would benefit most are usually poor ones (and not the speaker's), the motivation is apparently unselfish. It is casually presumed that every ubiquitous problem is a "global" problem. But "ubiquitous" is merely a descriptive word, whereas "global" has now become a prescriptive term, a term that implicitly prescribes political action, generally the commonization of costs.

Death, taxes, poverty, and sin are ubiquitous, but do we want to define them as global, in the new sense? Is it advisable to try to commonize the costs of these ancient ills?

To speak of "global poverty" is to imply that commonizing wealth will put an end to poverty. "Global hunger" implies that commonizing food resources will put an end to malnutrition and starva-

tion. To speak of the "Global Population Problem" is to imply that an overpopulated nation cannot control the breeding of its own peo-
55 ple. But if a unitary nation cannot control nature's reproductive force, what chance is there for a group of bickering nations? Or for people living under the anarchy of no nations?

Now that computers are in the ascendant, we are inclined to look to them for solving problems dealing with large numbers and many
60 groups. But detection of the folly of globalizing problems requires no more sophisticated a computer than the unaided human brain. Ancient wisdom is all the software we need.

Long experience has shown that local problems are best dealt with by local action. Increase in numbers brings an increase in the
65 necessity for delegating, and an increase in the ways that delegation can malfunction. Other things being equal, large agencies are less efficient than small. The reason for this is quite simple. Self-interest urges individuals to evade personal responsibility whenever they possibly can. The more distant the monitor, the more feasible evasion
70 becomes. Globalization favors evasion. The wise rule to follow should be plain:

> Never globalize a problem if it can possibly be dealt with locally.

All of this is so obvious that it should not need saying. However, the rise of environmentalism has been accompanied by a great
75 increase in the volume of voices calling for global attacks on all problems, great or small, extensive or localized.

Globalism is usually counterproductive. This is not to say that there are absolutely no problems that are truly global. There are: not many, but a few. And they pose difficulties far more serious than most
80 globalists realize.

"Never globalize a problem if it can possibly be dealt with locally." Once we have internalized this rule, we can accept the wisdom of the following conclusions:

▶ Though potholes are ubiquitous there is no "global pothole
85   problem."
▶ Though hunger is ubiquitous there is no "global hunger problem."

► Though overpopulation is ubiquitous there is no "global over-population problem."

All three ills – potholes, hunger, and overpopulation – are pro- 90
duced by local action, the common feature of which is expecting or
demanding too much of local resources. The mitigation of these ills
requires local action; difficult as it may sometimes be, it is more feasible and more reliable than a global approach.

Follow-up Answer the main idea question here: _____

_____

E. Read for more detail

Read the selection a second time. Use the questions to understand it better and
to bring your own experience to the reading.

1. What problem did the mayor face? Why was it seen as a global problem?
2. What solution did the genius recommend? Can you think of other problems
    that have been handled this way?
3. What practices and institutions does the writer make fun of here?
4. Why does Hardin make a distinction between local and global problems?
    Does his distinction make sense to you?
5. Which problems does Hardin think are purely local ones? Which of these
    problems exist in your country?
6. *Key words* Make a list of six words that you feel are important to the story.
    Be ready to tell why each word is important, and what it means, if neces-
    sary.

Follow-up Share your answers with a small group or the class.

2 RESPONDING TO THE MAIN READING

A. Journals: A private audience

Choose two of the following topics. Write at least 75 words on each of them in your journal notebook. Express your opinions and feelings honestly. These journal entries are for your eyes only, so do not spend a lot of time using a dictionary or worrying about grammar.

1. Does it bother you that Hardin makes an analogy between a humorous problem (potholes) and serious ones like hunger and overpopulation?
2. Did you like this reading? Why or why not?
3. Write a formal letter to Hardin giving your reactions to his piece on world problems.
4. Is your country affected by other countries' pollution or overpopulation? How?

B. Shared writing

Choose at least two topics and write for a total of 30 minutes. Your audience is your classmates, with whom you will share your writing. Your audience will be interested not only in *what* you feel but also in *why* you feel that way. Express your views clearly and support them.

1. Which problems do you feel need the world's attention immediately? Why?
2. Do you make the same distinction between local and global problems that Hardin does? Explain.
3. Whose responsibility is it to solve problems like pollution and hunger?
4. Do developed countries have the right to encourage poorer countries to practice birth control?

C. Feedback on your writing

Get feedback on how clear and logical your thinking and writing are. Select one of your writings from the previous section, "Shared Writing," and read it to a group of two or three classmates. Each member of the group will read one of his or her writings. Follow the instructions in "Peer Feedback Guidelines" at the end of this chapter.

Follow-up   In 5 minutes, evaluate in writing how well your audience received your paper. Could they summarize it accurately? Did they understand your points? How could you make your paper clearer? More interesting to your audience?

3 GOING MORE DEEPLY INTO THE TOPIC

Two American families

How many children do families in
your country typically have? Do you
think that having a large family is a
good idea? Why or why not?

A. Preparing to read

This selection, "What Are the *Real* Population and Resource Problems?",
by Julian Simon, is from the introduction to Simon's book, *The Ultimate
Resource*. Julian Simon is a controversial yet respected writer on economics,
the environment, and the population problem. If you have read popular period-
icals or seen TV documentaries on the environment, you will probably be surprised by what Simon has to say about natural resources, pollution, and overpopulation. Keep in mind that his view is based on *economics* and not on
science.

Simon refers to Thomas Robert Malthus, a famous nineteenth-century
British economist, whose work is still referred to today. Malthus said that the
world population, if unchecked, would increase faster than the means of subsistence. The result would be an inadequate supply of food and other goods
for the population until war, disease, or famine reduced the population. In this
selection, Simon discusses the ways a new child in a family is a *burden*, a
disadvantage, and in what ways it is a *boon*, an advantage.

Before reading, discuss these questions in pairs, small groups, or as a
class.

1. Do you agree with Malthus's theory? Give examples to illustrate your
   points.

2. Does modern technology play a role that Malthus did not foresee in the production of food and goods? Explain.

3. Which natural resources are becoming scarcer? Will these resources disappear in the future?

B. First reading

Read these excerpts from *The Ultimate Resource* the first time to answer this main idea question: *What is the ultimate resource referred to in Simon's title? In what way is it a resource?*

What Are the Real Population and Resource Problems?

JULIAN SIMON

Is there a natural-resource problem now? Certainly there is – just as there has always been. The problem is that natural resources are scarce, in the sense that it costs us labor and capital to get them, though we would prefer to get them for free.

5   Are we now "entering an age of scarcity"? You can see anything you like in a crystal ball. But almost without exception, the best data – the long-run economic indicators – suggest precisely the opposite. The relevant measures of scarcity – the costs of natural resources in human labor, and their prices relative to wages and to other goods –

10   all suggest that natural resources have been becoming *less* scarce over the long run, right up to the present.

How about pollution? Is this not a problem? Of course pollution is a problem – people have always had to dispose of their waste products so as to enjoy a pleasant and healthy living space. But on the

15   average we now live in a less dirty and more healthy environment than in earlier centuries.

About population now: Is there a population "problem"? Again, of course there is a population problem, just as there has always been. When a couple is about to have a baby, they must prepare a

20   place for the child to sleep safely. Then, after the birth of the child, the parents must feed, clothe, guard, and teach it. All of this requires

effort and resources, and not from the parents alone. When a baby is born or an immigrant arrives, a community must increase its municipal services – schooling, fire and police protection, and garbage collection. None of these are free.

Beyond any doubt, an additional child is a burden on other people for the first fifteen or twenty-five years of its life. Brothers and sisters must do with less of everything except companionship. Taxpayers must cough up additional funds for schooling and other public services. Neighbors have more noise. During these early years the child produces nothing, and the income of the family and the community is spread around more thinly than if the baby were not born. And when the child grows up and first goes to work, jobs are squeezed a bit, and the output and pay per working person goes down. All this clearly is an economic loss for other people.

Almost equally beyond any doubt, however, an additional person is also a boon. The child or immigrant will pay taxes later on, contribute energy and resources to the community, produce goods and services for the consumption of others, and make efforts to beautify and purify the environment. Perhaps most significant of all for the more-developed countries is the contribution that the average person makes to increasing the efficiency of production through new ideas and improved methods.

The real population problem, then, is *not* that there are too many people or that too many babies are being born. It is that others must support each additional person before that person contributes in turn to the well being of others.

Preview of the Book

Here are some of the topics covered in this book.

Food   Contrary to popular impression, the per capita food situation has been improving for the three decades since World War II, the only decades for which we have acceptable data. We also know that famine has progressively diminished for at least the past century. And there is strong reason to believe that human nutrition will continue to improve into the indefinite future, even with continued population growth.

Land   Agricultural land is not a fixed resource, as Malthus and many since Malthus have thought. Rather, the amount of agricultural land has been, and still is, increasing substantially, and it is likely to continue to increase where needed. Paradoxically, in the countries that are best supplied with food, such as the U.S., the quantity of land under cultivation has been decreasing because it is more economical to raise larger yields on less land than to increase the total amount of farmland. For this reason, among others, land for recreation and for wildlife has been increasing rapidly in the U.S. All this may be hard to believe, but solid data substantiate these statements beyond a doubt.

Natural resources   Hold your hat – our supplies of natural resources are not finite in any economic sense. Nor does past experience give reason to expect natural resources to become more scarce. Rather, if the past is any guide, natural resources will progressively become less scarce, and less costly, and will constitute a smaller proportion of our expenses in future years. And population growth is likely to have a long-run *beneficial* impact on the natural-resource situation.

Energy   Grab your hat again – the long-run future of our energy supply is at least as bright as that of other natural resources, though political maneuvering can temporarily boost prices from time to time. Finiteness is no problem here either. And the long-run impact of additional people is likely to speed the development of a cheap energy supply that is almost inexhaustible.

Pollution   This set of issues is as complicated as you wish to make it. But even many ecologists, as well as the bulk of economists, agree that population growth is not the villain in the creation and reduction of pollution. And the key trend is that life expectancy, which is the best over-all index of the pollution level, has improved markedly as the world's population has grown.

Pathological effects of population density   This putative drawback of population growth is sheer myth. Its apparent source is faulty biological and psychological analogies with animal populations.

The standard of living   In the short run, additional children imply

additional costs, though the costs to persons other than the children's
parents are relatively small. In the longer run, however, per capita   90
income is likely to be higher with a growing population than with a
stationary one, both in more developed and less developed countries.
Whether you wish to pay the present costs for the future benefits
depends on how you weigh the future relative to the present; this is a
value judgment.   95

Immigration   Immigration usually has a positive effect on most citizens. The few persons whom the immigrants might displace from
their jobs may be hurt, of course, but many of them only temporarily.
On balance, immigrants contribute more to the economy than they
take, in the U.S. and most other places.   100

Human fertility   The contention that poor and uneducated people
breed like animals is demonstrably wrong, even for the poorest and
most "primitive" societies. Well-off people who believe that the poor
do not weigh the consequences of having more children are simply
arrogant or ignorant, or both.   105

Future population growth   Population forecasts are publicized with
confidence and fanfare, but the record of even the official forecasts
made by U.S. government agencies and by the UN is little (if any) better than that of the most naive predictions. For example, experts in
the 1930s saw the U.S. population as declining, perhaps to as little as   110
100 million people, long before the turn of the century. And official
UN forecasts made in 1970 for the year 2000, a mere thirty years in
advance, were five years later revised downward by almost 2 billion
people, from 7.5 billion to 5.6 billion. Nor is the record better with
more modern statistical methods. Perhaps most astonishing is a fore-   115
cast made by the recent President's Commission on Population
Growth and the American Future. In 1972, the commission published its prediction that "there will be no year in the next two
decades in which the absolute number of births will be less than in
1970." But in the year *before* the prediction was made – 1971 – the   120
number of births had *already* fallen lower than in 1970. The science
of demographic forecasting clearly has not yet reached perfection.

Follow-up   Answer the main idea question here: _____

_____

_____

C. Additional readings

Read the selection again. Mark any places in the text that are still unclear to you. Then read these passages once more to improve your understanding of them.

D. Negotiating the meaning

Write at least 75 words on this selection. Write on any or all of the following:

▶ whether you liked it or not, and why
▶ whether you prefer it to the previous selection
▶ what you have trouble understanding

Follow-up   To a group of two or three, read what you have written. Read your reaction a second time if necessary.

Each group member will respond with (1) a question, (2) a comment, and/or (3) clarification. Every group member should read what he or she has written. As a group, choose one response to share with the whole class.

E. Discussion: Critical thinking

Discuss these questions in pairs, small groups, or as a class.

1. How do Hardin and Simon disagree about the "problem" of overpopulation?
2. Do you find Simon's analysis of the world's future too optimistic? How realistic is it in your opinion?
3. Which of the two authors would you like to read further? Why?
4. In other parts of his book, Hardin discusses global environmental problems, not only local ones like pollution and overpopulation. Which specific problems do you think he would consider global?

4 IMPROVING WRITING SKILLS

A. Using another's writing: Summarizing another's views

Under the heading "Preview of the Book," Simon lists the topics he will cover and gives a brief outline of the book. You may want to refer to his views on some topics in your writing assignment. To do so, you will need to summarize what he says. Practice summarizing Simon's views in the exercise that follows.

 EXERCISE 1   Writing one-sentence summaries

Write one-sentence summaries of Simon's views on each of the following topics: food, land, natural resources, and the standard of living.

Follow-up   Exchange summaries in small groups to see how others summarized the same ideas.

B. Meeting reader expectations: Answers to essay exams

On an essay examination, a question about a very specific issue can often be answered in one well-developed paragraph. A more general essay question, of course, requires a longer answer in the form of an essay with several paragraphs. (The shortest subjective exam questions are short-answer questions, which require only a sentence or two to answer. We will not discuss those here.)

PREPARING FOR AN ESSAY EXAM

The best way to prepare for an essay exam is to study the material that the exam will cover, in a logical way. A teacher wants you to demonstrate both a general understanding of the readings and a grasp of important details when you write an exam. Therefore, a good way to study is to look at the readings in terms of the main ideas and supporting points. Do *not* memorize reading texts. Do take notes in outline form so that main ideas stand out from less important ones.

Since an essay exam is written, prepare for it by writing sample answers to questions you know or expect will be on the exam. Of course, these sample answers cannot be used during the exam. Essay exams are traditionally *closed-book* exams: No notes or books besides a dictionary are allowed.

In one sense, an essay exam is a lot like free writing because you are expected to write a lot in a short time. However, in an essay exam your writing must be *focused* because you must answer the question and you will seldom have time to revise what you have written. Your first draft is your final draft.

HEADWORDS IN EXAM QUESTIONS

Characteristically, essay exam questions are in imperative form. Directions most often begin with headwords such as *discuss, compare and contrast, explain, criticize, list, summarize,* or *analyze*, among others. These headwords give you your purpose: to talk about a topic generally (discuss), to give similarities and differences (compare and contrast), to make something clearer to the reader (explain), to find the fallacy in the logic (criticize), to give examples (list), to reduce into a short form (summarize), or to break into parts (analyze).

STRATEGIES FOR TAKING AN EXAM

These strategies will help during an exam:

(1) Preview the exam   At the beginning of the exam, read all the exam questions. Then you know how much time to devote to each answer, and your mind can work ahead subconsciously on future questions. Pay careful attention to the headword in each question.

(2) Think and make notes   Take time to think and make notes before you begin to write. This is the hardest advice for students to follow because of the time pressure. But a few minutes of thinking will save a lot of time later. A few notes or a brief outline will help relieve tension; later you can concentrate on writing because you won't be trying to remember what you planned to say.

(3) Get started   For a paragraph response, write a topic sentence that addresses the question asked. For an essay response, formulate the thesis statement. Incorporating part of the question in the topic sentence or thesis statement is a useful tactic because it saves time and keeps you on the topic.

(4) Develop the answer   Continue by supporting your main idea sentence with relevant main ideas and significant details from the readings. Give your opinion only if it is asked for. Do not wander. Wandering, or leaving the topic and writing something you know rather than what the question requires, is the biggest danger to students in an essay exam. If you have no idea how to answer a question, devote very little time to that question. Write something, but devote more time to the other questions.

(5) Use the expected form   Answer in full sentences that make up complete paragraphs. Do not present the required information in a numbered list of incomplete sentences *unless you run out of time*. In an essay response, separate different points into paragraphs.

✎EXERCISE 2   Beginnings

Each numbered example contains an essay exam question on one of the readings in this chapter and three possible ways to begin an answer to the question. For each question, decide which of the three choices (a, b, or c) is the best beginning for an answer, by deciding which one:

▶ expresses a main idea that addresses the question,
▶ is consistent in purpose with the headword of the question, and
▶ shows an understanding of the reading.

Then compare your answers with a partner.

1. *Explain* how an additional child is both a burden and a boon, according to Simon.

    (a) All children are problems because they require care and resources and do not contribute very much in their early years.
    (b) An additional child is a burden because it must be cared for by parents and society to some extent, without giving much in return. When the child matures, however, it contributes its intelligence and talents to its society.
    (c) An additional child is a burden even in an underpopulated country because it consumes resources that could be used by overpopulated countries. The child is a boon in the emotional sense that it is wanted by its parents.

2. *Discuss* the distinction Hardin makes between local and global problems. Include causes and solutions.

    (a) Local and global problems are different. The former are problems for a few people only, and the latter are problems for the world in general.
    (b) Local problems like overpopulation are caused by local action that taxes local resources, and they need local solutions. Global problems like the greenhouse effect have more complicated causes and can only be solved by countries working together.
    (c) Local problems and global problems are really the same because both kinds of problems can be solved only through worldwide efforts.

3. *List* two environmental problems that in your opinion are truly global in nature and *explain* why each is global.

   (a) The depletion of the ozone layer and pollution of the seas are two global problems whose solutions can only be reached by a concerted effort of all nations.
   (b) Carbon dioxide in the atmosphere has been steadily raising the average temperature of the earth. Furthermore, many nations are dumping sewage and nuclear wastes into the sea, killing fish and decreasing world food supplies.
   (c) Hunger and overpopulation are the two main problems in the world; they afflict more people than any other problems.

4. *Summarize* Hardin's anecdote about potholes. What is his purpose in writing the anecdote?

   (a) The city's potholes needed to be fixed, but the citizens would not allow the mayor to raise taxes to fix them.
   (b) Global thinking about problems like potholes is a sign of a generous, civilized society.
   (c) In his anecdote about potholes, Hardin pokes fun at the tendency to globalize problems whose causes and solutions are really local.

✎ EXERCISE 3   Choosing the better answer

Read the following paragraph-length responses to question 4 in Exercise 2. Decide which one answers the question better. Be ready to explain why.

(1)   In his anecdote about potholes, Hardin pokes fun at the tendency to globalize problems whose causes and solutions are really local. When he was confronted with potholes in his city, the mayor hired a Genius to solve the problem. After a long, expensive study, the Genius reported that potholes were a global problem because every nation had them. Therefore, he proposed they establish a Global Pothole Authority to study the problem further before starting to fill potholes. Requisitions for the work would be sent to the central office. The work would be financed by commonizing the costs among the nations. The Genius convinced the mayor by saying this global approach was unselfish and civilized. International organizations supported the proposal. Unfortunately, the city's potholes were never filled, but the Genius was well paid for his advice. We see that a global solution to a local problem does not work.

(2)   In his anecdote about potholes, Hardin pokes fun at the tendency to globalize problems whose causes and solutions are really local. He takes the example of a city mayor who met resistance from citizens when he proposed raising taxes to fill potholes in the city streets. When the situation got worse, the mayor hired a Genius to solve the problem. The Genius studied the problem and concluded it was global because every nation had potholes. His recommendations were to set up a Global Pothole Authority to study the problem further and to start filling potholes under a centralized plan. The plan called for nations to make requests to the Authority, which would approve the work and pay for it with funds from richer countries. The plan didn't work very well, and the potholes in the mayor's city remained unfilled. The Genius bought an expensive house with the money he made for his advice.

Follow-up   Share your decision with a partner and then the whole class.

✎ EXERCISE 4   Outlining responses

Work with a partner to make a brief outline of points for an answer to each of these essay exam questions. Use an outline form that distinguishes (a) the topic sentence or thesis statement, (b) main supporting ideas, and (c) secondary supporting ideas.

1. Explain how an additional child is both a burden and a boon, according to Simon. (Outline a *paragraph* response.)
2. Discuss the distinction Hardin makes between local and global problems. (Outline a *paragraph* response.)
3. List two environmental problems that in your opinion are truly global in nature and explain why each is global. (Outline an *essay* response.)
4. Contrast Hardin's and Simon's views on overpopulation and hunger in the world. (Outline an *essay* response.)

Follow-up   Compare your outlines with at least one other pair of classmates.

C. Language conventions: Pronoun agreement and clear reference

Achieving correct pronoun agreement in writing can be hard because some constructions allowed in speaking are wrong in formal writing.

SPOKEN   Every student brought *their* own lunch.

Each of the brothers wants *their* own car.

If anyone has lost a book, *they* should check in the Lost and Found.

Every, each, and *anyone* are the antecedents for the italicized pronoun and possessive adjectives in the sentences above. Formally, possessive adjectives and pronouns should agree with their antecedent in number. In the cases above, they do not agree because *every, each,* and *anyone* are singular, whereas *their* and *they* are plural. (Remember that many indefinite pronouns are grammatically singular: *each, anyone, either, everybody, neither, no one, nobody, somebody, someone, something.*) Notice how pronoun agreement can be achieved in each case:

FORMAL   *All* the student*s* brought *their* own lunch*es*.

Each of the brothers wants *his* own car.

Anyone who has lost a book should check in the Lost and Found.
(The sentence has been rewritten; the pronoun has been eliminated.)

Note: Following the convention in most writing texts, the term *pronoun* will be used to refer to both pronouns and possessive adjectives in the exercises that follow.

EXERCISE 5   Achieving agreement

Underline the antecedent in each sentence; then circle the correct pronoun.

1. Both of my brothers have done his/their military service.
2. A woman who likes to work on cars won't find many other women among her/their co-enthusiasts.
3. Somebody left her/their lipstick in the restroom.
4. Neither Mr. Smith nor his son could find his/their car keys.
5. Each of the waitresses has to put her/their tips in a common pot.

GENDER BIAS

More and more people object to the use of singular masculine pronouns to refer to indefinite pronoun antecedents. The following sentence, although previously grammatical, is losing its acceptability in modern English writing:

BIASED   Everyone paid his own way to the movies.

People object to the use of the masculine *his* to refer to a group which contains women, too. The usage is called *gender bias*. Look at the following alternative construction:

BETTER   Everyone paid *his or her* own way to the movies.

His or her works here, but this construction can be awkward, especially when overused:

AWKWARD   Every student should pick up *his or her* schedule before seeing *his or her* adviser and before buying *his or her* books.

Did everyone turn in *his or her* homework?

Sentences like the ones above can be revised to avoid gender bias and awkwardness:

IMPROVED   *All* students should pick up *their* schedules before seeing *their* advisers and buying *their* books.

Did everyone turn in *the* homework?

Was the homework turned in by everyone?

Did *all* the students turn in *their* homework?

✎ EXERCISE 6   Avoiding gender bias

Rewrite these sentences to avoid gender bias.

1. No child in the class could tie his shoes without help.
2. Every teacher at the school had his own way of teaching.
3. A pupil who doesn't do all of his homework must stay after school to complete it.
4. A child who forgets his lunch can buy lunch in the cafeteria.
5. Any child can ask his teacher a question at any time if he doesn't understand something.
6. A parent who wants to visit his child's class is free to do so if he gives a day's notice to his teacher.
7. If a person who is not a parent wants to visit the school, he should get permission from the principal.

GROUP NOUNS

Singular group nouns like *class, family,* and *company* have a plural meaning but usually take singular pronouns in American English.

Our *family* takes *its* vacation in August.

The *company* was forced to close *its* doors.

✎ EXERCISE 7   Agreement with group nouns

Underline the antecedent in each sentence; then circle the correct pronoun.

1. The class will have its/their final exam on May 20th.
2. That new rock band is giving its/their next concert for charity.
3. All of the bands will donate its/their profits to benefit AIDS patients.
4. The jury is expected to give its/their verdict soon.
5. The women's basketball team increased its/their practice time.
6. Both the men's and women's teams are in first place in its/their divisions.
7. His family decided to sell its/their summer home.

AVOIDING VAGUE PRONOUN REFERENCE

A pronoun should have a clear antecedent. In speech, *this, that, it, which,* and *you* are sometimes used without clear antecedents. However, in writing it is important to be more precise.

(1) UNCLEAR   Bob used to drive carelessly and finally had an accident. *This* made his father angry.
(It is not clear whether Bob's careless driving or the accident made his father angry. We assume it is not both because *this* is singular).

BETTER   Bob used to drive carelessly and finally had an accident. The accident made his father angry.

(2) UNCLEAR   When *you* learn a foreign language, *you* benefit from listening to native speakers.
(Whom does *you* refer to? It is not clear.)

BETTER   People learning foreign languages benefit from listening to native speakers.

(3) UNCLEAR   Pam always wanted to be the top salesperson in her company. She was happy when she got *it*.
(There is no antecedent for *it*.)

BETTER   Pam always wanted to be the top salesperson in her company. She was happy when she achieved her goal.

(4)	UNCLEAR	*They* say time is money.
		(Who says this?)
	BETTER	People say time is money.
(5)	UNCLEAR	Janet wanted to interview someone about police work, but she doesn't know *one*.
		(There is no antecedent for *one*.)
	BETTER	Janet wanted to interview someone about police work, but she doesn't know a police officer.
(6)	UNCLEAR	Jack climbed the tree, *which* was hard.
		(Which was hard, the tree or climbing it?)
	BETTER	It was hard for Jack to climb the tree. (or)
		Climbing the tree was hard for Jack.
(7)	UNCLEAR	I try to walk two miles every day because *it* is good exercise.
		(There is no antecedent for *it,* because pronouns can refer to nouns and other pronouns, not to verbs.)
	BETTER	I try to walk two miles every day because walking is good exercise.

✎ EXERCISE 8   Correcting vague pronoun reference

Rewrite the following sentences to get rid of the pronouns with vague references and to make the meaning clear.

1. If Mrs. Smith's husband is jealous of their son, she should be kinder to him.
2. I forgot what he told me, which was rude.
3. Mr. Simms is on the golf course three times a week because it's good exercise.
4. You never know who your friends are until there's a crisis.
5. They are always raising taxes.
6. Jeff is sure he wants to be a lawyer even though he has never studied it.
7. My co-workers usually have pizza at the same restaurant every day even though they don't like it.
8. A lot of people point out to George that he is going bald. This embarrasses him.

✎ EXERCISE 9   Editing for vague pronoun reference

Edit the following passage for vague pronoun reference. First read it and mark problems; then rewrite the passage, correcting the vague references.

Ecologists today talk of a sustainable environment, one whose air, land, and water are not degraded further by human activity. The economist Julian Simon is more optimistic about this than most ecologists are. Ecologists have their own arguments with economists. One of them follows. There is a difference between the production cost of a product and the actual cost of the product. In the first place, the actual cost includes the costs to the air, water, and soil. How is this affected by the production of a pair of cotton jeans, for example? How much water is used to ensure a bigger cotton harvest? Does it mean less clean water for people, and do the pesticides pollute the environment? Has the soil been maintained to be suitable for further cultivation? It also includes the costs to workers' health, which can be a problem. Agricultural workers can suffer from exposure to pesticides, and garment workers from poor working conditions. In the end, ecologists advocate that the cost of a product reflect these actual costs in addition to the production costs. Only in recognizing actual costs can we achieve sustainability.

5   CORE WRITING ASSIGNMENT

A. Writing topics

In the remaining sections of this chapter, you will be asked to prepare for and then take an essay exam on some of the topics covered in the readings in this book. Review the list of possible questions now and choose the topics that you would like to write about. (Some teachers may wish to assign questions.)

TOPICS FROM CHAPTER 8

Paragraph responses

1. Explain how an additional child is both a burden and a boon, according to Simon.
2. Discuss the distinction Hardin makes between local and global problems.

Essay responses

3. List two environmental problems that in your opinion are truly global in nature and explain why each is global.
4. Contrast Hardin's and Simon's views on overpopulation and hunger in the world.

TOPICS FROM PREVIOUS CHAPTERS

Essay responses

5. Compare and contrast the environmental problems faced by developed and developing countries. Include solutions in your discussion.
6. Decide whether thinkers or feelers are more likely to find a solution to big problems like environmental pollution. Explain your decision. Or will the solution take a combination of the thinking and feeling approaches?
7. Compare or contrast a good friend and a good spouse. Are they basically the same or basically different?
8. Discuss the role of technology in improving our environment. Is technology the cause of, or the cure for, environmental problems?
9. Analyze the connection between good manners and whether a person is a feeler or a thinker. Is there a connection? If so, what is it?

B. Generating ideas: Reviewing the readings

We have already discussed the best way to prepare for an essay exam. (See Part 4, Section B, "Meeting Reader Expectations: Answers on Essay Exams.") Take time now to reread and outline those readings that relate to the exam questions you will answer.

C. Expanding your point of view

Get together with a small group of students who will answer the same questions that you will. Discuss each question separately with the aim of producing a brief outline of an answer to the question. Items to cover: (1) topic sentence or thesis statement, (2) main points of support, (3) secondary points of support.

D. Initial drafts

We have already pointed out that in an essay exam, your first draft is almost always your final draft because of the time pressure. For this reason, teachers will usually excuse a short introduction and conclusion. They will pay special attention to your content – to how well you answer the question.

Before the exam   Practice writing answers under the pressure of time. Use the outlines you prepared with classmates in Section C; revise the outlines if necessary. Begin with a topic sentence or thesis statement that addresses the question and add supporting points. Do not wander from the point. Read your answers over to see how well you have answered the questions.

During the exam   Follow the five "Strategies for Taking an Exam" that were presented in Part 4, Section B of this chapter. Do not use your book, outlines, or practice essays during the exam. If you use a dictionary, use it sparingly to save time.

E. Review or assessment

If your teacher chooses to use these essay responses as an exercise rather than a test, exchange essay responses with a partner, and follow the instructions under "Peer Feedback."

PEER FEEDBACK

Read a classmate's essay responses and answer the questions listed here. Record your answers on paper and then discuss them with your partner as you review the essays together.

1. Does the topic sentence or thesis statement express a main idea that addresses the question? Is the beginning of the response consistent with the headword of the question?
2. What main points of support does the writer provide?
3. Does the writer avoid wandering?
4. How completely and effectively has the writer answered the question?

TEACHER ASSESSMENT

Your teacher may choose to use the essay exam as a test. If so, your teacher will use the questions listed under "Peer Feedback" to evaluate your responses.

Appendix A
Grammar and punctuation guidelines

1 SUBJECTS AND VERBS

A. Subjects

The subject tells *who* or *what* the sentence is about, often who or what *does* something.

> *Istanbul* is not the capital but a very important city in Turkey.
>
> Many *tourists* visit Istanbul every year.
>
> *Autumn* is a favorite time for many people to visit Istanbul.

The subject is usually a noun or a pronoun. A noun is the name of a person, place, or thing: *tourists, Istanbul, autumn*. A pronoun can take the place of a noun. *It* is a pronoun that can be a subject. Some other subject pronouns are *we, they,* and *you*.

EXERCISE 1   Identifying subjects

Identify the subject in each sentence by asking who or what the sentence is about. Underline the subject only, not the words that describe or modify it. Some sentences may have more than one subject; underline them both.

1. My first trip to Istanbul was two years ago.
2. A friend and I went there in the summer.
3. The best hotels were all booked.
4. Fortunately, we found a comfortable hotel in the center.
5. Our ten vacation days went by very fast.
6. Both of us want to go back soon.

B. Verbs

ACTION VERBS

A verb can express the action that the subject performs. Most verbs are action verbs. Transitive verbs, which take a direct object, are action verbs; most intransitive verbs are, too.

> The child *threw* the ball into the street.
>
> The child *ran after* the ball.
>
> His mother *yelled* at him to stop.
>
> The child *didn't get hurt*.

LINKING VERBS

A verb can also link the subject to words that describe it. Look at these examples:

> The mother *was* terrified at first.
>
> She *seemed* relieved afterward.

Linking verbs include the forms of *be, seem, appear, look, become,* and *feel*. Some verbs can be either action or linking verbs, as in these examples:

> ACTION   She *felt* the wall for the light switch in the dark.
> LINKING   I *didn't feel* well last night.

✎ EXERCISE 2   Distinguishing linking and action verbs

Circle the verbs. Write *L* for linking and *A* for action verbs in the blanks.

_____ 1. Istanbul looks like an island.

_____ 2. Water is visible from most points in the city.

_____ 3. Tourists and residents enjoy the many beaches in summer.

_____ 4. Some travelers prefer short cruises on the sea.

_____ 5. The area offers a wealth of recreational possibilities.

C. Additional characteristics of subjects and verbs

SUBJECTS

1. The subject tells who or what the sentence is about and is usually a noun or pronoun.

2. The subject most often appears near the beginning of the sentence, but it can appear later.

    Taking too long to decide, she missed her chance.
    (*She* is the subject of the sentence.)

3. *There* is never the subject of a sentence.

    There were two students absent this morning.
    (*Students* is the subject.)

4. A word in a prepositional phrase may be a noun, but it is never the subject.

    Of all the people in my class, Tim is the brightest.
    (Neither *people* nor *class* is the subject; *Tim* is the subject of the sentence.)

5. A sentence can have more than one subject.

    His aunt and his cousin are going to visit Tim.
    (Both *aunt* and *cousin* are the subjects of the sentence.)

VERBS

1. Action verbs express what the subject does; linking verbs link the subject to words that describe it.

2. A sentence may have more than one verb.

    She did her homework and then went out with friends.
    (*Did* and *went out* are both verbs in this sentence.)

3. A complete verb can be more than one word: It includes the root verb and any auxiliaries.

    The wallet couldn't have been stolen from his car.
    (*Steal* is the root verb; *could, not, have,* and *been* are all auxiliaries.)

4. A verb form ending in *-ing* is not complete without a form of the auxiliary *be*.

    Setting in the west, the sun was surrounded by red clouds.
    (*Setting* is not a verb in this sentence; it is an adjective derived from a verb. *Was surrounded* is the complete verb.)

    The sun was setting just as we got to the beach.
    (*Was setting* is the complete verb in this sentence.)

✎ EXERCISE 3   Identifying subjects and verbs

Enter the simple subject (one word) and the complete verb (root verb plus auxiliary verbs) in the blanks. There may be more than one subject or more than one verb in some examples; write both, separating them with a comma.

1. The environmental movement is getting stronger every year.

    S _____   V _____

2. The origins of the movement go back decades, if not longer.

    S _____   V _____

3. A number of people from different walks of life are showing more interest in the movement.

    S _____   V _____

4. Scientists from different fields recognize the value of their contributions to the movement.

    S _____   V _____

5. Economists and even ethicists see their place in the fight against environmental degradation.

    S _____   V _____

6. Even among politicians there are some sincere advocates of a cleaner environment.

    S _____   V _____

7. Laws against polluting and misuse of resources are becoming more common.

    S _____   V _____

8. Of course, these laws are not always enforced.

    S _____   V _____

9. With huge business interests against most environmental legislation, enforcement is sometimes difficult.

    S _____   V _____

10. In the future, well-informed voters will undoubtedly demand and vote for a cleaner environment.

    S _____   V _____

2 WORD ORDER

English word order is rather rigid compared to word order in many other languages. Sections A–D which follow contain a review of the correct placement of adverbials, modifiers, the words *also* and *too*, and direct and indirect objects.

A. Adverbials

Guideline 1 A verb and its direct object are almost never separated.

WRONG   I like very much your new hat.
         (verb: *like;* direct object: *your new hat.* The adverbial *very much* cannot come between them.)

CORRECT   I like your new hat very much.

Guideline 2 Adverbs of frequency (*always, often, seldom, never*, etc.) come after *be* or the first auxiliary verb, if there is one, but before other verbs, even in the negative.

My sister is *never* on time for appointments.

Sally *seldom* writes to me anymore.

We have *often* had lunch there on weekends.

I didn't *always* hand my homework in on time.

Aren't they *usually* late with their rent check?

Guideline 3 Other adverbials typically come at the end of the sentence in this order: manner (How?), place (Where?), time (When?).

Jim usually does his homework alone at home after class.

Exceptions: The frequency adverbs *sometimes* and *usually* and adverbials of time can come at the beginning of a sentence.

Sometimes I like to sleep in on weekends.

This past winter, we had higher than normal heating bills.

The negative frequency adverbs *never, rarely,* and *seldom* can also come first but are then followed by inverted word order:

Never have I seen such a huge watermelon before!

Seldom does he help his wife with the housework.

Rarely have I felt so embarrassed.

The word order given in Guideline 2 is more common, however.

✎ EXERCISE 4   Using adverbials

Divide the following adverbs and adverbial phrases into three groups: *manner, place,* and *time.* Then write five sentences, each of which contains two of these adverbials. Use the guidelines to help you determine the correct placement of these words and phrases.

since Christmas	in a hurry
punctually	at home
without looking	on my birthday
late	recently
to the store	here
carelessly	on campus
early	meaningfully

✎ EXERCISE 5   Correct word order

Put the words in the correct order to produce good English sentences. Use question word order for items followed by a question mark. Use every word.

1. his / doesn't / brush / he / after meals / always / teeth .
2. time / at home / have / seldom / on weekdays / lunch / I / to cook .
3. rarely / in my country / snows / in the winter / it.
4. his / in a restaurant / at night / they / birthday / celebrate / usually / with a big party .
5. on the weekend / ever / you / do / with friends / to the movies / go ?
6. his strange behavior / to understand / I / the reason / never / been able / have / for .
7. likely / George / is / at home / again / to leave / his homework ?
8. in a quiet place / don't / I / without interruptions / usually / trouble / doing my homework / have .
9. too many / in line / aren't / at the post office / right now / people / there .
10. has / she / to go out / never / on the weekend / with them / wanted
11. time / to read / have / seldom / stories / do /a second time / I .
12. experienced / I / never / rude behavior such / had.

B. Modifiers

A modifier is a word or phrase that adds to the meaning of other words. Modifiers can change the meaning of a sentence by changing the meaning of one word in the sentence. Consider these examples:

(1) *Only* Susan said she liked spaghetti.
 (The others said they didn't like spaghetti.)

(2) Susan *only* said she like spaghetti.
 (She doesn't like it; she just said so to spare her mother-in-law's feelings.)

(3) Susan said she *only* liked spaghetti.
 (She doesn't love it.)

(4) Susan said she liked *only* spaghetti.
 (She doesn't care to eat anything else.)

Example 4 contradicts Guideline 1 from Section A, "Adverbials," which says not to separate a verb and its direct object. The guideline is still a good one to keep in mind, however. Exceptions to the rule occur with only a few adverbs: *only, almost, nearly,* and *even*, which must go in front of the words they modify.

(1) MISPLACED   He *only* drinks soft drinks at parties.
 (He does not talk, dance, eat, or breathe.)
 CORRECT   He drinks *only* soft drinks at parties.
 (He does not drink wine or beer.)

(2) MISPLACED   I *almost* spent two hours doing that assignment.
 (So I didn't do the assignment.)
 CORRECT   I spent *almost* two hours doing that assignment.

(3) MISPLACED   A child *even* knows how to do that.
 CORRECT   *Even* a child knows how to do that.

Relative clauses and prepositional phrases sometimes function as modifiers. And like the adverbs just discussed, they can cause confusion if they are misplaced:

(4) MISPLACED   He borrowed an egg from a neighbor *that was rotten*.
 (Which one was rotten, the neighbor or the egg?)
 CORRECT   He borrowed an egg *that was rotten* from a neighbor.

(5) MISPLACED   The teacher explained the error to the student *with a great deal of impatience.*
(Who was impatient, the student or the teacher?)

CORRECT   *With a great deal of impatience*, the teacher explained the error to the student.
(Now it is clear that the teacher was impatient.)

✎ EXERCISE 6   Correcting misplaced modifiers

Decide which modifier is misplaced in each sentence. Circle it and draw an arrow to where it should be.

1. The cosmetic salesperson sprayed perfume samples on the customer that smelled wonderful.
2. The postal clerk handed a package to the woman that was a little battered.
3. I almost played the piano all morning.
4. That student doesn't try very hard; he doesn't come even to class.
5. The used car that Jeff bought only goes 40 miles per hour.
6. Mary hardly eats anything for lunch.
7. A mother only knows what her children are really like.

✎ EXERCISE 7   Adding modifiers to sentences

Read the sentences and add the modifiers in parentheses.

1. (almost) I dropped my book on the floor.
2. (that are dependent) Children need their parents.
3. (nearly) It took most of the students three hours to write their compositions.
4. (only) Some of them spent 30 minutes doing it.
5. (that was so difficult) The students did not appreciate another assignment from their teacher.
6. (even) This task is so simple that a three-year-old can do it.
7. (without looking at them) The teacher asked a question of the students, who answered quickly.

C. *Also* and *too*

Also usually goes before a single-word main verb, but after *be* and after the first auxiliary. *Too* goes at the end of the clause.

They've registered for their required classes. They *also* want to register for a gym class.

Not only is he my cousin, he is *also* my friend.

Carl's grandparents will *also* be coming to visit him.

You will have to do homework and be ready for an exam, *too*.

EXERCISE 8   Adding *also* and *too* to sentences

Read the two sentences in each item. Insert the word in parentheses into the second sentence.

1. (too) Tony took his parents sightseeing last weekend. He took them to his favorite restaurant.
2. (also) His parents liked the places they visited. They liked the food at the restaurant.
3. (also) His parents usually visit Tony in May. This year they are coming in September.
4. (too) The Johnsons stay at a hotel when they visit Tony because he has a small apartment. He has a roommate.
5. (too) Tony is looking forward to their next visit. His aunt and uncle are going to visit.
6. (also) His parents usually drive when they visit. His aunt and uncle will drive, but in their own car.
7. (also) Tony likes his uncle a lot. He likes his aunt, but not as much.

D. Direct and indirect objects

When both direct and indirect objects accompany a verb, there are two possible patterns for most verbs:

Pattern 1   This pattern consists of the verb (V) followed by the direct object (D.O.), followed by preposition *to* or *for* and the indirect object (I.O.).

I wrote a letter to my best friend last night.
        D.O.   I.O.

My father bought a car for me.
                 D.O.   I.O.

Use *to* with indirect objects after verbs like *give, lend, bring, send, write, say* and *tell*. Use *for* with indirect objects after verbs like *buy, get,* and *make.*

Pattern 2   This pattern consists of the verb followed by the indirect object followed by the direct object.

I wrote my best friend a letter last night.
        I.O.   D.O.

My father bought <u>me</u> <u>a car.</u>
              I.O.   D.O.

Exceptions   When the direct object is a pronoun, only Pattern 1 is possible.

I sent it <u>to my cousin</u> last month.
  D.O.   I.O.

He got <u>it</u> <u>for me</u> at a discount.
  D.O.   I.O.

The verbs *say, explain,* and *recommend* take only Pattern 1.

Can you recommend <u>a good restaurant</u> <u>to us?</u>
                      D.O.   I.O.

He didn't say <u>"Good morning"</u> <u>to me.</u>
                 D.O.   I.O.

Jeff explained <u>his problem</u> <u>to her.</u>
                  D.O.   I.O.

✎ **EXERCISE 9   Adding indirect objects to sentences**

Insert the indirect object in parentheses into each sentence.

1. (me) My parents didn't give what I wanted for my birthday.
2. (for me) I had asked for a particular motorcycle, but they didn't buy it.
3. (them) I was disappointed because I had told which model I wanted.
4. (me) Fortunately, several friends remembered to send cards.
5. (for me) My mother also made a cake, so I was somewhat consoled about the motorcycle.
6. (me) My parents also bought a very nice sweater.
7. (to him) A friend has really admired the sweater, but I don't think I'll ever lend it.
8. (him) I was telling the truth when I said he could borrow anything else I had.
9. (to him) After I explained the situation, he was completely understanding.
10. (for myself) I'm working part-time so that I can buy the motorcycle.
11. (to me) I really don't expect my parents to give it.
12. (to them) I'll never say anything about the motorcycle again.

✎ **EXERCISE 10   Completing sentences with direct and indirect objects**

In each item, complete the second sentence by adding both an indirect and direct object and any other phrases or clauses necessary to finish the logic of the sentence. Use pronouns for the objects and the prepositions *to* and *for* as needed.

1. Mary gave John some flowers. She gave . . . reluctantly because . . .
2. I'm going to send my brother a birthday card. I'll send . . . even though . . .
3. I don't understand this equation. Could you explain . . . so that . . . ?
4. She told me a funny story. She had to tell . . . in a soft voice because . . .
5. I hope you take better care of my notes this time, or I won't lend . . .
6. That is a very pretty sweater. Who made . . . ?
7. I'm going to get my parents a TV for their anniversary. I'll try to buy . . . early so that . . .
8. My books are in your car. Could you bring . . . before you . . . ?
9. I don't especially like that restaurant, so I really can't recommend . . .

3 ADJECTIVES AND ADVERBS

Adjectives modify nouns and pronouns. They may occur just before the nouns or pronouns they modify, or they may be connected to them through linking verbs.

> The *big, healthy, blue-eyed* soccer player got a *black* eye in *her last* match.
> (The adjectives occur just before the nouns.)

> She felt *embarrassed* and at the same time *ashamed* because she had started the fight.
> (The adjectives are connected to the pronoun through a linking verb.)

Adverbs modify verbs, adjectives, or other adverbs. They usually follow the verbs they modify and precede the adjectives or adverbs they modify. Adverbs often end in *-ly*.

> Susan plays soccer *more skillfully* than most of her teammates.

> Which do you like *better*, coffee or tea?

> I'm *extremely* disappointed in you.

> He did his homework *very carefully*.

A. Adjectives and adverbs with the same form

Although most adverbs differ in form from adjectives, some have the same form.

(1) ADJECTIVE   *Fast* cars use a lot of gas.
     ADVERB   Jeff eats very *fast*.

(2) ADJECTIVE   I don't feel *well* today.
                 (*Well* is an adjective when it refers to health.)
    ADVERB   He usually does *well* on exams.
(3) ADJECTIVE   I have an *early* appointment with the doctor.
    ADVERB   I'll get up a little *early* to get there on time.
(4) ADJECTIVE   This will be a *hard* case for the lawyers to win.
    ADVERB   They will have to work very *hard* to convince the jury.

Note: The adverb *hardly* is different from *hard* and usually precedes the root verb.

I *hardly* know her.

I can *hardly* stay awake in that class.
(*hardly* = barely, almost not)

He knows he will succeed if he works *hard*.
(*hard* = with great energy)

✎ EXERCISE 11   Using adjectives and adverbs

Read the sentences and circle the correct choice for each pair of words in parentheses.

1. If you try (hard/hardly), you will (sure/surely) succeed.
2. The quiz was so (easy/easily) that I finished very (quick/quickly).
3. I'm not very (good/well) at tennis, but I swim quite (good/well).
4. You look very (handsome/handsomely) today.
5. Let's finish this assignment (quick/fast) so that we can go out.
6. He says he's got a cold, but he looks (well/finely) to me.
7. I can't treat you to lunch because I (hard/hardly) have enough money for myself.
8. The boss got (real/really) angry with the employees.
9. I will (glad/gladly) lend him my car.
10. The new boss expects the employees to work more (efficient/efficiently) than they used to.
11. She isn't as (friendly/nicely) as her brother.
12. Better (safe/safely) than sorry.

B. Forms of comparison

Adjectives and adverbs usually have different comparative forms.

Adjective	*Adverb*	*Comparative Adjective*	*Comparative Adverb*
slow	slowly	slower	more slowly
safe	safely	safer	more safely

Adjective	Adverb	Comparative Adjective	Comparative Adverb
nice	nicely	nicer	more nicely
easy	easily	easier	more easily
busy	busily	busier	more busily
noisy	noisily	noisier	more noisily

Compare these forms to the exceptions listed below.

Adjective/Adverb	Comparative Adjective	Comparative Adverb
hard	harder	harder
early	earlier	earlier
late	later	later
fast	faster	faster

✎ EXERCISE 12   Using adjectives and adverbs in comparisons

Read each sentence and circle the correct form in parentheses.

1. You can do this (easier / more easily) if you concentrate.
2. The (busier / more busily) he is, the more nervous he gets.
3. They moved to a (safer / more safely) neighborhood.
4. The class tends to get (noisier / more noisily) when the teacher leaves the room.
5. He's trying to live (healthier / more healthily) by eating better.
6. I'm afraid I have to ask you to work a little (quicker / more quickly).
7. Try to treat him a little (nicer / more nicely), and I'm sure he'll cooperate.
8. He is much (slower / more slowly) in reading than in math.
9. The composition was (easier / more easily) to do than I had expected it to be.

4   RELATIVE CLAUSES

Relative clauses modify the nouns they follow.

> The book *that I needed* was not available in the college bookstore.

> The woman *who runs the bookstore* said the book would be available two weeks from now.

> Unfortunately, the assignments *our teacher has given us* require reading the book.

The guidelines on the following pages will help you use relative clauses correctly.

Guideline 1 The relative pronouns *who* and *that* are used for people; *which* and *that* are used for things. *Whose* is the possessive relative pronoun; it takes the place of possessive adjectives in a relative clause. In formal writing, *whom* is used in place of *who* when it is the object of a verb or the object of a preposition in a relative clause.

The book *that you are looking at* is very expensive.

New Orleans is a city *which is known for its good food.*

The neighbors *whose children go to school with ours* are moving.

The two professors *whom you recommended* were excellent.

Most of the people *whom I went to school with* are in college now.

Guideline 2 Subjects and objects are not repeated in a relative clause.

(1) WRONG   The man *whom I met him at your party* didn't remember me.

     CORRECT   The man *whom I met at your party* didn't remember me.

(2) WRONG   It surprises me that people *who they seem so nice* can be so forgetful.

     CORRECT   It surprises me that people *who seem so nice* can be so forgetful.

(3) WRONG   Luis Rodriguez is the one *who his major is meteorology.*

     CORRECT   Luis Rodriguez is the one *whose major is meteorology.*

Guideline 3 A relative clause is either restrictive or nonrestrictive. A restrictive clause restricts the meaning of the noun it modifies; it tells you *which one* (or ones) is being talked about. Restrictive clauses are essential to the meaning of the main clause and are not set off with commas.

Nonrestrictive clauses are not essential to the meaning of the main clause, and they are set off with commas. Nonrestrictive clauses do not use *that* as a relative pronoun and never omit the relative pronoun. One test of restrictiveness is whether the sentence still makes sense without the clause:

RESTRICTIVE   Most foreign students *who don't study hard* don't pass the TOEFL.
               (Without the relative clause, the sentence is not factually correct, so the clause is restrictive and essential. It is a fact that most foreign students do pass the TOEFL.)

NONRESTRICTIVE   Foreign students, *who must have student visas to study at U.S. universities*, add diversity and a new perspective to U.S. campuses.
(The relative clause is nonrestrictive because it is extra, nonessential information; the sentence makes perfect sense without the clause.)

Guideline 4   The relative pronoun is often omitted in restrictive clauses where the relative pronoun is an object.

Most of the people *I went to school with* are quite successful.
(The omitted relative pronoun *whom* is the object of the preposition *with*.)

I can't find the tickets *we bought*.
(The omitted relative pronoun *that* is the direct object of *bought*.)

✏ EXERCISE 13   Recognizing good relative clauses

Underline the relative clause in each sentence. Put a check (✓) in the blank if it is grammatically correct and correctly punctuated. Put an ✗ in the blank if it is incorrect. Correct any mistakes you find.

_____ 1. The biology department needs a secretary who can do word processing.

_____ 2. Assignments which are handed in late will receive less credit.

_____ 3. I bought some notebooks on sale which they are not of very good quality.

_____ 4. When is that library book we used for our report due?

_____ 5. Professor Chen who you know as the author of our economics text will deliver a guest lecture next Friday.

_____ 6. I require all students they are enrolled in this course to attend the lecture.

_____ 7. The language tapes we used to listen to are no longer available in the library.

_____ 8. You can order the tapes from Cambridge University Press that is the publisher of the tapes.

_____ 9. Firefighters, whose work can be very dangerous, are often paid less than police officers.

_____10. I'm afraid that the cassette I am listening to is defective. Can I get another copy?

_____11. It is sometimes difficult to convince students who their only goal is to pass the TOEFL that ability is more important than test results.

_____12. Is that the company you wrote your letter of complaint to?

Follow-up Write two sentences illustrating each of the guidelines. Write about your English studies.

✎ EXERCISE 14   Adding relative clauses to sentences

Read each sentence. Then decide which of the two clauses in parentheses is a well-formed relative clause that correctly modifies a noun in the sentence. Rewrite the sentence, inserting this clause. (Commas indicate a nonrestrictive relative clause.)

1. Professor Norris is an excellent administrator.
   (, who used to direct the English language program,)
   (that is the author of our textbook)
2. Computers are becoming more widespread worldwide.
   (, which have come down in price,)
   (they are beneficial in education)
3. The police haven't been able to locate the witness.
   (her testimony is important to the case)
   (, whose testimony is important to the case)
4. I would like a car.
   (that it can hold five or six passengers)
   (that doesn't require a lot of maintenance)
5. The book bag isn't big enough for all the books I need this semester.
   (I bought)
   (that are quite useful)
6. People shouldn't throw stones.
   (who live in glass houses)
   (, who live in glass houses,)
7. Students usually find that their writing improves.
   (they like to read)
   (who read a lot)
8. Punctuation is not terribly difficult to learn to use correctly.
   (, which often frustrates writing students,)
   (that students don't like)
9. I gave him the letter.
   (that he asked for)
   (he asked for it)
10. My sister-in-law is coming to visit soon.
    (, who is also a good friend,)
    (she's my older brother's wife)

5 PUNCTUATION

Attention to the simple guidelines presented in this part will help you use punctuation correctly.

A. Commas

Guideline 1   Use a comma after an introductory clause or phrase.

INTRODUCTORY PHRASE	*To be honest*, I don't know where he comes from.
INTRODUCTORY DEPENDENT CLAUSE	*Because it rained last night*, it's cooler today.

Guideline 2   Use commas to set off nonessential clauses and phrases.

NONESSENTIAL   Jeffrey, *who didn't take the final exam*, failed his biology course.
(The independent clause *Jeffrey failed his biology course* makes sense without the relative clause. Commas are used to signal that the relative clause is nonrestrictive and nonessential.)

The final exam, *I assume*, will be comprehensive.
(*I assume* interrupts the main clause but is extra information and therefore nonessential. Other similar expressions are: *of course, it seems, I think, to be sure,* and *according to the author.*)

My wife, *Zelda*, earns more money than anyone else in her department.

ESSENTIAL   All students *who don't take the final exam* will fail the course.
(The independent clause *All students will fail the course* does not make sense without the relative clause; the relative clause is essential and needs no commas.)

My brother *Ronald* cooks better than I do.
(The absence of commas here tells the reader that *Ronald* is essential information; therefore the writer must have more than one brother.)

EXERCISE 15   Using commas for introductory and nonessential elements

Read the sentences. Add commas to set off introductory phrases and clauses and nonessential elements.

1. On their vacation the Smiths are going to go to India which they've both been interested in visiting ever since an Indian family moved in next door.
2. Because of busy work schedules they won't be able to spend more than two weeks there.
3. They'll visit the Taj Mahal I'm sure as well as two or three major cities.
4. Since the Smiths live in a warm climate they already have suitable clothes for their trip.
5. They'll want to buy presents which are typical of the places that they visit.
6. In my opinion they will have a wonderful time because both are good travelers and interested in other cultures.

Follow-up   Write two sentences illustrating Guideline 1 and two sentences illustrating Guideline 2. Write about plans for a visit to another country.

Guideline 3   Use a comma to separate two independent clauses joined by a coordinating conjunction (*and, or, but, so,* etc.)

TWO CLAUSES	I have a lot of homework, but I'll be able to finish it.
ONE CLAUSE, TWO VERBS	I'll write my report tonight and revise it tomorrow.

Guideline 4   Use commas to separate a series (three or more) of similar items.

SERIES OF SUBJECTS	Frank, his brother, and I are going to Mexico together.
	Swimming, walking, and jogging are all good forms of exercise.
SERIES OF VERBS	We hope to swim, sunbathe, relax, and eat good seafood.

Note: Some writers omit the comma before *and* in a series. If you omit the final comma, do so consistently in your writing.

 EXERCISE 16   Using commas to separate independent clauses and items in a series

Read the sentences. Add commas to separate independent clauses and items in a series.

1. Jack his brother and I are going hiking and fishing this weekend.
2. We had wanted to go to the beach but couldn't get hotel accommodations.
3. We decided to go to the mountains instead and enjoy the cooler weather.
4. We'll probably hike for a few days and then we'll relax by fishing at the local lake.
5. We'll take food sleeping bags a few changes of clothes but little else.
6. Would you like to come along or are you busy this weekend?

Follow-up   Write two sentences illustrating Guideline 3 and two illustrating Guideline 4. Write about a recent vacation.

Guideline 5   Use commas to set off items in an address or date.

> I was born in Chicago, Illinois, U.S.A. on February 5, 1978.
>
> Chadwick's of Boston, Ltd., is at One Chadwick Place, Box 1600, Brockton, Massachusetts 02303.

Note: No commas after the country name or between the state and the zip code.

Follow-up   Write sentences to answer the following questions, and separate items with commas.

1. Where and when were you born?
2. Where and when were your parents or other relatives married?
3. Where and when did you send your last letter? Whom did you send it to?

B. Periods, semicolons, and colons

Guideline 6   End a complete sentence with a period.

> He cried.
>
> She tried to comfort him.
>
> They made up.

Guideline 7   Use a semicolon to separate independent clauses that are closely related and not otherwise joined. This rule applies even if the second clause contains a transition word.

> He cried; she tried to comfort him; they made up.
>
> He cried, she tried to comfort him, and they made up.
> (No semicolon is needed because the series is joined with *and*.)

He cried; therefore, she tried to comfort him.

He cried, and she, therefore, tried to comfort him.
(No semicolon is needed because the two clauses are joined with *and*.)

Guideline 8 Use a colon after a complete sentence to announce a list, a long quotation, or an explanation of the sentence.

LIST	You'll probably need to bring these items on the hike: a tent, a sleeping bag, and food and water for three days.
LONG QUOTATION	In *America as a Civilization*,* Max Lerner says: "What holds America together? A democracy, De Tocqueville wrote, cannot function without a religion and a philosophy. Which is to say that while every civilization needs some principle to hold it together, a democracy has a special problem of cohesion."
EXPLANATION	There is something I have never understood about Jeffrey: his inability to arrive anywhere on time.

EXERCISE 17 Using periods, semicolons, and colons

Read these sentences. Add periods (and capital letters if necessary), semicolons, and colons where needed.

1. Students who wish to improve their writing can do so in three ways reading more, studying English rhetoric and sentence structure, and heeding their writing teacher's comments.
2. Punctuation is not very interesting to study correct punctuation does, however, make writing easier to read.
3. The semicolon and the colon look similar, and, therefore, are sometimes used incorrectly by students.
4. The period and the semicolon are almost identical in function each signals that an independent clause lies before and after it.
5. There is an important difference between the period and the semicolon the semicolon is used within one longer sentence, while the period breaks up two independent clauses into separate sentences.
6. Students should be careful to use the right transition word it is better to omit a transition word than to use it incorrectly.
7. By far the most mistakes are made with commas they are often used unnecessarily.

*H. Holt and Co., 1987.

8. An understanding of the basic rules of punctuation and a little practice are sufficient for most students to master punctuation, however.

C. Apostrophes

The apostrophe has two functions in English: It is used to replace missing letters in contractions and to indicate possession. What letter(s) does the apostrophe replace in these examples?

they're   We'd better go.
didn't   She'd rather stay.
it's   There's going to be a party.
I've   There's been an accident.

To indicate possession with an apostrophe, follow these rules: (1) Add *'s* to singular nouns, indefinite nouns, and plural nouns with irregular plurals.

John*'s* car   everyone*'s* friend
my father*'s* car   the men*'s* room
somebody else*'s* sweater   children*'s* books

(2) Add only an apostrophe to plural nouns ending in *s*.

the boys' room
the Smiths' summer house
ten dollars' worth of stamps

(3) Add an apostrophe only or *'s* to singular nouns ending in *s*.

the waitress' tips *or* the waitress*'s* tips
James' car *or* James*'s* car

Note: Whether written or not, the possessive *s* is pronounced in words like *James'* and *waitress'*.

Do not use apostrophes with possessive pronouns. The possessive pronouns *its* and *whose* are easy to confuse with their homonyms *it's* and *who's*.

POSSESSIVE PRONOUNS   Jane's composition was longer than *ours*.
                       The others' papers got better grades than *hers* did.
CONTRACTION   *It's* a pretty day.
POSSESSIVE PRONOUN   The cloud cast *its* shadow on the lake.
CONTRACTION   *Who's* coming to dinner?
POSSESSIVE PRONOUN   He is the teacher *whose* lectures have been
                       videotaped for TV.

✎ EXERCISE 18   Differences in meaning and punctuation

Working with a partner or as a class, look at each pair of correctly punctuated expressions. Explain the differences in meaning and punctuation.

1. Joan and Mike's car / Joan's and Mike's cars
2. the boy's toys / the boys' toys
3. the waitress's uniforms / the waitresses' uniforms
4. the lady's room / the ladies' room
5. the wings of the airplane / the bird's wings
6. my brother-in-law's work / my brother-in-law's working

✎ EXERCISE 19 Adding apostrophes

Read the sentences and add apostrophes where necessary.

1. Peg and Sues Diner doesnt open until eight oclock in the morning.
2. The students assignments in Professor Browns section are longer than ours.
3. My roommates class schedules are easier than mine.
4. This years winter lettuce crop was ruined by heavy rains.
5. Whose dress is Helen going to wear, yours or hers?
6. Whos going to meet Phyllis flight tomorrow night – her husband or her sons?
7. Stewardesses working hours are just as long as pilots.

D. Quotation marks

Direct speech is someone's exact words and requires quotation marks.

DIRECT   "But I hate spinach," he protested.

The counselor asked, "Whom do you take after more – your mother or your father?"

Indirect speech is the writer's report of what someone said and does not have quotation marks. *That* is often used to introduce indirect statements. Questions in indirect speech occur as dependent clauses with subject-verb word order. They are reported without question marks, but the main clause can be a question that requires a question mark.

INDIRECT   He protested that he hated spinach.

The counselor asked whom I took after more – my mother or my father.

Did he ask you whom you voted for?

Guideline 9   Quotation marks come after periods and commas.

"Your grades will be sent to your home address," the letter said.

Guideline 10   Question marks go inside quotation marks when they apply to the quotation. They go outside quotation marks when they apply to the whole sentence.

"Where do you live?" he wanted to know.

Who said, "Birds of a feather flock together"?

Guideline 11   A quotation begins with a capital letter if it is a complete sentence, or if it comes at the beginning of the sentence that it is a part of.

"I don't care about grades," Peter said, "but I need the credits to graduate."

Guideline 12   Words reporting a quotation (like *he protested*) are not inside quotation marks.

The coach proclaimed, "We have the best soccer team in the league!"

EXERCISE 20   Adding quotation marks

Read the sentences and add quotation marks and capital letters where needed to direct speech. Add necessary punctuation to all sentences.

1. He asked me where I had been living
2. I told him I have the same apartment that I had when I met you
3. Are you eating well my mother always asks when she calls and do you have nice friends
4. I assure her that I can take care of myself and that she shouldn't worry
5. The police wanted to know what we had seen during the accident
6. We said we weren't really paying attention, so we don't know which driver was at fault.
7. A stitch in time saves nine our history professor is fond of telling us.

Guideline 13   Names of stories, songs, chapters, and articles (i.e., parts of a larger work) appear in quotation marks. Names of books, magazines, and movies should be either underlined or printed in italics.

```
"The Ant and the Grasshopper" also appeared in
a collection entitled Collected Short Stories by
W. Somerset Maugham.
```

Margaret Meade's "Different Lands, Different Friendships," which was published in *Redbook* magazine in 1966, discusses cultural differences in friendship.

✎ EXERCISE 21   Editing for punctuation

Add quotation marks, underlining, periods, and commas to this paragraph.

In the essay Whether, How, and Why to Spank[1], author David Dempsey presents his case in favor of physical punishment of children. David Dempsey explains Better to punish children than to be indifferent to them, since it is the neglected child who is more likely to grow up to be a problem. On the other hand, in his book Dr. Spock on Parenting, a respected doctor comes out against physical punishment. If we are ever to turn toward a kinder society and a safer world, Dr. Spock writes, a revulsion against the physical punishment of children would be a good place to start. Whose advice should we follow? parents raising children often ask. The answer to this question is not easy.

[1] *The New York Times Magazine*, July 6, 1958.

Appendix B
Complete essay assessment guidelines

The Complete Essay Assessment Guidelines that begin on page 272 have been provided for you and your teacher to use in assessing your work. Like the guidelines in Chapters 3–7, they list the criteria of a very good essay in three main areas: (1) content and ideas, (2) organization and form, and (3) writing conventions. This set of guidelines also describes the characteristics of an average and a weak paper. Assess papers by following these steps:

1. *Content and ideas* Read the criteria listed under "Content and Ideas" for a very good, an average, and a weak paper. Carefully read the essay you are assessing and assign a maximum of five points and a minimum of one point for the elements in this area, depending on which of the three sets of criteria describe the essay best.*

2. *Organization and form* Read the criteria listed under "Organization and Form" for a very good, average, and weak paper. Reread the essay and assign a maximum of five points and a minimum of one point for the elements in this area.*

3. *Writing conventions* Read the criteria listed under "Writing Conventions" for a very good, average, and weak paper. Reread the essay and assign a maximum of five points and a minimum of one point for the elements in this area.*

4. *Total score* Add up the points you assigned in steps 1, 2, and 3 above. The maximum score is 15/15 (15 out of a possible score of 15); the minimum score is 3/15.

   Weighting the elements If your teacher decides to weight one area of elements, e.g., content and ideas, that area can be worth ten points instead of five. Double the points you assigned to that area (4/5 would become 8/10, and the total possible score would be 20 instead of 15).

*Five points indicates the essay elements for this area are very good; three points indicates a paper with average elements; one point indicates a paper that is weak in the elements being considered. If you decide the elements are better than a 3 but not good enough to be a 5, assign a 4, for example.

COMPLETE ESSAY ASSESSMENT GUIDELINES

Content and ideas

Very good (5 points)

- ☐ The writer has thought about the topic and has a clear main idea or thesis.
- ☐ The writer discusses each main point enough to give the reader a reason to believe it.
- ☐ The writer supports each main point, and no important point is left out.
- ☐ There are no logical fallacies used to support the writer's thesis.
- ☐ The writer's voice is clear because he or she writes in a sincere way, with the audience in mind.

Average (3 points)

- ☐ The writer needs to think more about the topic to make his or her ideas more convincing.
- ☐ The points need more support to become clear and meaningful.
- ☐ The writer may be writing what sounds good, not what he or she believes and knows.
- ☐ The writer's logic is not clear.
- ☐ The writer's voice is not very strong. In addition to generalities, the writer needs to include details that show familiarity with and understanding of the topic.

Weak (1 point)

- ☐ The writer needs to think more about the topic because it is not clear what point he or she is trying to make.
- ☐ The writer needs to explain and develop points and not repeat the same ideas.
- ☐ The writer's argument is weakened by faulty logic.
- ☐ The writer's voice will be stronger if his or her own beliefs are included.

Organization and form

Very good (5 points)

- ☐ The paper has a clear beginning, middle, and end, with separate introductory, body, and concluding paragraphs. It moves logically in a straight line.

☐ The reader wants to continue reading and can understand the thesis and other main points fully after one reading.

☐ It is clear which are the main points and which are secondary points.

Average (3 points)

☐ The paper has all the right parts but does not have balance. The introduction may be too long, or the conclusion may be too short.

☐ The writer needs to make sure that important details get more attention than less important details. The writer may need to omit irrelevant information.

☐ The reader has to read the paper twice to understand it because of a lack of coherence between the parts of the paper.

Weak (1 point)

☐ The paper needs a clear beginning, middle, and end in order to move in one direction.

☐ The writer needs to organize the paper so that the main points are separated from each other.

☐ The reader gets lost because the writer changes directions: The writer needs to add coherence.

Writing conventions

Very good (5 points)

☐ The writer uses a variety of sentence lengths and types to add interest to the writing.

☐ The writer chooses vocabulary carefully to communicate clearly.

☐ The writer uses cohesive devices to make the relationships between the ideas clear.

☐ The writer avoids problems of sentence structure including fragments, comma-splices, run-together sentences, and lack of parallel structure.

☐ There are no illogical shifts in tense, person, or number, and the tone is consistently formal.

☐ The writer uses English grammar effectively to convey the message. There are few problems of verb tense, subject-verb agreement, word order, count/noncount use, or word forms.

☐ The writer follows rules for spelling, capitalization, and punctuation.

Average (3 points)

☐ The writer uses mainly simple and compound sentences.

- ☐ Some vocabulary is inaccurate, causing the reader to stop and question.
- ☐ Relationships between ideas is sometimes unclear.
- ☐ Sentence-structure problems require that some sentences be read twice for a good understanding.
- ☐ There are confusing shifts in tense, person, and/or number.
- ☐ The tone of the writing occasionally shifts to the informal.
- ☐ Grammar mistakes interfere with meaning.
- ☐ Errors in spelling, capitalization, and punctuation slow the reader down.

Weak (1 point)

- ☐ Sentences are mainly simple ones, and some of them are badly formed. Compound sentences are long and rambling.
- ☐ Poor choice of vocabulary leaves the reader confused in several places.
- ☐ The writing lacks cohesive devices to tie the ideas together.
- ☐ Sentence structure is poor; the reader must reconstruct the sentences to understand them.
- ☐ Illogical changes in tense, person, and/or number make the writing confusing.
- ☐ The writer uses an informal tone that is inappropriate for academic writing.
- ☐ Grammar mistakes make the paper difficult to read.
- ☐ Errors in spelling, capitalization, and punctuation distract the reader from the writer's message.
- ☐ The reader has trouble focusing on meaning and must reread to understand the paper.